# Cognition and Extended Rational Choice

One of the most exciting recent innovations in the social sciences has been the emergence of "behavioral economics," which extends the notion of rational choice to allow for both motivation beyond self-interest and intuitions that cannot be reduced to the logic of a situation. This new book by Howard Margolis demonstrates how an account of widely discussed topics, from tipping points in social choice to cognitive illusions and experimental anomalies, can be brought within a coherent framework.

Starting from Darwin's own comments on the origins of moral concerns and from a review of notorious cognitive illusions, Margolis shows how rational choice theory can be extended to incorporate social as well as self-interested motivation, but allowing for the cognitive complications that can be expected in domains well outside familiar experience. This yields a coherent account of many otherwise mystifying results from cooperation experiments. A concluding chapter illustrates how the argument can be applied to the salient empirical topic of jihadist terrorism.

"Twenty-five years ago I strongly recommended Margolis's 'Selfishness, Altruism, and Rationality." Now, five books later, it is exciting to see how much farther he's taken that theory, supported it with an extensive review of laboratory experiments, and applied it to groups, large and small, resolving numerous puzzles along the way."

*Thomas C. Schelling, 2005 Nobel Prize Laureate in Economics*

This book will be of great interest not only to students and researchers in behavioral and experimental economics but across the social sciences.

**Howard Margolis** is a Professor in the Irving B. Harris Graduate School of Public Policy Studies and the College. He has taught at the University of California-Irvine, and has held research positions at the Institute for Advanced Study (Princeton), the Russell Sage Foundation, and the Massachusetts Institute of Technology.

For Norman Bradburn

# Cognition and Extended Rational Choice

## Howard Margolis

 Routledge
Taylor & Francis Group

LONDON AND NEW YORK

First published 2007
by Routledge
2 Park Square, Milton Park, Abingdon, Oxon OX14 4RN

Simultaneously published in the USA and Canada
by Routledge
270 Madison Ave, New York, NY 10016

*Routledge is an imprint of the Taylor & Francis Group, an informa business*

Typeset in Times New Roman by
RefineCatch Limited, Bungay, Suffolk
Printed and bound in Great Britain by
TJ International Ltd, Padstow, Cornwall

*British Library Cataloguing in Publication Data*
A catalogue record for this book is available from the British Library

*Library of Congress Cataloging in Publication Data*
  Margolis Howard
  Cognition and extended rational choice / Howard Margolis
     p. cm.
  Includes bibliographical references and index.
  ISBN 978–0–415–70197–6 (hb)
  1. Rational choice theory. 2. Social choice. 3. Social perception.
  4. Cognition. I. Title.
  HM495.M37 2007
  302′.1301–dc22
  2007018401

ISBN10: 0–415–70197–X (hbk)
ISBN10: 0–415–70198–3 (pbk)
ISBN10: 0–203–93902–6 (ebk)

ISBN13: 978–0–415–70197–6 (hbk)
ISBN13: 978–0–415–70198–3 (pbk)
ISBN13: 978–0–203–93902–4 (ebk)

# Contents

vi   *Contents*

# Figures

# Tables

# Acknowledgements

It has been twenty-five years since I published the account of what I came to call "NSNX": a "neither selfish nor exploited" account of how social and self-interested motivation interact. Near the end of that book (*Selfishness, Altruism and Rationality*, 1982), I commented on the need for complementary work on cognition and persuasion, which indeed has been the focus of a series of books since then. But I had never joined the two endeavors. This book started from my interest in finding a topic which would fill in that gap. I expected that exploring the data accumulated in cooperation experiments in experimental economics would let me make some progress on that large task. So here is the result.

I am greatly in debt to the National Science Foundation, and especially to its Small Grants for Exploratory Research initiative for support (SGER 0344130). This allows program managers, in this case Robert O'Connor (Program Director for Risk and Decision, Risk and Management Science, NSF), some flexibility in supporting work far enough outside the mainstream to be otherwise difficult to fund.

Then early on a visit from Rob Langham of Routledge persuaded me to broaden the project to include the occasional work I had done on NSNX since 1982. Except for a paper on religion and norms (1991) invited by Timor Kuran for a conference on institutional economics, and another on what I called "incomplete coercion" written for an IRS conference on tax compliance (1991), everything of any consequence since 1982 is covered here. Chapter 2 is drawn from a volume on social motivation organized by Jane Mansbridge, Chapter 3 from a conference on norms organized by Russell Hardin, and Chapters 4 and 5 are developed from my paper for the Schelling *Festschrift* organized by Richard Zeckhauser (details throughout References). Glenn Harrison and Duncan Snidel provided many useful comments.

The project could only proceed with the help of many people in the experimental economics community, who provided not only all the data I use in the later chapters, but also many profitable discussions of the experiments. This extends far beyond the relative handful of experimenters whose work comes into the detailed analysis, though of course I owe a special debt to them.

Most of the actual drafting of the book was done as a 2005–2006 fellow at the Woodrow Wilson International Center for Scholars in Washington. I thank that splendid institution.

# Introduction

It is now more than twenty years since I published a proposal (Margolis 1982) for broadening the standard model of economic theory to build in what few people would want to deny: that human beings respond to interests that go beyond self-interest. Even then, what I later labeled NSNX ("neither selfish nor exploited" and pronounced "niz-nex") was not the only proposal on the table.[1] But at the time *Selfishness, Altruism and Rationality* (hereafter SA&R) was published, among "rational choice" social scientists (most conspicuously, economists) the prevailing view was still that the standard account of self-interested choice would ultimately prove adequate to deal with the accumulating evidence against that. Indeed, until recent years, and even today for many writers, "rational choice" was by definition self-interested choice.

But by the early 1980s, allowing for motivation beyond simple self-interest had at least moved to the second stage of an often-noticed sequence in science: from "it's too absurd to be taken seriously" to "it's not crazy but it's wrong." The end of the sequence, which may or may not be reached in any particular case, is "we knew it all along." My sense of the situation as this book was written was that broadening a rational choice model to allow for motivation beyond self-interest was well into the third phase of this transition from "it's crazy" to "it's wrong" to "we knew it all along." But the NSNX approach, which is the focus here, was a step behind the broader trend of extending the notion of rational choice to allow for social ("other-regarding" or "norm-obeying") as well as self-interested motivation.[2]

What makes NSNX seem odd is that it violates something ordinarily taken to be so obvious that it seems incoherent to even suppose it *could* be wrong. A formal (mathematical) model of rational choice has always entailed maximizing a utility function. The crucial word in the previous sentence is the shortest: "*a*". For as you will see, NSNX does not do that. On the Darwinian logic that underpins the theory a person would not have *a* utility function. What in a more conventional account would be a utility function with additional arguments to capture other-regarding motivation here *turns out to be* – for it is not an assumption underlying the account but something that follows from the argument to be introduced in Chapter 1 – a pair of utility functions. Each meets the usual conditions of a utility function, but there are *two*: one capturing the self-interested motivation that used to be referred to as "economic man," and the other capturing the person's social preferences.

That a person has distinct social and self-interested preferences is a very old idea, easily traced back not only to Adam Smith's *Theory of Moral Sentiments* but all the way to the Greeks. But the simple equilibrium condition you will encounter shortly, as a purely mathematical property, does not permit the two utility functions (self-interested and social) to be merged into some total utility function. As a scientific point, there is nothing at all surprising in that. Science is full of equilibrium conditions where competing forces tend to come into balance though nothing is being maximized. In the Darwinian argument to come here, it would be rather a miracle if there was some quantity that was being maximized by the tendency towards equilibrium.

Further, although NSNX turns on an unexpected mathematical property, it happens to have a very respectable precedent. For the linked dual-utilities (social and private) inherent in NSNX relate to the standard approach to rational choice in a way that parallels the generalization that long ago expanded the notion of number to allow a second dimension, creating complex numbers. No one would look for it. But when it crops up as the resolution of a technical problem, and if it turns out to have some power, it is hard to sustain refusal to allow that the world can be what it wants to be even if that goes against what we expect it to be.

What can be said to someone (I have run into such someones many times) who says that if it is actually true that there is no single utility function in NSNX then that shows NSNX has to be wrong? An important part of the answer is that while it is hard to draw firm lessons from the history of science, one thing that does stand out is that it does not work to put prior constraints on what Nature is allowed to do.

But to someone thoroughly immersed in a universe of discourse where rational choice *means* maximizing a utility function, the NSNX failure to provide this will seem as unreasonable as seeing cars drive on the "wrong" side of the road seems to someone from America or the Continent on first encountering traffic in Britain. So in due course I give that substantively trivial but psychologically potent concern the attention it needs.

The book is organized as follows. The first five chapters are based on my occasional papers on NSNX since the 1982 book, but prior to my current effort to use the extensive accumulation of data from cooperation experiments to test and refine the NSNX account. Since the 1982 book remains in print, I do not attempt to cover here anything like the full range of topics discussed there. But everything needed to support the discussion in this book will be covered. What is new here, in particular, is an account of how the *individual* equilibrium developed in SA&R, balancing self-interest and social motivation, can be elaborated to yield an account of how a *social* equilibrium emerges out of the interactions among many individuals. This elaboration of NSNX as explored in SA&R emerges from applying the NSNX logic to extend the range of the ingenious diagram for analyzing simple social choices devised by Tom Schelling. This turns the Schelling diagram into what I call the "S-diagram," which turns out to capture some fundamental dynamics of social change.

But the title divides attention between NSNX and cognition. And the cognitive effects of special interest here are those that channel intuition in ways that violate what on reflection the chooser would judge sensible in the situation. Mostly, cognitive shortcuts take us quickly to some reasonable approximation of where step-by-step reasoning would get us. But sometimes, of course, the shortcut must go awry. Cognitive effects of that perverse sort play no role at all in the first five chapters. But if the NSNX proposal captures something essential about interaction between social and self-interested motivation, that must further interact with cognition in the response of individuals to social issues and through them affect the response of societies. Cognitive effects which are sometimes perverse are likely to be of particular concern in social contexts, where they may be harder to correct, and where adverse effects can be multiplied.

NSNX turns on a balancing of propensities to self-interested choice against propensities favoring socially motivated choice. But social choices will often turn on how a person sees large-scale contexts which are far from transparent to the individuals whose aggregated interactions determine the social result. Analysis of social cooperation is then not likely to be adequate without insight from both of what developed as two separate projects but are here brought together. The NSNX project seeks to define how individuals achieve a balance between their propensity to act in self-interest and some propensity to act in the interest of a salient group. But, very prominently in the later chapters here, that NSNX account interacts with the *habits of mind* view of cognition I've pursued in other work.

Chapter 6 begins with a bit more discussion than I have given here of why cognitive effects that are usually benign but occasionally adverse can take on special importance in contexts of social choice. But it quickly turns to a particular kind of cognitive shortcut (what I will call *neglect defaulting*) which has not played any role in the very extensive attention to cognitive effects that has developed since Kahneman and Tversky's work in the 1970s. As with cognitive shortcuts generally, neglect defaults usually are effective as well as efficient, but not always. They are usually benign, but sometimes adverse. Then the individual would have done better to plod through in the time- and attention-consuming step-by-step alternative to the shortcut, but she is unlikely to notice that.

The argument starts from simple puzzles which overwhelmingly elicit responses which are not smart even from subjects who are. Cases of "adverse defaulting" will play a direct role in later discussion of social contexts. But seeing how defaulting can have remarkably strong adverse effects in the context of the simple puzzles in Chapter 6 prepares the ground for consideration in Chapter 7 of another sort of defaulting effect which is intrinsically tied to social contexts.

The analog of the simple puzzles in Chapter 6 is experimental data in Chapter 7 which defies reasonable interpretation in terms of either self-interested or social motivation or of any plausible mix of the two. Experimental data in which *most* choices are of that puzzling sort turn out to be unexpectedly easy to find. And the account of what is happening suggested by NSNX turns on noticing that *adverse defaulting* akin to the neglect defaults of Chapter 6 must have counterparts in the cognitive structure I call the NSNX cascade. The cascade governs how a social context is seen (as competitive or cooperative, with the secondary distinctions you will see in Chapter 7). Parallel to the neglect defaults encountered in Chapter 6, the NSNX cascade entails a defaulting structure that can be expected to influence social intuitions in contexts that are ambiguous or unfamiliar, or otherwise difficult to interpret. But contexts of large-scale social choice, where individuals must make choices about matters far outside their normal range of experience, often have that character.

Chapters 8, 9, and 10 then consider how the cognitive effects introduced in Chapters 6 and 7, interacting with NSNX, can be applied to further experimental data. I try to show how NSNX + cognition effects can yield insight into data from Public Goods and related games that is interesting but not bizarre (Chapter 8), and how it can produce what seem to me even more striking results when applied to experimental data that are also interesting but verging over to choices that sometimes looks quite bizarre (Chapters 9 and 10). But even bizarre choices come from somewhere. The subjects in the experiments are not ordinarily bizarre in their behavior outside the lab. Somehow in the lab they are being cued into choices that ordinarily would not be made.

The experiments are intended to show us something about what is surely the fundamental problem of the social sciences, which is understanding cooperation among agents whose behavior is ordinarily conspicuously marked by pursuit of self-interest. What is novel here is not the notion that experiments can show us something about how cooperation works. That has been the point all along. But here new tools are applied to the data, yielding what I (of course) hope can be seen as substantial new insights.

This puzzle of how cooperation can be (sometimes) sustained is mostly a puzzle about the extended cooperation of large-scale societies. If we want to understand how the simplest human societies work, we can learn a good deal by treating them as more sophisticated versions of other animal societies, and especially other primate societies. The culture of even the simplest human hunter/gatherers is vastly more complex than the culturally richest non-human community. But anyone who has been to a zoo can see there is no absolute divide between the social behavior of chimps or gorillas and human behavior in small kin groups. Whatever insights can be gained from cooperation among primates, however, does not get us very far at all in trying to understand the vast scale of human cooperation since (at least) the emergence of literacy 5,000 years or so ago. Somehow cooperation can be sometimes sustained even when it extends far beyond small group interactions among people who know each other and have continuing interactions, and often with strong kinship relations. We can see substantial cooperation extending to people who are strangers but not enemies.

In social choice experiments, subjects are recruited to play games, usually for non-trivial amounts of real money, that are arranged to mimic incentives characteristic of important social interactions. The data produced by these experiments therefore provide us with the choices human beings have made, faced with carefully organized incentives, and conditional on variations in the structure of the games, conditions of the game, players' characteristics, and so on. But interpreting what is going on in the games is a challenge.

Choices in the lab do not always look very much like the choices we see in the world among people who are strangers but not enemies. But in contexts outside the range of everyday experience, cues that would ordinarily correct faulty intuitions might be missing or blurred. Anomalous behavior in the lab might be showing us something about real behavior in unfamiliar conditions outside the lab, where large-scale political and social cooperation is *mostly* about issues beyond familiar experience. How issues are perceived can stray from how things will someday look to historians. In a concluding chapter, I try to give some flavor of how the formal insights of earlier chapters and the insights tied to experimental data in later chapters might be put to work.

That concluding chapter sketches applications of ideas from both the social equilibrium discussion developed through to Chapter 5 and from the NSNX + cognition discussion of Chapters 6 to 10 to the particularly salient (as this is written, and perhaps long after it is written) context of fundamentalist terrorism. I will be considering how the "tipping point" dynamics of the S-diagram can yield insight into the recruitment and longer-term prospects of terrorist movements, and then of how these dynamics could be expected to interact with the defaulting effects developed in the later chapters.

All this is followed by two appendices. One describes software (the *template*) for data analysis developed for use in this project. This tool for analysis is not at all tied to the theoretical and empirical arguments that comprise the bulk of the book. I present it only as an appendix to the main text. Until you have seen some results from use of the template, you are unlikely to be interested in this software exercise.

The second appendix concerns a prominent topic in the experimental economics literature (quantal response equilibria as a correction where Nash equilibrium falls short), whose connection to NSNX only became apparent to me after seeing a paper published in the *American Political Science Review* (Levine and Palfrey 2007) while this book was already in press.

# 1 The NSNX model

Almost a century and a half ago, Charles Darwin (1871: 166) argued that natural selection would support the evolution of social behavior, since there would be selection between competing groups as well as selection between competing individuals within groups. In competition between groups, groups in which individuals cared something about what was good for the group, not only about what was good for themselves, would be favored. For biologists, claims of this sort went very much out of fashion after Williams's (1966) classic critique of group selection. This was not because there is something wrong with Darwin's claim that between-group selection would favor some measure of social motivation. The argument that between-group as well as within-group selection must occur has never been in dispute. No competent biologist doubts it, nor that such selection would favor group-oriented rather than self-interested behavior where the two conflict. The counterargument is rather that the intermittent between-group advantage to social motivation would be swamped by the routine within-group advantage to self-interest. In the language of economics, the argument leaves open the possibility that the result will be a corner solution, or something very close to it.

But even within biology there has been some revival of interest in group selection in recent years. Among other things, it is hard to make sense of the existence of sex in terms of the self-interest of mothers, who squander half their genes in favor of a father. Even where fathers help with child-rearing (in most species they don't), why would not a self-interested female cheat? This is not a knock-down argument for group selection. But it has never been decisively answered, and various models that respond to Williams's critique of group selection are now in play.[1] But whatever the standing of group selection in biology generally, that possibility is of particular interest for the special case of our own species, since the human ability to communicate and to improvise novel behavior makes the potential gains from a capacity for cooperation vast compared to other vertebrates. And we can observe that indeed human beings manage to cooperate (sometimes) under conditions and on a scale far beyond anything that could be accounted for by motivation reducible to direct self-interest augmented by indirect self-interest (kin selection or reciprocal altruism).[2] Since cooperation far beyond plausible self-interest exists, it apparently is possible. So it is worth considering *how* it is possible.

What is required is an account of how (even in the especially favorable human case) the conflicting between-group versus within-group selection pressures might yield a non-trivial sustainable component of social motivation A key to that (going now beyond Darwin's brief remarks) might be noticing that between-group selection would favor not only some element of social motivation, but more specifically social motivation qualified in ways that would increase the *sustainable* level of social motivation, given the always-present within-group pressure favoring self-interest.

## The NSNX rules

Social motivation favors what is good for the group, even when what is good for the group is not what is best for the individual. And any Darwinian process will tend to favor efficient use of resources. But the competition here between within-group versus between-group selection would make that tendency toward efficiency particularly strong with respect to making the most of that special resource of social motivation. It would "economize on love" (Robertson 1956). Which suggests:

> Rule 1 (NSNX efficiency): Other things equal, the more good a bit of resources would do if used socially (compared with what it could do if used for private interests), the more likely an individual will use that bit of resources socially.

Without a rule of this sort, whatever social motivation can be sustained despite within-group selection favoring self-interest could be squandered, which would reduce whatever capacity this motivation had to resist the contrary pressure from within-group selection. Clearly one aspect of how social motivation would work which would be favored by between-group selection and which would *not* be undercut by within-group selection is the propensity captured by Rule 1. Sustainable social motivation would tend to conserve whatever reservoir of social motivation is available for when it would be most likely to be well used.

But Rule 1 itself needs some qualification. *Sustainable* social motivation must operate in some way that shields the most socially oriented members of the group from fatal exploitation by those most inclined to self-interest. I give a detailed discussion of this in Chapter 3 of SA&R. But the outcome is that an essential element of how social motivation is likely to be governed would include a second rule making social behavior less vulnerable to exploitation (hence the label for the model: "neither selfish nor exploited"). Specifically:

Rule 2 (NSNX equity): Other things equal, the more an individual has already used resources socially relative to what others – in particular what others who look "like me" or "in my situation" – are doing, the more weight will go to private interests in spending the next bit of resources.

Rule 1 would incline a person towards cooperation to the extent that her contribution looks (to that person) to be socially useful relative to its private cost. Other things equal, the more socially useful the behavior seems to an agent, the more willing she would be to do more. But the greater the private cost of that contribution, the less willing she would be. No plausible account of social behavior could fail to incorporate some functional equivalent of this rule, turning on the perceived ratio between the social values versus the private cost of a contribution to social goals. The private cost must include expectations about rewards or punishments associated with a choice as well as "out of pocket" costs. The (net) cost of giving needs to be reduced if there is a prospect of reward and the net gain from free-riding needs to be reduced if there is a prospect of penalties. And we need to allow that actual social choices commonly involve some private as well as some social value. SA&R treats this in some detail, and some aspects of this will come into the discussion in Chapter 5.

But Rule 2 says that an individual response to social concerns will also depend on how a person's sacrifice of private for social values compares with what others are doing. Complementary to that, when almost everyone is cooperating, it will usually be less risky to sacrifice some self-interest in favor of social cooperation than when few are cooperating, and also with usually better prospects.

Neither rule is novel. Their equivalents have a long history. With respect to Rule 2, for example, more than two centuries ago James Madison remarked (about federal arrangements): ". . . distrust of the voluntary compliance of each other may prevent compliance of any, although it should be the latent disposition of all" (Madison 1787, note 7). He would not have been puzzled by Rule 2 here. And although a skeptical reader need not accept the Darwinian argument as more than an "as if" story, I want to discourage that, since thinking about the Darwinian logic often proves to be useful in interpreting the rules.

The simplest specification of an equilibrium condition consistent with the two rules would be:

$$W = G'/S' \quad \text{(NSNX equilibrium)}$$

where $G'$ is the value to the group of a contribution to the group (as perceived by the individual facing the choice), $S'$ is the marginal private cost to the chooser, and $W$ is the weight (never less than 1) given to self-interest.[3] The value ratio (G'/S') can be thought of as especially tied to the "neither selfish" aspect of NSNX, and the weight to self-interest (W) especially tied to the "nor exploited" aspect of NSNX. This oversimplifies, but perhaps helpfully as a first cut. NSNX emerges from the interaction between the two rules, not as "NS" from G'/S' and "NX" from W. But thinking in terms of this simplification may make it easier to see why, if W < G'/S' then an increased allocation to group-interest, which increases W (from Rule 2) and ordinarily also decreases G'/S', moves the player towards NSNX equilibrium, though perhaps over- or under-shooting the equilibrium. And the converse for W > G'/S'. From choices observed in entirely unrelated settings (not involving the group-interested versus self-interested tension), we might expect that the guiding ratio of group-interested versus self-interested spending will be some "local" (context-dependent) sense of that rather than a global accounting. So when we consider revealed behavior in Public Goods games (Chapter 8), it is not surprising that we see "neither selfish nor exploited" responses heavily influenced by what has been happening in the game at hand, though that must be wholly inconse-quential in terms of some global accounting.

This NSNX equilibrium looks like, but (as already stressed in the Introduc-tion) *is not*, the usual first-order condition for optimizing a utility function. The topic is treated in detail in Chapter 2, where I show (among other things) that *any* model which stays with the fundamental commitment of the standard theory to maximizing a single utility function implies empirically implausible behavior.

The "see-saw" figures here illustrate this equilibrium notion. Consider a sample citizen (call her Ellie), and simplify a bit by considering dollars the only resource at issue. From Rules 1 and 2, Ellie will allocate the dollar to social G-spending if W < G'/S', and to self-interested S-spending if W > G'/S'. Figure 1.1 provides a picture of the intuition that drives the model (the balancing of the conflicting pressures from the *value ratio* in Rule 1 and the *participation ratio* (how much the agent is already spending socially), which governs W in Rule 2. Alternatively, we could write the same equi-librium condition as WS' = G', which prompts allocation to self-interest if WS' > G', to group-interest if W < G'/S', and is just in balance (in equi-librium, and so Ellie is not moved to shift the balance of her spending one way or the other) when WS' = G'. Later on, we will have occasion to use that form in working out the notion of social equilibrium mentioned in the Introduction, to complement the notion of individual equilibrium being developed here.

In Figure 1.1, the value ratio (G'/S') is on the right of the see-saw, and the

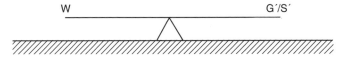

*Figure 1.1* Balancing W against G'/S' in NSNX equilibrium.

weight to self-interest (W) is on the left. As Ellie uses resources, or as things happen to Ellie or to Ellie's society, G′, S′, and W all may change. If the see-saw is tilted down to the left, then she would allocate a marginal dollar to self-interested S-spending; if tilted down to the right, she would allocate it to group-interested G-spending. She is in equilibrium, feels she has done her fair share, feels neither selfish nor exploited when the see-saw is in balance. SA&R shows how the account generalizes to treat various complications, especially the common (in fact usual) situation in which a choice provides some value to both group- and self-interest.

A second see-saw diagram shows the dynamics of the situation in an alternative way. Here (Figure 1.2) S′ is on the left, G′ on the right, and W is the fulcrum. As you will remember from playground days, the heavier person does not necessarily tilt the see-saw her way. How the allocation goes depends on how far the fulcrum favors S′ over G′. The farther to the right the fulcrum is, the greater the leverage given to S′. Other things equal, if Ellie allocates the dollar to G-spending, that pushes W more to the right (Rule 2), increasing the leverage of S-spending in allocating the next dollar.

*Figure 1.2* Another way to think of balancing to reach NSNX equilibrium

Or, finally, Figure 1.3 shows (on the vertical axis) scales for both the weight (W) and the value ratio (G′/S′). On the horizontal axis, we have the fraction of Ellie's resources that have been allocated to G-spending (*g*). At the origin Ellie is spending nothing at all socially, and at the right she is spending 100 percent of her resources socially with nothing left for her private interest. So Figure 1.3 plots both W and G′/S′ curves on the vertical axis against the fraction of resources allocated to group-interest on the horizontal axis, where the

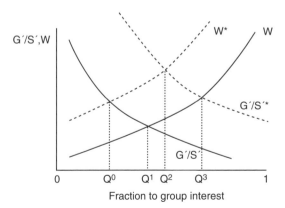

*Figure 1.3* NSNX equilibrium comparative statics.

horizontal axis runs from 0 (complete free-riding) to 1 (everything is spent for the group). This yields a diagram that looks like the familiar supply/demand diagram. In that market equilibrium diagram, the axis that carries two variables (quantity supplied, quantity demanded) is the horizontal axis. Supply increases with increasing price, demand decreases, yielding the market equilibrium at their intersection. The NSNX rules yield an equilibrium at the intersection of the W and G′/S′ curves. But here the intersection defines an individual equilibrium between self- and group-interested spending, not the social equilibrium of market prices and quantities of a supply/demand diagram. The Schelling diagram mentioned in the Introduction does define a social equilibrium, but as you will see (Chapter 5), it does not look anything like a supply/demand diagram.

I've drawn the figure with two W-curves (solid W and dashed W*) and two value ratio curves (G′/S′ and G′/S′*). But for now consider only the solid curves.

The G′/S′ curve illustrates the usual situation, where diminishing marginal utility holds. For that usual case, G′/S′ must decline as we move to the right in the diagram. For Ellie is spending less on herself, so S′ (marginal utility of private spending) must be increasing as the contributing individual digs deeper and deeper into what otherwise would be her private spending. And although in the usual situation, G′ will also be decreasing, so long as Ellie is one person in a large society, G′ would not ordinarily be noticeably affected by her own spending. For any single person, G′ is ordinarily perceptibly constant, as in the standard supply/demand diagram, the spending of an ordinary individual by itself has no perceptible effect, though the equilibrium is determined by the aggregate effect of all. But with G′ perceptibly constant and S′ increasing as Ellie's allocation moves to the right (towards more for the group, hence a smaller share of spending on herself), the marginal disutility of giving up even more is increasing. The value ratio (G′/S′) consequently will be getting smaller. The curve for G′/S′ will be downward-sloping, as shown.

The rising curve measures W, since by definition W increases as $g$ increases. We can set W = 1 when the share of Ellie's resources allocated to G-spending is zero (so the participation ratio is zero). But from Rule 2, other things equal, W must increase as the participation ratio increases. Equilibrium in the figure occurs at $Q_1$, where W = G′/S′.

Suppose Ellie found herself at $Q_2$, where for the solid curves W > G′/S′. She is out of equilibrium on the high side of social spending. By shifting resources to favor her private interests (moving left in the figure, allocating less to G-spending), she could restore herself to equilibrium. For moving her left in the figure would decrease W and increase G′/S′, reaching equilibrium at $Q_1$.

Alternatively, suppose Ellie's wealth increases. Then for any fraction of wealth allocated to G-spending, the amount left for S-spending will be larger, hence S′ smaller. As before, if Ellie is an ordinary citizen in a large society, G′ would still be sensibly constant. So with G′ unchanged but S′ decreased at any share allocated to G, the increase in Ellie's wealth would shift her value ratio upward (say to the dashed G′/S′ curve in Figure 1.3), and her equilibrium allocation would therefore shift to the right, to $Q_3$, where the shifted value ratio (G′/S′) intersects the solid W-curve. So an almost immediate implication of NSNX is that, other things equal, as wealth increases, the share of resources spent on what an individual takes to be group-interested spending increases. Social spending turns out to be a superior good, though in another sense Ellie is also becoming more selfish: the weight to self-interest, W, is increasing.

The two W-curves (solid, dashed) and similarly two G′/S′ curves allow some simple comparative statics. Of the two W curves, the solid is more favorable to contributing. Since it is lower, it intersects a downward-sloping G′/S′ curve further to the right, where social spending is higher. Both W-curves (repeating that point) necessarily slope up, since W is the weight to self-interest (always ≥ 1), which (from Rule 2) increases as the fraction committed to social spending (on the horizontal axis) increases.

Parallel to the remark about the two W-curves, of the two G′/S′ curves shown, the dashed is more favorable to social spending, in the way required by Rule 1.

Suppose again that Ellie's initial situation is that of the solid curves, with equilibrium at $Q_1$. Now her neighbor's house catches fire. On any plausible account, the value of acting socially must increase when your neighbor's house catches fire. G′ must increase. The W-curve is not shifted, but the G′/S′ curve must shift up (G′ is bigger but S′ is the same), here to the dashed G′/S′* curve, implying the shift to the less self-interested equilibrium at $Q_3$.

Alternatively, suppose an actor is initially on the solid W-curve as before, but on the dashed G′/S′ curve. He is in equilibrium at $Q_2$. But now his own house catches fire, which suddenly increases the marginal value of effort in his own self-interest, shifting the G′/S′ curve down, say to the solid G′/S′ curve, with an obviously reasonable implication for how the actor will react. Perhaps he was going to take his Boy Scout troop on a hike. But now he finds he has better things to do with his time.

Next, suppose again the initial situation finds an agent facing the dashed W and solid G′/S′ curves, with equilibrium $Q_0$. But now his country is attacked. G′ shifts abruptly up, moving the actor to G′/S′* with equilibrium $Q_2$. But this "social emergency" shift in marginal value of social effort affects everyone, and the W-curve depends on how much social effort this actor is making relative to what others are doing, and now others are doing more. Consequently, the whole W-curve must shift down, say to the solid W-curve, resulting in the even higher equilibrium allocation at $Q_3$.

Simple illustrations of this sort show the basic NSNX mechanics, and the results are easy to interpret as the kind of behavior we would expect if the model is workable. For more extended discussion, see SA&R.

And what if there is a hurricane or earthquake so all houses, including your own, are simultaneously damaged? Now the model is ambiguous. G′ is sharply increased. But since your own situation is worse, S′ is also increased. What happens to G′/S′ will be contingent on the local circumstances. And in fact communities are observed to react in dichotomous ways to such calamities. People do not go on behaving (with respect to competing social and private concerns) as if nothing had happened. Many but not all communities exhibit an exceptional amount of cohesion and commitment to common interests. On the eve of the first game of a World Series, an earthquake near San Francisco forced cancellation of the game (in Oakland, across the bay). Around the same time, a hurricane struck Charleston, SC. News coverage showed people in San Francisco rushing into the streets to help their neighbors, and people in Charleston rushing into the streets to loot. The dichotomous response to such calamities is very well documented (as in Quarantelli and Dynes 1977). So that the model does not give a general result on this point is not a weakness. The it-could-go-either-way implication corresponds to what we see in the world.

As already mentioned, a later chapter works out an extension to dynamic social situations by way of Schelling's ingenious diagrams. This yields a set of tipping-point processes which find ready application to real cases as varied as evolution of novel social norms, establishment of new religions, ethnic conflict, and political revolutions. The could-go-either-way implication for a situation of general calamity also applies to all these cases, as indeed it must unless there is something wrong with the model.

Another way to sharpen intuitions about how NSNX works is to consider what happens, on the logic of the model, under odd conditions. It sometimes happens that $G'$ is negative. Under circumstances in which it is awkward or risky to say "no," a person might be asked to contribute to a political campaign that she privately intends to vote against. Or with vastly more severe consequences, she might be asked to collaborate with an occupying army she passionately hopes will be driven out. So she sees the social value of cooperation ($G'$) as certainly negative. But the net private cost ($S'$), considering adverse consequences that can be escaped by cooperating or a reward that might be obtained by cooperating, might make that less negative. It is then declining to cooperate, not cooperating, that accepts some positive cost. So although $S'$, like $G'$, is ordinarily positive (there is usually a social gain, as judged by the chooser, in cooperation, but a private cost), this can be reversed.

And sometimes there may be sufficient offsets to the direct cost of cooperation to make $S'$ negative when $G'$ is positive. You must contribute to what you regard as a good cause to attend a party. But if you are keen enough on the party, the price of contributing may be more than offset by what you would pay even if no cause you valued was to benefit. So here, the value ratio ($G'/S'$) in the NSNX equilibrium condition could be negative.

This yields three atypical cases ($G' < 0$ but $S' > 0$; $G' > 0$ but $S' < 0$; and $G' < 0$ and $S' < 0$). In each, either the value ratio is negative (because $G'$ or $S'$ but not both are negative), or the value ratio is positive in an unusual way (because both $G'$ and $S'$ are negative). But each implies easily interpreted and appropriate behavior. For either of the first two cases, $G'/S'$ is negative, hence less than W, since W by definition is $\geq 1$. So the chooser will allocate to self-interest. But for $G' < 0$, $S' > 0$, it makes sense that a chooser will not sacrifice privately to damage her sense of group-interest. And for $G' > 0$, $S' < 0$, a self-interested choice again makes sense, since now there is no conflict between choosing in self-interest and choosing in group-interest. Cooperation in this case has a negative cost: it is actually profitable. So NSNX equilibrium choices in both these cases are self-interested (since $W > G'/S'$), but in the first case, chooser does not cooperate, and in the second she does cooperate, in both cases as makes sense.

For the $G' < 0$ and $S' < 0$, for sufficiently small negative cost we would have $W < G'/S'$ (since for $S' = 0$, $G'/S'$ would be infinite, and for an arbitrarily small negative increment to $S'$, $G'/S'$ would still be greater than W). So up to some point (until $W = G'/S'$), the chooser will favor her sense of group-interest. She will not cooperate with an activity she sees as socially perverse, even though she could gain by doing so. But for sufficiently large negative $S'$, we must eventually reach $W > G'/S'$. Then the chooser will cooperate even though she recognizes that it is inconsistent with her sense of group-interest. If what made $S'$ sufficiently negative (what made the cost of cooperation negative) is a reward for cooperation, we could say she was bribed. If what made $S'$ sufficiently negative (what made the cost of cooperation negative) is avoiding a punishment by cooperation, we could say she was coerced.

But that overstates the case. We can observe, not often but unmistakably, that even the most severe cost to self-interest does not necessarily make cooperation the dominant choice. An exceptional chooser may see $G'$ as so extremely negative that cooperation would leave that chooser even further from NSNX equilibrium than would a choice that would avoid cooperation with what (to this chooser) is a highly perverse mode of cooperation. And we can recognize such extreme situations, most clearly for individuals who choose extreme suffering or death rather than cooperate with their captors. This becomes highly relevant when we come eventually to think about application of the argument to the challenging case of terrorism.

Since the S-function in the denominator of the value ratio ($G'/S'$) is just the self-interested utility function of standard theory, nothing needs to be said about it beyond stressing that point. The S-function is indeed strictly self-interested. All compromises of self-interest in favor of other-regarding motivation enter through the G-function as moderated by the weighting function, W.

The G-function needs to be explored, but its salient components are entirely unsurprising. There are three inputs: (1) We can look at the norms that rational individuals might adopt if they could mutually bind themselves. Most obviously, social preferences that would make everyone better off (pareto-improvements) must have positive value in the G-function. (2) But on many matters, multiple equilibria are available, so we would often need to observe revealed social preferences in the actor's society. And (3) path-dependence will certainly sometimes yield prevalent behavior that fits neither

(1) nor (2) but an acceptable explanation calling on path-dependence must offer a plausible story (or better, but it is not always even a possibility, actual historical evidence). Plausibility may lie in the eye of the beholder. But the qualification is not vacuous. If a phenomenon is seen widely across many cultures, it will not be easy to find a path-dependent explanation. And concerns that this is too loose (in particular, any looser than allowances taken as reasonable within standard theory for path-dependent oddities in the realm of markets and auctions) only arise if turning to path-dependence to account for anomalies turns out to be common. But it doesn't.

So the G-function is not open-ended. Individuals will vary in what they see as social value, but (without embarrassing the theory) not in ways that would easily violate both (1) and (2). And falling back to (3) is something that is inevitable even if the theory as I am presenting it should be perfect, but it is something that cannot happen very often. The complications should not require any more generous allowance for context-dependence and path-dependence than would be taken as unobjectionable in the case of mainstream economic theory applied to core domains such as markets and auctions. To give a couple of presumably uncontroversial examples: no one feels bound by social norms against deception while playing poker; and while tipping is common to many societies, the appropriate amount and occasion for tips emerges in a path-dependent way that leads to different expectations in different societies. I will say a bit about both examples in Chapter 3 (on norms) as well as about some odder cases, such as why in no society is it treated as reasonable for people to sell their place in line to a late arrival. If you have plenty of money and I have plenty of time, we may find a deal to make. But we know it is not really the way people are expected to behave, and we will keep it out of sight. On the other hand, people are almost always more tolerant of ticket scalping, which is close to the same thing. So can we say why that might be so? I will try to do that in Chapter 3.

What do criteria (1) and (2) of the previous paragraphs imply? At the most general level, they imply that NSNX agents will value *efficiency* and *equity* and (of course) *self-interest*: *efficiency* because, other things equal, more resources for group-interest are better than less; *equity* because a sense of unfairness in distribution of resources could only harm group solidarity and increase resource-dissipating conflict; and attention to *self-interest* follows directly from the basic Darwinian argument.

Here are some rules of thumb that develop these ideas, always subject to the *other things equal* proviso.

A.  A bigger pie for the group is better than a smaller (which just restates the bare efficiency principle).
B.  Equally deserving members of the group ought to get equal slices (since nothing could be as fair). This leaves a lot of context-dependent and path-dependent room for interpretation of "equally deserving," but not unlimited room since interpretations are constrained by criterion (2).

C. Diminishing marginal utility implies that the value of helping a member increases as that member is worse off than others in the group.

Criteria (1) and (2) also imply that norms of fairness and reciprocity will be positive values in the NSNX G-function. But just how they operate in practice here (or, equally, within a more standard model where fairness or reciprocity might be arguments in the individual utility function) is not implicit in the theory, especially allowing for cognitive complications, which might be severe, as will be grossly apparent in some of the experimental data we will take up in later chapters.

Allowing for complications (like the possibility of overshooting, of gestalt shifts, and others) a prediction could be only that the tendency (with $W < G'/S'$) will be to allocate more to social values, or in a comparative statics inference across situations, give as much or more as in the comparison situation. But as will be seen, comparative statics is sufficient to yield many predictions with bite.

To conclude this introductory sketch of the model, here are some simple illustrations of the NSNX logic. Each deals with some familiar puzzles for economists.

Suppose you are in a restaurant in a distant city and the people you are with are trying to figure out why they will tip even though they happen to be people who tell each other they know it is irrational to tip in such a situation. But if normal motivation is NSNX, then there is no puzzle here. A waiter's tip is part of, indeed most of, his compensation. Everyone knows that. So not leaving a tip, even though it is legal not to leave a tip, is unfair, and everyone knows that. A society in which people feel free to abuse elementary standards of fairness would not be a nice place to live, so there is special social value (elevated $G'$) to resources used for an appropriate tip relative to just giving some of your money to a stranger. Since leaving the usual tip is virtually universal, W will be low: a person who doesn't will feel selfish, and a person who does will not feel exploited. And a tip, being a tip, is not a great compromise with self-interest, so $S'$ will not be high. But as will be discussed in Chapter 3, this equilibrium would be under stress when many people – restaurants seem to always judge *six* as where "many" begins – share a common check, and voluntary tipping comes under stress.

Or consider the puzzle of repeated games of Prisoner's Dilemma. Suppose there will be 100 plays, with a payoff of $100 for each play when both cooperate; $0 for both defecting; and $110 for a defector against a cooperator, with $1 for the cooperator. On a backward induction argument, perfectly rational players would defect every time, and end up winning nothing, since they would realize that at play 100, with no future opportunity to be punished, each will defect. But since defection is certain at play 100, there is no reason to cooperate at play 99. And so on. But two naive players would be likely to win $10,000 each. Bringing this puzzle to wide attention half a century ago, Luce and Raiffa (1957) allowed that rationality here leads to a recommendation that would be stupid, but they were not able to explain exactly why. The favored explanation (of why a rational person could cooperate, contingent on the other player also cooperating, at least up until some point near the end) is that it is not certain that the other player will be rational (Krebs *et al.* 1982). This "trembling hand" account provides a rather shaky foundation for a model of rational choice. It implies that the more confident players are that they are playing with someone competent, the less money they will make. This seems neither reasonable nor true. That the trembling hand account has become the standard explanation reveals how difficult it is within the standard account to avoid a pragmatically intolerable inference (that the rational play is to defect at move 1).

In terms of NSNX, the dilemma does not arise. The backward induction that creates the dilemma has each actor seeing it as obviously rational to prefer $110 for himself and $1 for the other player to $100 for each, even if they had cooperated fully for the first 99 plays. That each player has just won $9,900 by cooperating on the previous 99 plays is irrelevant. But one of the things that generates a sense of group loyalty (borrowing a bit from a cognitive discussion to come) is working together on a project – especially working together against a common adversary, though that frequently important aspect is irrelevant here. If NSNX is right, players who have been enjoying enormous success from cooperation will not be indifferent to the other player's situation.

By now they are partners in a very successful enterprise, and it would seem quite bizarre if either was seriously tempted to want to end by defecting since he had no further use for his reputation for cooperating. Perceived G′ would be high relative to a game played only once; and with both players far ahead of their starting point, perceived S′ (the cost of cooperation relative to the gains in hand from cooperation) would be low. And W would be low. Neither player is doing a bit more than everyone else is doing. Cooperation would be likely to feel easily more comfortable (closer to equilibrium) than defecting. And supposing the contrary to be sufficiently certain to warrant defecting on move 1 would seem quite idiotic, with no trembling hand needed. It is failure to cooperate that would be a puzzle, which indeed sometimes occurs in experiments with this game. We will see later other examples of failures of cooperation under conditions where cooperation should not be very difficult. That poses a puzzle for NSNX, with interesting consequences. But nothing as fragile as the trembling hand is needed to manage the difficulties.

Finally, consider a more elaborate situation which has been the focus of recent discussion in the *American Economic Review*. The "traveler's dilemma" (Basu 1994) engages two players who must (without communication) choose a number between 180 and 300. Each will get a payoff equal to the lower number chosen, but unless both make the same choice the payoffs are adjusted to punish the player who bids more and reward the player who bids less. Some amount – call it R – will be taken from the payoff of the higher chooser and given to the lower. So this is a mixed motive game akin to the

Prisoner's Dilemma. And again on the standard theory, a backward induction argument yields as the unique Nash equilibrium that no matter how small R might be, both players should choose 180.[4] So again, completely rational play, on the standard account, yields each player the lowest possible payoff. Basu observed that this hardly makes sense in terms of how people would plausibly behave when R is small.

Subsequent discussion has tried to resolve this difficulty and other apparent departures from strict rational choice by a process (QRE: see McKelvey and Palfrey 1995) which turns on each player calculating optimal responses on the assumption that other players are *not* making optimal responses. So there is a bootstrapping effect in which everyone assumes that everyone else is vulnerable to error (akin to the "trembling hand") on their primary response in a simple situation, calculates a sophisticated response and then trembles away from it.

But convolutions of that sort would not be needed if players behave as NSNX would require. With small R, the potential gain to both self and group of choosing high is large and the risk of exploitation is low, but the converse when R is large. So while standard theory predicts 180 as the equilibrium choice whatever the value of R, with NSNX "neither selfish nor exploited" motivation, for sufficiently low R both players become likely to choose high. Both numerator and denominator of the NSNX equilibrium condition (W = G'/S') move interactively in favor of the socially better choice in a comparative statics assessment of G'/S' for R = 180 versus R = 5. Where it is an embarrassment for standard theory that players choose high for R = 5 but low for R = 180, the same result is just what must be expected if NSNX is right. Goeree and Holt (2001) ran trials with R = 180 and R = 5, finding that the very high penalty indeed yielded a modal response of 180, but R = 5 produced a modal response of 300, with a bit more than two-thirds of all responses at 300 or 299.

On the other hand, puzzles like the three reviewed here do not provide a sufficient argument for taking NSNX seriously. NSNX easily handles them. But so would some other model that broadens the strictly self-interested motivation of the standard theory to allow for other-regarding motivation. In general, if we are focused on some particular case, or some restricted range of cases, it will always be possible to define a less radical departure from received theory than NSNX that will do whatever is needed to handle what is on the table. Postulate a propensity to value reciprocity, for example, and either puzzle just discussed has a solution without any departure from standard theory as drastic as the dual-utilities of NSNX. So if there is a case to be made for NSNX, it has to turn on how this theory is able to handle the full range of other-regarding choice we can observe *better* than a more conventional alternative.

## Appendix: Similarities and contrasts

A few comments on a particularly prominent review of models that allow for motivation beyond self-interest (Fehr and Fischbacher 2003) may be useful, noticing both some points where NSNX coincides with and where it contrasts with this survey and interpretation of experimental work.

As already discussed, we certainly must expect that pareto-improving choices would be favored in a NSNX world: obviously so given a neutral effect on self-interest (on the S-function), and significantly so even when there is a cost to self-interest. And we should expect that pareto-damaging choices would be discouraged. Both points follow from the earlier discussion of the G-function: clearly, rational actors explicitly agreeing on norms to guide a group would agree on these. Although we can find what seem to be pareto-damaging norms (potlatches, and a few other cases), these are certainly odd, as their notoriety attests.

Positive reciprocity, which allows a society gains from trade which transaction costs would otherwise render infeasible, should certainly be favored. Further, criteria (1) and (2) from the earlier discussion require that this extend to a *strong* form of reciprocity, where a socially motivated choice helps someone (possibly a stranger) who is never likely to be in a position to repay the choice, but in a context where prevailing norms warrant anticipation that on another occasion, were the situation reversed, someone would return the help. And we would expect negative reciprocity also to be evident but less marked. The social value of punishing those who fail to follow social rules (second-order norms) has often been noticed in discussion of rational norms. But for norms of punishment the possibility of errors is more serious (perhaps there was a misunderstanding, perhaps there were extenuating circumstances), and if that might be so, there is an enhanced possibility that the punishment will turn out to be socially perverse, or that it will turn out to have unexpected costs to the punisher. Risk aversion would play a role here as well. For positive reciprocity, uncertainty about possible secondary effects is essentially all on the upside: good behavior might have been noticed beyond what the actor expected. But for negative reciprocity, there is a clear downside risk as well: socially motivated punishment might be seen by some (and not only the target) as unreasonable or mean or badly judged. Overall, negative reciprocity ought to be less well marked than positive reciprocity.

Finally, on two other possibilities often discussed in the recent literature, a propensity toward allocating marginal resources to favor equality across equally deserving people ought to be clear, but not ordinarily a propensity toward harming those well-off merely to move toward equality (difference aversion). For the former favors helping those most in need, which would ordinarily be pareto-improving in utility, but the latter will be pareto-damaging.

Fehr and Fischbacher do not explicitly comment on the last of these points. The experimental evidence is mixed (see the discussion in Charness and

Rabin 2002). But as in a NSNX world, they find clear and persistent evidence for strong positive reciprocity, and somewhat weaker effects for negative reciprocity. This in fact is sometimes grossly defied in experiments, with the just-mentioned Charness and Rabin paper a striking example. Experiments which seem to defy reciprocity norms need an explanation given the Fehr and Fischbacher survey, and for our purpose they especially need an explanation consistent with NSNX. I will take up the really striking example provided by Charness and Rabin in Chapter 9.

Fehr and Fischbacher stress the potential of a minority of free-riders to, over time, lead to the disintegration of cooperation when no opportunity for rewards or punishment is available, and they see strong evidence that the ability of others to reward cooperation or punish free-riding can sustain coopera-tion (as in the lessened sharing propensity in dictator as against ultimatum games).

On the most fundamental points, NSNX is consistent with the Fehr and Fischbacher reading, and both also are largely consistent with what shrewd observers have noticed over the centuries (as in the Madison quote earlier). For example, the drop in sharing which Fehr and Fischbacher note (but not nearly to zero) between the ultimatum and dictator games necessarily holds under NSNX. For in "ultimatum" the net cost of sharing is *less* (relative to "dictator") due to the risk that what the chooser keeps she might not actually get. In other words, for any given level of sharing, $S'$ adjusted for risk is smaller in "ultimatum" than in "dictator," where there is no risk. But $G'$ is not smaller. Hence in terms of the NSNX diagram (Figure 1.1) the $G'/S'$ curve is shifted up in "ultimatum" relative to "dictator." And to the extent that a player's expectation of what others – including the very recipient in this choice! – would give in this situation is (correctly, after all) higher for "ulti-matum" than for "dictator," then from Rule 2 the W-curve would be shifted down. So the situation would be parallel to the "wartime" illustration in the comparative statics exercise earlier, with the clear effect on propensity to give that Fehr and Fischbacher observe.

Fehr and Fischbacher see the theory and evidence they review as suggest-ing "that a combination of altruistic and selfish concerns" is what motivates choice; "if this argument is correct, we should also observe that altruistic acts become less frequent as their cost increases" (Fehr and Fischbacher 2003: 788) as is transparently correct if the pair of NSNX rules and the equilibrium they define are sound.

But on two points there is some contrast between the NSNX and Fehr–Fischbacher views. The first concerns the important role given to contrasting "types" in the Fehr–Fischbacher account and in many other economic models; the second concerns the role of gene-culture interactions.

On the NSNX account, pathological cases aside, there is only one "type." Players may vary a great deal, contingent on individual differences, on con-ditioned expectations of how others will play, on (perhaps subtle and unintended) differential reading of contextual cues, and more. But in terms of NSNX, there is no division between selfish types who cooperate only if severely enough threatened with punishment, and cooperative types who are willing to bear costs to punish free-riders. All players are NSNX players. This claim has consequences, and those immediately at hand seem to me to favor it. For example, as will be seen in Chapter 8, there are very large differences in the frequency of complete free-riding, contingent on game parameters, even when players are randomly drawn from a common pool. This makes sense in terms of NSNX, but hard to explain on a notion of fixed types. A more familiar kind of evidence is the powerful effect of communication in these games. This usually yields a huge increase in cooperation, which makes sense in terms of NSNX, where the usual decline of cooperation over a sequence of rounds is substantially due to coordination problems: players who want to be neither selfish nor exploited face difficulties in feeling confident about how far others are playing the same game they are. But it may be hard to make sense of this powerful effect of "cheap talk" if there are fixed selfish and altruistic types. We will see (in Chapter 9) a striking example of how far from what might be expected from stable types experimental evidence sometimes reveals.

On the gene-culture point, Fehr and Fischbacher argue that Darwinian influences alone cannot account for socially motivated departures from self-interest. But on the NSNX argument these are deeply entrenched human propensities that surely are influenced by gene-culture interactions but do not fundamentally depend on that. Indeed, how could we otherwise explain why the propensities Fehr and Fischbacher report are found in *all* cultures for which solid documentation is available? One possibility is that what we see may be a result not of group selection as usually thought of, but of higher-order selection at the species level. Of the several (or perhaps even many) proto-human species in the past several million years, one turned out to dominate all others. But since the advantages of cooperation are vast for a species able to communicate and improvise, a species which was genetically bound to a socially motivated component of behavior would have an enormous advantage over sibling species for which the inevitable and persistent within-group competition favoring self-interest could swamp the between-group social advantage. The cross-group migration that makes it difficult to model Darwinian social motivation would be absent when it is migration across species that would be needed.

# 2  Dual-utilities

The NSNX dual-utility structure requires a substantive defense, since why bother (as stressed at the end of Chapter 1) unless it performs *better* than a model that does not require it. But before taking that up, consider some concrete situations which have nothing to do with the NSNX proposal, but which exhibit just the structure that appears in NSNX.

Suppose a real person (call her Ellie) was asked to organize a reception for her school's major contributors. Among other things, she decided to spend $500 on floral arrangements: which she knew was in fact a rather modest amount for the occasion. What would Ellie say if we asked what the floral arrangements were worth to her, and claimed that Ellie would be irrational to allocate that $500 unless the value to her (allowing of course for her altruistic interest in the organization) is at least $500? Her reaction would surely be that the $500 reflects her view of how some money entrusted to her to be spent for the organization could best be spent. It is what (she judges) the spending is worth to the organization, which will routinely be far more than she sees it as worth to herself, even allowing for her altruistic interest in the organization.

For Ellie and the flowers, however, Ellie is morally (and legally . . . she could be sent to jail!) bound to treat the $500 as the organization's money, not her own, so the example doesn't show that a person must ordinarily have the divided preferences required by the dual-utilities model. That empirical claim is not seriously tested by the flowers example. Rather, the example only illustrates how the standard tradeoff argument might be misleading if preferences, in fact, have the dual character I've sketched. For NSNX, resources allocated to G-spending are used to obtain social benefits, and it would be odd to try to think of them as fungible with private value to the individual. If we put the question only in private terms, we shouldn't be surprised to get an answer that understates the actual willingness to spend resources dedicated to social spending.

But consider a country that wishes to impose restraints on overseas investment. Whether that is a good idea or not is beside the point here. In fact, many governments have done it. So it can happen. And suppose that to allocate the quota of exportable capital, the country adopts a rule that, other things equal, makes overseas investment by a firm easier to the extent that the investment would yield a higher rate of return than investment at home. Call this Rule A. Rule A seems reasonable, but the essential point here is just that obviously a government might adopt such a rule.

Yet for political or equity reasons, the country also wishes to avoid allocating all the overseas investment it judges tolerable to one or a few firms that happen to face the most favorable opportunities at the moment. So a second principle is adopted (call it Rule B) that says that, other things equal, the more a firm has already been allowed to invest overseas, the more difficult it ought to be for it to export even more capital.

And if you compare Rules A and B here with NSNX efficiency and NSNX equity Rules 1 and 2 in Chapter 1, you will see that the parallel is exact. The $G'$ and $S'$ of the dual-utilities set-up would here be reinterpreted as rate of return on overseas and domestic investment, respectively. The weighting function can take a mathematically identical form $[W = f(g/s), W' > 0]$, but now $g$ and $s$ are, respectively, a firm's overseas and domestic investment, rather than on individual's social and private spending. The equilibrium condition is the same for both cases $[W = G'/S']$, and with trivial adjustments the whole discussion of the figures in Chapter 1 then carries over into this mainstream economics example.

For this case, although the mathematical set-up comes out identical to that of the dual-utilities model, we are unlikely to think of the firm as having dual preferences. Each firm would ordinarily prefer to be free to invest wherever it wants. We would interpret each firm's choices as maximizing subject to a government-imposed constraint. So here the same formal structure proposed to account for individual choice has a perfectly conventional interpretation. No economist would see anything bizarre in the situation, or suppose that the way to deal with the problem would be to reformulate the framework in terms of some overall, ultimate firm maximand, within which the analogues of $G'$ and $S'$ (here, they would be rate of return on overseas versus domestic investment) were subsumed. Although an individual firm would see the situation as maximizing subject to a constraint, in its observed behavior over time the firm would choose as if it held dual preferences.

And now carry this one step further. Situations could arise in which the dual structure is the actual preference structure of the firm. Suppose the firm wants to ward off pressure for government controls or unfavorable publicity. Then it could plausibly, that is, without condemning its management as unreasonable or irrational, indeed perhaps demonstrating the sophistication and prudence of management, choose to adopt an investment policy governed by Rules A and B. Now the dual-utilities balanced by the exact NSNX equilibrium condition captures the actual preference of the firm, though still there is no overall firm utility function, nor is any economic theorist likely to propose one. Analogously, a really zealous proponent of both evolutionary arguments and canonical notions of rational choice might even interpret the dual-utilities NSNX set-up as a pragmatic outcome like this economic example, arising *as if* from a calculated effort to produce a species capable of large-scale, open-ended cooperation, given the constraints on what is feasible for that metaphorical rational actor, Mother Nature.

Or consider another, entirely different, example with the same result, but now it will unambiguously involve the unconstrained preferences of a single individual. Suppose Ellie has two children, one of whom could gain more from her financial help than the other. This child (G) might be handicapped, so he needs more help; he might be exceptionally talented, so he can make better use of whatever help he gets; or as a struggling artist he might have much less income than his otherwise equally deserving businessman brother (S). Thinking of G's greater gain from her help, Ellie might wish to use almost all her spare resources to help G. However, Ellie also feels she ought to treat both children equally. She might resolve her difficulty by adopting versions of NSNX Rules 1 and 2 (or, equivalently, Rules A and B of the investment example): (1′) Other things equal, the larger the value to G of a marginal dollar compared to the value of that marginal dollar to S, the more likely the dollar should go to G. But (2′) other things equal, the more Ellie has already given to G than to S, the less likely it is that the next dollar will be spent to further help G.

We would once again get the mathematical structure of the dual-utilities model. Now $G'$ and $S'$ are the marginal values of dollars to help son G and son S, respectively; $g$ and $s$ are the amounts she has spent on G and S; and the weighting function, W, tells Ellie how big the marginal value ratio ($G'/S'$) has to be to warrant allocating still more to G over S. Once again, all the figures used in Chapter 1 to illustrate the NSNX equilibrium are readily reinterpreted to cover Ellie and her children.

And as with the firm's choices for the voluntary constraint version of the capital export example, there is no ambiguity about whether the structure represents the authentic preference structure of a single individual. Plainly it does. Some such structure no doubt captures the essentials of choice for many parents, and occasionally for some firms as well.

So however odd the dual-utility structure might seem as a model of individual choice, these examples show that formally equivalent analogues either easily could exist or in fact do exist in actual societies. They are not examples that look especially bizarre, or that look in any plausible sense irrational. When I label NSNX an extension of standard rational choice theory, that is more than just arbitrarily claiming access to the honorific label "rational." Unless you want to claim that Ellie and the business firm in my examples are behaving irrationally, then NSNX *is* an extension of rational choice theory to cover a crucial aspect of choice in important empirical contexts.

And to conclude with a particular simple application before proceeding to a more abstract and technical discussion of general cases, consider the long debate over why (or whether!) it is rational to vote in an election with many millions of voters. The exclamation is warranted. For not only would a large proportion of the population have to be considered irrational (and if irrational in this, why suppose they are rational on other issues routinely analyzed with rational choice apparatus), but since a propensity to vote increases with increasing education, it would be the most sophisticated segment of the population which is most likely to choose irrationally. Might there not be some flaw in this assessment?

But the expected value to self-interest of one vote could not amount to as much as a penny when that vote is one among many millions. Noticing the low payoff to self-interest yields the notorious "paradox of rational voting." But would allowing for social (not just self-interested) motivation resolve the paradox? If Ellie were voting out of social concern, she might reasonably see a large social gain (easily $1 billion or more) from the election of a particular presidential candidate. For $1 billion is a small number compared to the trillion-dollar federal budget a president shapes, smaller still compared to the GNP his policies influence, and trivial compared to the costs should a president blunder into a nuclear war.

Hence if Ellie were to attach a numerical value to the advantage to the country of electing what she judges to be the better president, that number could easily be in the billions. Ellie's one vote would provide only a tiny increment (one part in tens of millions) to the probability that Ellie's candidate actually wins. But since the social value is very large, the expected value of her vote can still be perfectly respectable (some tens of dollars) compared to the cost of voting.

So there seems to be no great puzzle about how to account for rational voting if Ellie were moved by social, not only by self-interested, motivation. Yet the puzzle returns when we carry the analysis one step further.

Suppose it were possible to show that Ellie doesn't attach a value of anything like $1 billion to the outcome? Then she could not be acting rationally (consistently) if she acted as if she did. There may be realistic levels of social valuation large enough to make a vote rational. But such values apparently aren't Ellie's values in the sense relevant for the standard sort of rational actor analysis. What counts for that purpose is the personal sacrifice Ellie would make to promote those values. If Ellie is guided by a single preference structure which incorporates her social as well as her private preferences (if she is guided by the single utility function of standard theory), what the presidential election is worth to Ellie is just what she would give up to secure the result she takes to be socially valuable.

So from that standard point of view, consider how much of a private reward Ellie would require to make her prefer an election outcome in which her presidential candidate loses. Before an election, we might ask Ellie how much money in her own pocket it would take to make her hope for the defeat of the candidate she favors. The dollar amounts you will find if you ask people about this will rarely exceed $10,000. And that is far too small to make Ellie's vote rational when discounted by any reasonable estimate of the effect of her vote on the election (Margolis 1977).

So, on this argument, if Ellie is rational, and if she reports she would begin to hope her candidate would lose if some rich rascal were to give her $10,000 in that event, then in terms of her preferences the election is worth no more than $10,000. The point is not that Ellie is insincere if she says that the social value is vastly larger than $10,000. But in terms of what that large social value is worth to Ellie – in terms of what Ellie would personally give up to obtain that large gain for society – the smaller number ($10,000, not $1 billion) is alone relevant. When that smaller number is discounted for the effect of one vote on the probable outcome, what is left of the value of Ellie's vote could hardly be enough to explain her bothering to vote. It would be a small fraction of a penny. But we are not surprised to find Ellie voting. And if we ask her whether she thinks the chance that she will be killed in an auto accident driving to the polls is as large as the chance that her single vote changes the election outcome, she will almost certainly allow that must be true. I give a detailed discussion in Chapter 7 of SA&R. But we are still not surprised to find Ellie voting. Similarly, my colleague Gary Becker assures me that he is both rational and votes. And, alas, I feel the same myself. So are we all (probably you too) deceiving ourselves?

But this argument I've just given does not work if the way human beings actually behave fits the NSNX dual-utilities model. Rather, I want to claim that this Ellie argument is just another of the empirically somehow-crazy inferences that can be deduced from the standard model when that model is used in the context of social choice.

In the standard model, a person maximizes utility by choosing an allocation such that the utility of the last dollar allocated to social utility just equals that of the last dollar allocated to private utility. Hence asking Ellie how much money in her own pocket it would take to get her to prefer the election outcome she thinks socially perverse would give us logically certain knowledge about the actual value *to Ellie* of the social gain she expects from electing one candidate over another. And that should guide her choice if Ellie is rational and the standard model correctly captures human preferences.

But in the dual-utilities model that logic does not hold. Equilibrium is determined by a condition that, however much it may look like a usual first-order equilibrium condition for maximizing utility, in fact works on an entirely different principle. Its roots lie in competing Darwinian pressures favoring group versus self-interested behavior. And resources won to the social side of the individual balance are not spent to satisfy Ellie's private preferences any more than the money she spends on flowers in the very first example of this chapter. Ellie privately might allow she couldn't resist (or at least suspects she couldn't resist) hoping for what she takes to be the socially perverse outcome if it would put $10,000 in her pocket. But she will not vote that way, since the voting comes from resources to satisfy her G-preferences, where $10,000 to Ellie does not begin to affect her judgment of which candidate would be better. The G-preference is about what would (in Ellie's judgment) be good for society, not about what would be good for Ellie. Ellie

counts in that G-function, for she is part of society, but in the G-function she counts for no more than other people like herself.

So in the dual-utilities context, the marginal allocation is not one that balances marginal returns to some hypothesized grand preference function across self-interested and group-interested spending opportunities. Instead, it is the allocation that brings the individual as close as feasible to a "fair-share" balance, feeling neither selfish nor exploited, between spending to satisfy private versus spending to satisfy social preferences. And resources allocated to G-spending of course are spent to maximize G-preferences.

So even if Ellie would truly give up no more than $10,000 to guarantee her presidential choice, she will also rationally treat the social value of that choice to be very much more than she personally is willing to pay. There are simply two distinct questions: (1) about Ellie's social judgment, and (2) about how large a share of her personal resources she would spend to support that judgment in a context where she has the power, if she is willing to make a large enough sacrifice, personally to determine the social outcome.

Suppose (as is reasonable) that Ellie in fact would ordinarily devote only a small share of her resources to social G-preferences. Even so, the cost of voting will be very small as a fraction of her total G-spending. How much of her personal resources she would sacrifice is irrelevant to the voting context. No choice remotely on that scale is at stake. In terms of the see-saw diagrams of Chapter 1, any shift in S' or G' or W contingent on whether or how Ellie votes would be very small.

The two questions – about Ellie's judgment of the social value, and about how much Ellie would personally sacrifice to gain that value – must be connected. But they are not the same question. To take the answer to the question about personal sacrifice as the answer to the question about Ellie's true assessment of the value of the election is not a necessary condition for rational choice. Rather, it's a mistake.

The NSNX rules require that as the price Ellie must pay for voting her social preference gets larger (hence the share of her resources required gets larger), her reluctance to sacrifice that much must grow, to the point at which she eventually takes the money offered for changing her vote. Somewhere between the amount she would pay out of pure self-interest (the S-value of the election) and the vastly larger social value (the G-value), she will feel that she personally is being asked to do too much.

A side point not really essential for the discussion here, but foreshadowing the importance of cognitive issues later on, is to notice that it would be embarrassing for the dual-utilities model if in fact a voter who feels strongly about a presidential election would actually prefer $10,000 in her own pocket to what she takes to be the clearly better social outcome. This could be tested only in a situation where Ellie believes the actual outcome somehow will really be determined by whatever she prefers. That would be hard to arrange! But some reasonable analog might be constructed in an experiment of the sort we will be examining in later chapters. If we found support for Ellie really being unwilling to accept a large but far from devastating cost in that case, that would be an embarrassment for NSNX.

However, from the actual evidence we have about what happens when people face choices between large private sacrifices and social gains they judge very important (behavior in time of war, for example), it is apparent that sacrifice of self-interest in such contexts frequently – even routinely, though not universally – is very much greater than we notice in everyday situations, and often far greater than the individuals themselves could anticipate.

In general, we make judgments by a process of anchor-and-adjust, starting from patterns of response that are already in our cognitive repertoire. But in the Ellie thought experiment, there is nothing familiar to anchor on which is anywhere near the hypothetical situation in which Ellie's vote decides a presidential election. So she can be expected to anchor unconsciously on something far removed (on a situation in which her choice does not decide for all of society), and the adjustment is then likely to fall far short. If we could actually put Ellie in the situation, she might be surprised at her willingness to spend for a social cause when her choice alone determines what happens.

More is at stake in this rationality of voting discussion than accounting for why a citizen might spend the modest resources (the bit of time) required to vote. How a person votes can't be plausibly assumed to be independent of why she is motivated to vote in the first place. So although the cost of voting is ordinarily very small for any individual, and far from enormous even for the whole electorate, the social consequences of how people vote are enormous. And the same pattern of argument can be extended to social choice generally. Your G-preferences might include a preference for helping me, but your sense of what would be good for me might be very different from my sense of that. I might be mightily pleased with my recent behavior, and you might think what I have earned is a good kick in the ass. But my sense of what is good for all of us is going to be compatible with my sense of what would be good for me, and the same for you.

Return now to the main point of this chapter. So long as you suspect that NSNX *can't* be right, you will not be very open to the possibility that it might be right. Suppose it just cannot make sense that agents do not have *a* set of preferences but two related but irreducible sets, with no overarching total preference which mediates whatever compromise might emerge. Then you would suppose NSNX can't be right. But the S-function is the usual self-interested utility function of standard theory, and the G-function is also familiar under the label of a Social Welfare Function (SWF), as in Harsanyi (1955). But Harsanyi's SWF (like Adam Smith's much earlier "higher self") invokes preferences for, so to speak, special occasions, when individuals rise above their everyday propensities. But the NSNX G-function is always in play. Choices may not show much effect from it in routine situations. But it is always there, while the Harsanyi or Adam Smith notion might be only what a person responds to when little or nothing is at stake for them personally. But since we can sometimes observe that choices that do not appear to be purely self-interested occur even at non-trivial private cost, surely we ought to be interested in how we might organize our understanding of what conditions evoke this higher self, and how it might interact with the self-interested economic man that we easily notice as we go through a day.

Nevertheless, what might seem the right way to proceed with the NSNX equilibrium ($W = G'/S'$) is to set $U' = WS' - G'$, expecting to integrate that expression to find a NSNX total utility function. But there is no such function. Total utility so defined would be path-dependent, with no stable value, hence not a viable mathematical function. And on the Darwinian logic that underpins the model, there is no reason to suppose that any such function would exist. Logically, given the Darwinian foundation, this is not a problem at all. For all the actual work in a standard choice model is done by the equilibrium condition obtained by differentiating the utility function and setting it equal to zero. So to pick an especially simple example where there is no ambiguity, if $U = 8x - x^2$, where x is the agent's location in some space, then (taking the derivative) agent will want to be where $0 = 8 - 2x$, hence at $x = 4$. When $x = 4$, utility $= 16$, and agent is in equilibrium. She cannot do better. Making x either larger or smaller will lower utility. That is what we want to know. Given her utility function and her menu of feasible choices, what would she do?

In contrast, for the dual-utilities model the equilibrium condition appeals directly to the pair of Darwinian rules developed in Chapter 1 (or also to the exact analogs of those rules illustrated in this chapter with the capital export and Ellie's children examples). Even if a sufficiently complicated mathematical function could be devised with the property that, when differentiated, it approximates $W = G'/S'$ as its first-order condition, it would be only a mathematical freak, having no useful role to play in the logic of the model.

Someone well accustomed to working with the standard model will be tempted to suppose that, unless the theory is just wrong, there really ought to be a single maximand hidden somewhere but I have missed it. The dual-utilities argument will then look like a proof that $2 + 2 = 5$: you know there is something wrong with it, even if you haven't put your finger on just where the error lies. But if you think about the capital export example and the Ellie example, you have a way to test that intuition (however clear it may seem) against actual cases which have a structure identical to NSNX. It is unlikely, I think, that you will end up feeling it would be sensible to demand some total utility function for either case.

I conclude on a polemical note. We now have half a century of post-Downs (1957) efforts to account for voting within the standard model of rational choice. The record is coming to look like one of the psychologists' *Umwelt* experiments. Put a starving chicken, then a starving dog, on one side of a wide glass wall, with food visible on the other side. Each animal starts out by trying to bang through the wall. Eventually the dog seems to catch on and, after some searching, finds its way around the wall. The unfortunate chicken starves to death, banging its head against the wall. To me it seems about time to consider alternatives to the standard model. But I observe that the chicken is still hard at work.

I don't want to claim that giving up the notion of rational choice as maximizing *a* utility function ought to be pain-free for someone with a deep commitment to the standard view. NSNX agents do not meet the fundamental criterion of standard rational choice, which is consistency. If they did, it would be possible to design a single utility function that encompasses the dual utilities. NSNX agents meet the usual criterion with respect to how they allocate *within* the S-function and also with respect to how they allocate within the G-function, both of which are built on the standard axioms of rational choice. And allocating *between* the S- and G-functions, NSNX agents follow a different sort of consistency criterion in choosing to move as close as they can to NSNX equilibrium. It is certainly not clear how they are deficient in rational choice understood as reasonable choice, as can be seen in the examples earlier in this chapter. And in a wide range of contexts (a profit-maximizing firm, for example) perfectly standard analysis remains appropriate since allocating between self-interested and social values is ordinarily not at issue. The stark "money pump" argument used to show the necessity of consistency for rational choice in standard treatments would not work with NSNX agents. Also, in a variety of familiar cases, revealed behavior is consistent with NSNX not with the standard theory, as with the paradox of voting discussed in this chapter and the several puzzles discussed at the end of Chapter 1. Indeed, if there is a consequential example of a case where standard utility maximizing conflicts with NSNX and revealed behavior favors the standard theory, I am not aware of it. But if such a case were conjectured, that woud be entirely welcome, since we could look for what happens and see which model works better.

# 3 Equilibrium norms

In one sense a norm is a statistical notion. It is just whatever people on average do. In another sense, a norm is what people ought to do. We can imagine a community in which people commonly drink and drive, but if we ask about it, everyone says it's wrong to drink and drive and they wish the police were stricter so they wouldn't do it. So here, the statistical norm would be entirely different from the "normative" norm. Is there, nevertheless, a connection between the two senses, and if so what does it involve? An inquiry of this sort might reveal nothing more in the case of an interesting word like "love" or "rationality" or "norm" than in the case of an ordinary word, like "foot" or "bank." For either sort of word, we will find comparable examples of how the meanings of words evolve by extension and analogy, or merely by migration from another language. However, for norms, if NSNX is sound, it becomes tautological that something deeper is involved. After some definitions and preliminary remarks, I want to consider how NSNX implies a way of thinking about norms, in which there is an essential connection between various senses of the term, and this connection yields insights into how norms change over time, why some behavior comes to be covered by formal regulations backed by police power while other activities are left to voluntary compliance, and so on.

Norms understood as what usually happens characteristically fall short of norms understood as what people in the society think would be socially best (what a good person would want to do if he could rise above his self-interest). But norms as what usually happens also sometimes go well beyond what a person guided only by self-interest would do. In terms of NSNX, we would look for some "neither selfish nor exploited" balance between these two competing tendencies (what would be best for me, what would be best for all of us). And since norms in either the statistical or normative sense are intrinsically social, they must emerge from a social process, as prices in a market emerge from a social process. In either case, we get a social equilibrium emerging from the interaction of many individual choices. For prices, this emerges from an interaction among many choices about what to buy and what to sell. For NSNX and norms, the social outcome must grow from individual choices seeking a "neither selfish nor exploited" individual equilibrium. We want to say something about how that might work.

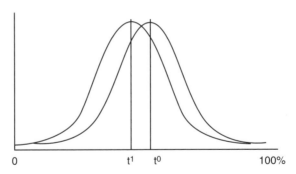

0                                     t¹   t⁰                    100%

*Figure 3.1* Norms of behavior.

The horizontal axis shows prevalence of compliance with a norm about how people ought to behave. At the origin, compliance is 0 (the norm is universally ignored); on the far right, compliance is perfect. The vertical axis is the probability density. The curve to the right shows the state of things at time $t^0$, with the *statistical* norm for this (*normative*) norm at its mean. But if behavior was strictly self-interested at the next time period ($t^1$), the norm will have declined, say to the curve on the left, since from self-interest alone, each person will want to do no more than necessary to avoid sanctions. Everyone would want to be in the lower half of the right-hand curve: not conspicuously below the mean, but certainly not intentionally above the mean. But if everyone chooses that way then at each period compliance must slide to the left. Indeed, before long, compliance must slide all the way to the left, and we face the puzzle of how compliance could ever have reached the level of the right-hand curve to begin with. So supposing that self-interest can account for norms leads to a contradiction. Somehow, apparently, people are not behaving out of strict self-interest.

There are statistical norms for everything – bowling scores, rainfall, and suchlike, but we are interested in norms of good behavior. We can notice that statistical norms (with respect to good behavior) always look like a compromise between purely self-interested and purely social motivation. And if the NSNX rules govern that compromise, what we see should be the current state of a process in which individuals move toward some balance (equilibrium) in their behavior, which at the social level aggregates to some social equilibrium characteristic of the society as a whole. We want to consider in more detail how that might work.

The categories we need are:

1   *Aspirational norms*, like the Golden Rule.
2   *Pragmatic norms*, which people are expected by their fellows to obey, and which elicit disapproval (or worse) if a person is seen to violate them. This is the primary sense of the word in ordinary usage, and the sense we are principally concerned to explicate here.
3   *Statistical norms*, or what typically is done.
4   *Personal norms*, by which a person judges his or her own behavior, and which may vary (in any particular case) toward more strictness or toward more laxity from the same person's sense of pragmatic norms.

Norms in the second and third senses (pragmatic and statistical) are irreducibly social. They are characteristics of a society, not of any particular individual. Norms in the personal sense are intrinsically attached to some individual, though always under the influence of social interactions. And a connection between personal and pragmatic norms is inevitable, since the principal factor in what makes one individual see the behavior of another as a violation of social norms must be just that if she were in the same situation she expects she would have behaved better. Someone living in the community would acquire a sense of prevailing *pragmatic norms* which as a first cut might be taken as reflecting the mean, or typical, personal norms in the community.

A clue to the character of pragmatic norms is that, as the reader will be aware, no one will scowl at you for driving 10 miles over the speed limit when everyone else is doing the same. But the corresponding norm in the statistical sense could be either higher or lower, contingent on the intensity of highway patrols and the scale of fines. So by itself, compliance tells us nothing one way or the other about the *normative* status of a rule. But scowls, sneers, and the like tell a lot.

Strictly speaking, *aspirational norms* could also be individual, like personal norms: they represent an individual's judgment about ideal behavior. But they are ordinarily widely shared across a society and, indeed, for the most important of such norms (favoring honesty, fairness, and so on), they are even widely shared across cultures, as indeed must be the case by the criteria for NSNX social preferences in Chapter 1. A common remark is that all the major religions have similar moral codes. And although there are certainly major idiosyncrasies across cultures, for many aspirational norms, any society that lacked them would not be a nice place to live, nor a place where cooperative behavior would be sufficiently common to make it a prosperous place to live. On the other hand, plausibly universal norms (like treating equally deserving cases equally, keeping promises, and so on) will be sufficiently general to inevitably run into conflict with other such norms (as when keeping a promise turns out to conflict with treating equally deserving cases equally). Shweder *et al.* (1997) provides an excellent discussion.

Even an outsider might give a good account of aspirational, pragmatic, and statistical norms familiar to everyone within a community, even though he has never met any individual member (like a scholar who can use documents, myths, and literature to give a good account of norms in some long-vanished society). But even a member of the community, entirely familiar with prevailing aspirational, pragmatic, and statistical norms, might personally regard some of those norms as irrational or perverse. So there can be personal norms which depart a long way from norms in the social sense.

The personal norms of individuals within the community would also be subject to some "local" variation, in the sense that even under fixed external conditions (the environment is not in any way unusual) no one exactly lives up to (or down to) his own standards all the time. In particular, an individual who feels at the moment out of NSNX equilibrium will be influenced by that, inclined to do more than usual if the disequilibrium is on the selfish side, and the converse if on the exploited side.

To see how equilibrium norms (in the various senses of "norms" now at hand) might evolve, start by noticing that although we today live in communities that readily sanction self-interested behavior, people nevertheless act as if there were limits to what is *appropriately* self-interested. It is alright to be self-interested but not to be selfish. On the other hand, there is also a sense that a person can go far enough in the opposite direction to be exploited. It is right to be socially concerned; but it is not wrong to avoid being exploited, even for a good cause.

So there will be the tension NSNX expects between the propensity not to be selfish and the propensity not to be exploited. Ordinarily, social motivation is less conspicuous than self-interested motivation. But the extent of social motivation in ordinary life may be much larger than is commonly recognized, masked in part by the empirical fact that socially motivated choices rarely are absolutely in conflict with private (self-interested) motivation. Even the very best thing socially is rarely an unqualifiedly bad thing privately. And as developed in some detail in SA&R (Chapter 5) NSNX choices will commonly be neither the best thing socially nor the best thing for self-interest, but a choice that combines elements of both. Consequently, it is often easy to see behavior in terms of self-interest even when very little analysis would be needed to show that the strictly selfish gain is too small to make that plausibly rational. Further, behavior that is social with respect to some community may be perverse, and hence be seen as selfish, from the perspective of a wider community, or a different community. Two people may both think: in my group, people respect norms; in your group, people don't know how to behave decently.

But if humans have any social motivation at all (they do not want to be merely selfish), they will have some rational concern about the right way (the socially sensible way) to behave in various circumstances, just as their rational self-interest assures that they will be concerned about the right way (the financially sensible way) to behave in buying a car. On the other hand, if people are also concerned not to be exploited (not to sacrifice much more of private interests for social values than others in similar situations), then they must be concerned about what other people in fact usually do. The first leads to concern about what behavior is most socially valuable (*aspirational* norms); the second leads to *personal* norms and then to an influence on personal norms of how the rest of the community is behaving (*statistical* norms), all of which in the aggregate will shape the pragmatic norms of the community.

From the discussion of Chapters 1 and 2, this should have a familiar ring. If we wanted to make all this more explicit, give it foundations, we would be led back to the formal NSNX set-up already introduced, as indeed will be done in Chapter 4. Overall, we can expect to see the emergence of personal norms which qualify aspirational norms in the light of statistical norms, but where there obviously will be linkage between the aggregate of personal norms and the pragmatic norms, which in turn will influence statistical norms.

We want a sense of how these relationships might represent an equilibrium outcome (or a tendency toward equilibrium) among the various contending influences at work, most obviously, the selfish versus exploited tension fundamental to NSNX. As in standard economic theory, an individual seeks an equilibrium allocation of her own resources. Here, the individual exhibits personal norms that reflect a balance between the competing motives of some degree of social motivation (which favors doing what seems socially best) as against self-interest (which favors ignoring norms except to the extent that either risk of punishment is sufficient to deter violations or promise of reward sufficient to elicit compliance).

For markets, social equilibria (prices and quantities) emerge which are characteristics of the overall situation, not of any individual. But the prices that emerge are contingent on individual equilibria governing how budgets are spread across the menu of goods on offer, which in turn are influenced by the social equilibrium. So an individual's equilibrium allocation of spending between, say, bread and beer is contingent on the relative prices, but the prices – in particular, whether an equilibrium has been reached and which direction things will move if not – are contingent on the aggregate of individual allocations. Personal norms are individual equilibria; pragmatic and statistical norms are social equilibria (like market prices and supply), with interactions between individual and social equilibria analogous to the connection between individual preferences and social outcomes in the context of markets.

Norms appear in several varieties, some of which may look hard to assimilate to a view which stresses their essential role as promoters of social value. But the most promising tactic from the NSNX perspective is to take the essential role as fundamental and then see how far the apparently non-functional or only weakly functional sorts of norms can be dealt with (on one side) as derivative of the primary function, or (an alternative also consistent with NSNX) as peripheral in some reasonably transparent way to the main argument. In other words, atypical norms might be side-effects which do not conflict with NSNX but are not directly part of a NSNX story. Or they might be actual anomalies for NSNX but sufficiently inconsequential that social motivation within the community would not be mobilized against them. Or they might be actual anomalies for NSNX that indeed challenge the theory. But before considering such complications, I want to work through what I take to be the core case.

From the discussion of criteria and derived rules of thumb in Chapter 1, we can specify some aspirational norms that ought to be present in every society, since they are so obviously helpful to promoting social life. Salient examples would be norms favoring telling the truth, keeping promises, and helping those in need, but all focused on members of the community. But from the Darwinian perspective, what counts as my group will be people who emit cues (or are embedded in a context containing cues) that look familiar to me from contexts of social cooperation. In a world of cheap global communications, there is ever more opportunity for "like me" cues to develop, but also more opportunity for adversarial cues. Whether "like me" or "not like me" cues are more salient is likely to depend especially on whether in my relation to this person, cooperative or adversarial relations are more salient.

Since it is socially valuable for members of a community to act in accord with aspirational norms, it must be socially valuable to encourage that. In terms of the selfish/exploited tension, people who are too selfish deserve to be punished. Similarly, people conspicuously useful to the community ought to be rewarded. So we should expect "second-order" norms, promoting adherence to primary norms and favoring individuals who seem particularly valuable to the community. But like effort devoted to first-order norms, enforcement and rewarding would be subject to NSNX Rules 1 and 2. So the issues affecting second-order norms are just those involved in assessing primary norms. Questions will turn on how reliably a person is able to recognize behavior that ought to be punished and on the burden accepted in being a punisher. That would conspicuously include the risk of retribution from the target or even from non-targets who, perhaps mistakenly, perhaps not, see the punishment as excessive or unwarranted, so that pragmatic norms for second-order compliance would be less stringent relative to first-order norms since they entail this additional element of cost.

But contrary examples can be found when failing to punish involves a *sacrifice* of self-interest because "everyone knows" what is going on, who is being sanctioned, and what is expected to happen (as with shunning). And indeed, it is just here that it is easiest to find striking cases of personal norms that diverge from pragmatic norms in a community, where individuals at real risk of penalties on themselves may nevertheless help a person the community treats as morally undeserving.

As the NSNX rules make explicit, merely allowing for social motivation does not make self-interest incentives irrelevant. The private incentive comes from the risk that failure to comply will be punished, or that visible compliance will be rewarded. The social component comes from the perceived social value of complying. It is the two together that must be sufficient to overcome the temptation to neglect a norm. Second-order norms say to punish someone seen to unreasonably violate a first-order norm. But what defines an "unreasonable" violation? There must be a standard of how good social behavior has to be to be good enough. In the language I am using, there must be pragmatic norms (good-enough-to-pass norms) as well as aspirational norms. In contrast to accounts in which individuals are dichotomized into stable "types" (norm-followers and norm-neglecters), it would be an embarrassment for NSNX to find many people who either always or never obey norms when evasion would serve their self-interest.

And a final point setting up a NSNX account of what governs the social equilibrium: it would also be an embarrassment for NSNX to find people to be simply incapable of violating a pragmatic norm without some easily detected revelation of their misbehavior (like a person who cannot tell a lie without blushing). Rather, on the account here, such involuntary self-revelation would be tied to violation of the individual's *personal* norms. For if violation of a norm would move a person closer to individual equilibrium than compliance (on this occasion), then it would be implausible (that is, it would make no sense in terms of the Darwinian argument) to suppose that such a person would turn out to be unable to conceal that non-compliance. Empirically, substantial ability and also some propensity to engage in conscious deception on what seems to the person appropriate occasions seems to be universal. Good poker players are not necessarily persons of bad character, though the heart of the game is deception. So on the argument here and also, I think, on the evidence, we would not suppose that compliance turns on something like a simple inability to avoid looking guilty other than when the agent actually *feels* guilty (is ashamed of himself, is plagued by conscience, and so on). Exactly what the notion of personal norms is intended to capture is the standards which a person ordinarily feels guilty not to meet.

However, since pragmatic norms represent qualified, or less demanding, versions of aspirational norms, they intrinsically allow variability in terms of their range of applicability and their relative weight as against other aspirational norms and also in terms of private costs that are appropriately borne in order to comply. Aspirational norms take the form of explicit principles not made relative to the details of circumstance, as in the Ten Commandments. But their associated pragmatic norms depend a good deal on the tacit knowledge of members of a community to recognize how much less demanding a pragmatic norm is relative to its aspirational counterpart. Boundaries are intrinsically fuzzy. So we need to account for how standards so hard to make explicit can actually be effective. Certainly, cases occur that leave us unsure, or where we see it one way on one occasion but might see it otherwise on a different occasion, or where someone whose judgment is ordinarily very similar to our own sees the situation one way and we see it another. Still, even though the boundary is fuzzy, we apparently by and large learn to recognize behavior that looks acceptable even though that often falls far short of idealized aspirations. But that is not the only important example of such coordination. The most important example is the ability of members of a community to coordinate on their understanding of *language*, down to subtleties of context-dependent nuance.

A further issue turns on questions of enforceability, as discussed a few paragraphs back in the context of second-order norms. Compliance, again, will reflect some mix of self-interest and social motivation, where the self-interest arises because there are often rewards to being perceived as a complier or penalties to the opposite. The most obvious point is that as behavior becomes more anonymous, the effectiveness of given penalties against non-compliance must fall, and rewards become impractical. Whether you have bothered to vote is usually essentially anonymous. On the other hand, sometimes identifying non-compliers is easy, such as a norm in my summer neighborhood – understood by all but, so far as I can recall, never explicitly expressed – that people shouldn't use lawnmowers before ten o'clock on weekend mornings. If someone did not comply, everyone in the neighborhood would notice.

A subtler but essential enforceability issue arises out of ambiguity. Even if behavior is easily observable, are violations well defined? In fact, they are never exactly so, though for some things (the "only after ten" lawnmower norm) the range of ambiguity may be inconsequential. Often, though, that is not so. There are various good reasons for non-compliance: "nobody told me," "I had a prior obligation," "I was sick," and so on, where for the most part each good reason might also be a bad reason – malingering in one form or another. Further, often norms overlap. It is bad to lie and also bad to harm other people. But sometimes the main effect of telling the truth would be to harm some innocent person. Many less familiar examples could be given. So no one could possibly obey all norms all the time. There will often be some zone of ambiguity about which norm takes precedence when there is conflict. All of this is essential to understanding pragmatic norms.

We ordinarily see a spectrum, not a dichotomy, between compliance and non-compliance. Academics feel an obligation to do some reviewing for journals and presses, but how much is enough? So, aside from anonymity (the chance that no one will notice whether you have complied), there are at least the further possibilities of (1) partial compliance and (2) good, or at least not obviously bad, excuses for non-compliance, which blur the line between socially acceptable and socially perverse behavior. Plainly, all these allow the gradual erosion of a norm. A slide to the left in the compliance curve of Figure 3.1 is easy to understand. But if you look around, for nearly all pragmatic norms, that is not happening. Far more typically, the situation seems stable. Norms are not noticeably either eroding or growing stronger, as the nuanced meaning of language is mostly stable, though also always in some flux. For norms, somehow we also have a mostly stable equilibrium.

To sum up, an empirically plausible view of what norms and compliance are really like will note, not neglect, that individuals are not dichotomously either norm-followers or norm-neglecters; that norms themselves – in particular, pragmatic norms – are not dichotomously either applicable or non-applicable to a particular case, but sometimes are only more or less, or marginally or debatably, applicable; and that (in addition) compliance itself allows a good deal of ambiguity, as we have just been noticing. Finally, of course, there is the fundamental ambiguity which was the starting point for the whole discussion: a pragmatic norm is intrinsically fuzzy, since it reflects how people in general are expected to behave as judged by individuals "like me" in the society. Although people within a community have a good sense of prevailing pragmatic norms, there is no great scoreboard in the sky – no heavenly normative Dow Jones – that makes available to everyone the *exact* state of norms of the moment.

Indeed, new norms or stricter versions of old norms occasionally appear, as with various environmental norms which have taken hold in recent years. Apparently, people can sometimes be moved to do more as well as be tempted to do less than the prevailing pragmatic norm requires, so that uncoerced compliance does not monotonically slide downhill. In particular, apparently an equilibrium can arise in which the tendency to erosion of a norm is offset by the tendency to comply more than minimally. We want to get a sense of the connection between the individual equilibrium (setting *personal* norms) and the social equilibrium (governing *pragmatic* and *statistical* norms). *Aspirational* norms, being absolute in character, are not part of the equilibrium process, but being socially shaped they will eventually re-enter the argument.

Consider some just-recognized environmental threat, such that once a person becomes aware of this threat, the intuition is reliably that people ought to work to contain it. But at the moment we are choosing to inquire, people are only beginning to be aware of the situation. Yet some individuals would be more sensitive to this issue (for example, because they believe they know more or because they care more) and some will be in a position to support the norm at relatively low personal cost (for example, because they are richer). Or both. So through an effect on $G'$, or on $S'$, or both, the value ratio $(G'/S')$ for these people will be atypically large. From NSNX Rule 1, we would expect such people to be first to feel some personal responsibility for recognizing the norm even though others are doing nothing. Since others are doing nothing, there is as yet no pragmatic norm. But for some people there is a personal norm to do something about neglect of a socially important opportunity. From Rule 2, we expect compliance to be limited even for individuals who recognize that "something ought to be done" unless opportunities for a favorable impact from their effort are exceptional, or if they happen to be in a position to do something at exceptionally low private cost – the conditions which would make the value ratio in Rule 1 exceptionally high.

But once some compliance is occurring, others – not quite such good prospects as the initial recruits – can more easily be drawn into some degree of compliance, which would (via Rule 2) tend to increase compliance by those already engaged. So there would be positive feedback until some equilibrium level of compliance was reached within the community, balanced between the perceived importance of the issue and the increasing cost of stricter behavior. Eventually people with an unusually high personal norm might start to relax that norm, noticing that they are taking more trouble on this matter than others, though probably not to match the statistical norm (the value ratio would remain higher for them than for most others). We could sketch an analogous story starting from the other extreme, where a once significant pragmatic norm (e.g. against premarital sex) has begun to deteriorate. What had been a well-entrenched aspirational norm (it is intrinsically wrong), weakens as a pragmatic norm (sanctions become less serious), and eventually doubt that it is even a proper aspirational norm become more widespread. The Pill sharply reduced possible costs, which increased the net cost of compliance ($S'$ = appeal of sex, forgone by abstention, net of risk of sex).

Since $S'$ is net cost to self-interest of behavior constrained by following the norm, $S'$ is smaller (other things equal) when risk is higher. So as risk (of unintended pregnancy) decreases, $S'$ (net cost of constraining behavior) increases. Temptation is not as much offset by risk. And this also undermines a source of perceived social value of the norm (its importance for avoiding unintended pregnancies). Hence $G'$ decreases. So $G'/S'$ is weakened top and bottom (the numerator is smaller, the denominator larger) with a now-familiar consequence for sustaining a norm against premarital sex. As $G'/S'$ decreases, the personal norm weakens, which in the aggregate weakens the pragmatic norm, which always fell well short of the aspirational norm. And when social consequences of that do not seem terrible, confidence that $G'$ is high for conforming to this norm then begins to erode, as once occurred for women's not smoking and is now far along in the other direction for anyone's smoking. In large parts of society, what had been an unquestioned aspirational norm and a much weaker but very significant pragmatic norm turns into a matter of individual choice, like deciding whether or not to take up skiing. Chapter 4 provides a more formal diagrammatic treatment of the process, applicable to norms and many other matters.

But now another puzzle appears, which happens to have the same form as a famous problem for Darwin, though here the solution must be entirely different. Near the outset I mentioned that pragmatic norms might be taken to be just the typical or average value of personal norms in the community. So in analogy to the blending inheritance problem that beleaguered Darwin, why should not any favorable social mutation be swamped – have no perceivable effect – on prevailing pragmatic norms, or at least such a minute effect that any significant shift in norms would take place far too slowly to account for what we see?

Darwin allowed he could not answer what seemed to him the reasonable criticism that the accumulation of slight advantages faced the difficulty that a slight advantage would be diluted to an insignificant advantage as it was transmitted to successive generations. He could only point to evidence that somehow the difficulty was overcome. Mendel's papers were available by then, but like everyone else Darwin did not recognize their significance. But Mendelian (particulate, not averaged) inheritance resolved the paradox. Here the correction comes from noticing that, although the foundation of the underlying NSNX rules is Darwinian, the cultural evolution at issue now is intrinsically Lamarckian, in the rough sense that variation is not random but very often directed (at least some actors are looking for an opening in a certain direction), and can be easily contagious across persons and groups in ways that would make no sense at all in a Darwinian context (since these agents can talk to each other about what would be good and indeed broadcast ideas to others they will never meet). Or using Dawkins' fashionable label, we can notice that memes very commonly propagate and evolve through mechanisms not available to genes.

We have (at least) three possible complementary contributors:

1   As with the smoking example, or as with the emergence of new fashions or new ideas of all kinds, this is likely to be a segmented process, with certain sections of a society first affected (and, of course, with the possibility that the novelty never becomes general and perhaps eventually disappears within the lead segment itself). The internal structure (classes, sects, and so on) of a society may not only play a role in the initiation of a change in prevailing norms but occasionally the converse may also be true. Individuals or small groups attracted early to a novelty may now see something more in common with others so moved, so that adherence to certain norms – even more than with adherence to novel social knowledge of other sorts – may either reinforce or undermine existing social alliances or create new ones.
2   Either in the society at large, or within a lead segment, there may be opportunities for magnifying the effect on general perceptions of the choices of a few people. In contemporary societies, this possibility has become especially striking through the influence of television, and more recently accentuated by the availability of imagery through the internet.
3   Finally, there is the quite different kind of possibility of political action (aiming at a centralized decision of some sort) to push the new norm. This last possibility leads us to the issue of norms supported by rules, meaning here explicit obligations imposed by some authority with penalties for non-compliance. In terms of the NSNX formalism, sanctions (and also rewards) *decrease* the opportunity cost of complying with a norm.

So, underlying and interacting with all these possibilities, a norm of the sort that concerns us here (which requires some subordination of self-interest to group-interest) will usually appear in gradually stronger form, not all at once, starting from shifts in personal norms, as described earlier, with the mechanisms just mentioned making it sometimes possible for modest shifts in personal norms to accumulate rather than dissipate.

All these possibilities can be seen more clearly in the diagrammatic analysis coming in Chapter 4.

Suppose that in terms of self-interest, I would prefer ignoring a norm on this occasion even if I were paid $10 to comply. I might (or might not, contingent on my personal norm and other NSNX-relevant context) ignore the norm. But now I learn that there will be a $100 fine if my non-compliance is noticed, with a 1 percent chance that it will be noticed. You still can't say whether I will comply. If I were risk-neutral, the threat would be $1, but if I were risk-averse the perceived deterrence might be equivalent to quite a bit more. But even without risk aversion, on general economic reasoning (not bound to

NSNX) you can only say I am more likely to comply than without the sanction. In terms of the NSNX formalism, $S'$ was at least \$10 without the threat. It now must be less (given the risk, I have to discount my gain from evasion – or, the same thing, decrease the opportunity cost of not evading), hence whatever $G'/S'$ was before, that ratio now must be larger, making me more likely to comply.

Out of such simple exercises, we could elaborate a discussion of principles that might govern – in fact do seem to govern – when and how far various norms are left to purely voluntary compliance (supported only by weak, informal sanctions like scowls) and how far norms are made formal rules backed by legal sanctions. If, for example, a norm seemed socially important ($G'$ is high) but also costly ($S'$ is high), compliance would tend to be low, but support for enforcement might be high. Each of us would be tempted to evade, but all of us agree we would be better off if all complied. But effective enforcement would increase compliance, which (by Rule 2, since W would increase) would increase willingness to comply, which would allow enforcement to be focused on the reduced numbers of offenders. We might reach a state where compliance was nearly universal and penalties rare, but the situation would deteriorate if penalties were rescinded as unnecessary.

Cases obviously could arise – empirically, we know they very often arise – in which a voluntary equilibrium would leave the society with statistical norms that fall far short of a good social outcome. We have the familiar free-rider dilemma, which is only qualified, not eliminated, by allowing for social as well as private motivation. Where anonymity and ambiguity are endemic, the same factors that keep the voluntary equilibrium too low will make the enforcement costs of securing compliance merely through coercion too high. No large society functions either way (only by voluntary compliance or always through coercion). There are no anarchic societies organized on any substantial scale. On the other hand, horrendous special cases aside, there is always a measure – usually a very substantial measure – of what can be called "incomplete coercion" or "partially voluntary compliance," as discussed in Levi (1988) and Margolis (1991).

From Rule 1, people will tend to comply with their own personal norms at some private cost, but the larger the private costs, other things being equal, the weaker those personal norms will be (the narrower the range of conditions will be in which the person behaves the way aspirational norms say a person should aspire to behave). But to the extent that failure to comply can be made costly, then the effective (net) private cost of compliance decreases. As has been noticed several times, the private gain from a violation is not the gain from evasion without qualification but only the gain after discounting for the risks of evasion. So, of course, the amount of social motivation required to secure any given level of compliance falls as the effectiveness of coercion increases.

What is not so obvious, but has now been inserted into the discussion, is that pragmatic norms, not merely statistical norms, may be strengthened by coercion. Under appropriate conditions, norms and rules can interact such that the norm becomes stronger, which makes the rule easier to enforce. The most important conditions are that both the nature of the coercion and the behavior mandated by the rule are seen as supporting aspirational norms. If so, the costs of policing (the costs of effectively imposing the rule) may decline over time – to some equilibrium level, not to zero – because pragmatic norms are becoming stronger.

As an example of the several ways in which that favorable interaction might occur, consider the case of socially useful behavior resisted simply out of the common tendency to feel uneasy with behavior that runs contrary to what we are accustomed to seeing. In a moment I will say something about this tendency to conform. The puzzle there is to see how mere conformity would fit into the general argument about compliance with norms. But that the propensity to conform exists is empirically obvious. Given that it exists, then simply making some novel behavior commonplace and familiar may be very important, even if at first compliance is mandated by a rule. The US civil rights legislation of the 1960s appears to be a case where enforced breaking of customary practices sharply accelerated an important shift in social norms.

The possibility of feedback between rules and norms (coercion and voluntary compliance), of which I have mentioned only the simplest mechanism, illustrates the complexity of a thorough analysis of equilibrium norms. We are trying to understand societies with complicated social structure, subgroups with subnorms, conflicting loyalties, and, of course, criminals and at least a scattering of psychotics. Yet the core process is not itself complicated, though even a reasonably simple core account will seem complicated until some familiarity with it is in hand.

Individual equilibrium with respect to personal norms, governed by NSNX Rules 1 and 2, should ordinarily lead to the appearance of (intrinsically social) pragmatic norms. But pragmatic norms tautologically cannot be so demanding that they fail to secure compliance across a group that a person holding a personal version of that norm sees as "people like me." Perceptions of social value will play a large role in the story (from Rule 1), as will perceptions of what others in the community are doing (from Rule 2). Overall, equilibrium norms will be socially important even when not backed by rules (enforcement). Norms weak enough to secure general compliance even without legal sanctions do not always mean norms too weak to be important. But (especially) when a socially adequate norm would involve large private costs, we expect to see norms bundled with rules (voluntary compliance bundled with coerced compliance).

I have been considering here only partial equilibrium at the individual level, taking commitment to the norm under discussion as independent of other social commitments by the individual. That is all right for this preliminary sketch. But there must be many circumstances where neglecting those interactions would be misleading. The aggregate burden on self-interest of complying with pragmatic norms that hold within the various groups that a person in some contexts sees as "people like me" must eventually have an effect on inclinations. The aggregate is not fixed. If everyone is doing more, everyone will feel more comfortable about doing more. But the expansion of commitment is not unlimited.

On the logic of the Darwinian argument, norms apply to dealings that affect others the person sees as part of her community or, with qualifications, to others who might have cooperative interactions with the community. So as suggested earlier, what is cognitively seen as the community is an important aspect of understanding norms, and a difficult one. It is consistent with the Darwinian argument and easily observed that for individuals living in large, complex societies, what is seen as the relevant community is context-dependent. The relevant community is sometimes seen as wider than would ordinarily be expected (extending far beyond the immediate community). But boundaries may also turn out to lie between classes or sects within what an outsider might consider one community. Two people who see themselves as part of a shared community in some context may see themselves as part of adversarial communities in another context, with consequences for which norms seem binding on their interactions.

As with scientific and historical, or any other, knowledge that reflects what people have learned on a wide scale (across the experience of many people), knowledge of norms will ordinarily have a dominant social component. For all but narrowly personal knowledge, the primary determinant of what a person feels he knows is simply what it seems that "everybody knows" in his society. In their most fundamental significance, aspirational norms are rules of thumb about what "everyone knows" would be socially best. Pragmatic norms are what "everyone knows" is socially acceptable.

Articulation of the social character of knowledge (of how it comes about that intuitions, habits of mind, and so on are coordinated so that "everyone knows" certain things) is not something to be pursued peculiarly in the context of norms. The paradigmatic context already mentioned is the evolution of language. To a remarkable degree the members of a language community fluently understand each other down to fine shades of meaning, though for words as well as norms, there is no billboard in the sky to account for that remarkable sharing of meaning. We have dictionaries, but it is unlikely that you will exactly catch the intended sense of a word by looking it up in a dictionary. And of course people with no access to dictionaries can communicate with subtle nuances of meaning anyway.

Empirically, no one can doubt that coordination of intuitions does occur. Somehow common notions, meanings, gestures, and so on become very well established. They are what "everyone knows" who is a member of the community and, indeed, not to know them, unless you are an outsider, is taken to be a sign of some mental affliction. The process of becoming established as something that "everyone knows" is not beyond analysis. But for the present purpose, it is sufficient to notice that such a process operates for many categories of social knowledge and there is no reason to suppose that something unique is required to account for the social character of knowledge of pragmatic norms. Rather, noticing that norms provide only one of many examples of the coordination of intuitions across a community lets us see that a secondary role of norms could arise as the coordinator of merely conventional social rules regarding dress, manners, gift giving, and so on.

The propensity for coordination that facilitates socially critical functions, such as communication, helps account for a taste for coordination even on matters, such as dress, where no essential functional point seems to be at stake. But even on such mere matters of convention, we should not neglect the extent to which such matters contribute to mutual identification of conformers as members of a community or at least have roots of that sort. The point is important, since we have already noticed that what an individual sees as the relevant community is often crucial to the judgment of what to do.

On the NSNX argument, the tendency to prefer anticipatable, familiar behavior makes some sense. For it is important for coordinating expectations, communication, and so on with respect to language and many other sorts of intuitions other than those about norms. Norms would not have a sharp boundary but, rather, would tend to carry over to other matters. Hence, we can get pragmatic norms without an immediate link to aspirational norms, where what makes the norm socially valued is not some functional contribution to social efficiency, but only the looser propensity to value social coordination for its own sake. We get a norm that amounts to: "unless you have good reason not to, do the usual thing, since it easily causes trouble when unexpected things start happening."

So we get norms that say you ought to dress in the usual way for various social occasions, with "the usual way" varying from context to context. The essential distinction to be made here is between customs (the usual thing) and norms (the right thing), which mostly but not always coincide. Tipping customs vary from context to context; the norm is to leave the customary tip. Similarly, if coordination is seen as usually beneficial, then the norm is to do the customary thing unless there is good reason not to, where the final proviso makes this a pragmatic rather than aspirational norm.

An instructive example is the possibility of selling a place in line. That is just not done, though there is no explicit rule against it. Few people have even thought about it. But there was no explicit rule about lawnmowing before ten o'clock in my summer neighborhood. It just is not done, and if you ask about it, people who have never given the matter a thought readily know that "everyone knows" it isn't done. What of people with a high value of time? Wouldn't it be efficient to let them trade money for time with people who have more time and less money? So does this not violate NSNX expectation that norms will favor social efficiency? And in a case like this, the equilibrium process I have been describing doesn't explain where the norm comes from. But for NSNX or any other plausible view, norms favor efficiency but also other social valuable concerns such as fairness and morale. So there are contexts where buying and selling is what we want to be able to do (conspicuously, a market), but ordinarily we do not want to be bothered with that. I mow my own lawn, but I would not welcome a neighbor inquiring how much I would want to mow his lawn, or take out his garbage, or rent my wife.

It is socially useful to have conventions (common understandings) of where naked cash is all that counts, and where offers to buy and sell are appropriate. And treating a place in line as a marketable commodity would create a socially wasteful occupation of standing in line with no intention of buying a ticket, but only intending to extract some money from someone who would be further back in the line. And why not when waiting in any other line, or sitting in a bus when there are standees, and endless further cases?

So it is not surprising that custom develops about when buying and selling is socially appropriate, supported by a general norm against upsetting social conventions without sufficient reason. Without spelling out more, it is easy enough to see that although a norm against a place in line being treated as for sale does not immediately look like the result of the equilibrium process I've sketched, it is easy enough to see just such an equilibrium process yielding social understanding of where the distinction might be that sets off contexts where offers to buy and sell are appropriate and where they aren't, with selling places in line clearly on the "not done" side of that line.

Another issue is that for the equilibrium process to work, an individual must be able to get some sense of the social value of compliance. The emergence of social knowledge must start with individual judgments. So how might a person get a sense of the social value of his individual behavior when he is only one of millions of people in a large society? But this is probably not so very different from the same issue for a member of a small hunter-gatherer band. For many social acts, even within a small community, involve effects too small to be individually perceptible, as, indeed, is also the case for many purely private acts. What is the effect of taking a vitamin pill today?

Such questions often yield confident intuitions if asked on a larger scale: is it worthwhile taking the vitamin pill in a habitual manner? If I am in a position to make that judgment, it is not surprising that my intuition is that it is worthwhile today, even though on any particular day (like today) the bother may be noticeable while the benefit from that day's effort is wholly imperceptible. Similarly, with social judgments it will often be easy enough to reach confident intuitions if the Kant-like question is of "what if everyone in my position did this?" For both the private and social judgments, "seeing" the question in terms of a larger-scale question, where personal experience and common knowledge within the society can be brought to bear, makes things far more manageable. Russell Hardin has pointed out to me that the problem is complicated by the possibility that what would be good if we all are doing it may be worthless if I alone am acting. And the converse case can also arise, where there would be no particular value in my acting if the rest of you are already doing your share, but if you are not, there may be some special social value in someone's taking the initiative. So the point of this paragraph is not the end of a discussion, but it is a significant start, and as much as needed for the discussion here. Return to the question of what defines a pragmatic norm, which is that violations arouse resentment in others. But how does a person judge whether another person's behavior warrants resentment?

In thinking of how to answer that question about pragmatic norms, which is essentially a question about what is ordinarily regarded as excessively self-ish behavior in the community, we can start by asking how a person recognizes when his own behavior would be too selfish. For the two questions (the first about the self, the second about others) may amount to much the same question. A person has a sense of what feels neither selfish nor exploited with respect to himself (personal norms), which yields intuitions about how another person ought to behave in terms of "how would I behave if I were in that situation?" This amounts to supposing that moral resentment remains quiet provided others behave about as well as we expect we would behave in that context. But we are offended to see others fail to do that. Pragmatic norms then emerge from the experience of individuals about what arouses resentment (provokes scowls, nasty remarks, and, occasionally, worse) in the many interactions a person encounters (not just those involving himself) in which people look with approval or disapproval on others' behavior. Empirically, that is a powerful influence on choice, commented on (for example) by Maynard Smith and by Robert Sugden (1988), by Jon Elster (1989), and in Chapter 8 of SA&R.

But there will also be "second-order scowls," where A is offended but B responds with a look that reflects a sense that A's scowl is unwarranted, and it is out of the aggregate of such interactions that a generally shared sense of the pragmatic norm emerges. So there is (of course) no place where you can look up what the pragmatic norm is in this situation. Rather, there is a social process out of which emerges a roughly shared sense of what looks like appropriate behavior, akin to the many other cases of shared social intuitions discussed earlier. In a completely homogeneous society, equilibrium *pragmatic* norms would straightforwardly determine how far *statistical* norms go beyond what is coerced. Even in large and complex societies, within a reason-ably homogeneous subgroup we should expect almost the same. In general, we can expect a strong propensity (shared with many other aspects of social knowledge) to follow the usual way of seeing things, though, as in the earlier discussion, individual variability is always present and critical in accounting for the possibility of changes in prevailing norms.

On this account, the effect that a mere glance of disapproval can have (even a waiter's imagined scowl on finding a stingy tip after you have left) should not be understood as a punishment effectively inflicted. If a person believed that a certain pragmatic norm was, in fact, socially perverse (as, for example, a white liberal in the old South or, even more obviously, a black activist there), scowls of disapproval would hardly be painful. But when a per-son's personal norms with respect to whatever is at issue are not radical or rebellious, then the person ordinarily wants to do the usual thing: it is ordinarily what leaves him comfortable (in individual equilibrium). Consequently, a person would be looking for indications of what people around him see as reasonable or unreasonable behavior. Hence, the latent function of the scowls is to signal to a target (and others) that the behavior does not appear good enough (or, in the opposite case, smiles function to signal that the behavior is to be admired). After all, what could any effect achieved by the scowl consist of unless the object of the scowl really wanted to behave in a way that would ordinarily avoid scowls?

But, as with many other issues touched on in this survey, the point is not that the deep question can be settled with a quick remark, but only to suggest how the NSNX point of view I have been sketching might be able to yield principled answers to a wide range of such puzzles.

# 4   The Schelling diagram

We are better off with a government that collects taxes and provides public services than with no government and no services. But individually I would be even better off if the government collected taxes from everyone else, but somehow neglected to collect from me. The overall level of public services would look the same whether I paid or not (provided the rest of you continue to pay), but what I could spend on myself would be noticeably larger. So why pay?

In terms of what is still standard economic theory, the answer is not so obvious as might first be supposed. Of course, I can get into serious trouble by not paying. Yet the tax system depends on a very significant measure of "voluntary compliance" (Roth *et al.* 1988). More broadly, no society could survive if its citizens violated its rules whenever a favorable opportunity arose: that is, whenever the risk of punishment was small enough to make the gamble tempting as a matter of narrow self-interest. On the other hand, beyond small communities, no society elicits such a high degree of voluntary compliance that it can get along without police and tax audits.

In general, understanding how societies function depends a great deal on how compliance with social rules is sustained and at what cost that compliance is secured. How that works will vary across sorts of rules and across conditions under which individuals might be tempted to violate the rules. Under some circumstances, as noticed earlier, normal levels of compliance can break down, although calamities (such as earthquakes) that produce social disorder in one community may elicit exceptionally cooperative behavior in another. There is always tension between forces favoring compliance with social norms and forces favoring narrowly self-interested behavior. Somehow a balance ordinarily prevails that allows a stable basis for social life. But that stability is not automatic or unchallengeable. Sometimes the balance is upset, and not always for the worse.

I want to construct an abstract model of how social coordination is usually sustained, but nevertheless is subject to change, and sometimes revolutionary change. In fact I will do that twice, interpreting the same geometry developed in the next section first (and briefly) in a way entirely independent of the NSNX argument, and then (in detail) in a way entirely contingent on that argument. The first reflects social contagion effects which parallel those of epidemics, and which have been brought to especially wide popular attention through Malcolm Gladwell's *The Tipping Point*. But the principal concern here is with parallel dynamics that arise out of the NSNX tension between self-interested and group-interested motivation. So there are parallel processes, one whose striking effects are too visible to be doubted (contagion of epidemics and social contagion of fads and fashions) and the other not so easily seen (NSNX effects on social coordination and cooperation), since unlike fashions, motivation is not something on easily visible display. NSNX effects are unimportant for understanding cycles of fads and fashion, but the reverse holds for the effects of social contagion in NSNX dynamics. I will return to that point at the end of the chapter.

The convenient way to start is again by way of an analog to the trading equilibrium of a market. In the market context, the equilibrium that emerges at the social level (conspicuously, prices) is contingent on and interacts with the equilibrium personal spending choices of individuals. So the analysis of market equilibrium is built up from the properties of equilibrium individual choices. We want to consider an analogous dual equilibrium, with individuals allocating between social and self-interested use of their resources, yielding a social equilibrium contingent on but also interacting with those individual allocations.

The analytical device I will use is derived from Schelling's (1978) simple but very rich diagrammatic treatment of the relation between individual and social choice, but with various changes to suit the purpose here.

## The basic diagram

Start from the standard model of strictly self-interested choice and from the stark case of strictly voluntary choices by these strictly self-interested individuals with respect to a pure public good.

The horizontal axis in Figure 4.1 measures the extent of cooperation on a scale that runs from 0 (no one is making the cooperative choice) to 1 (everyone is). And the vertical axis indexes value to the *marginal chooser* at the corresponding point on the horizontal axis, contingent on that chooser's choice between free-riding (the FR curve) and cooperation (the C curve). In contrast to Schelling's original, where the chooser is everywhere an average chooser, here the marginal chooser would ordinarily be a different individual at each point. So (again in contrast to Schelling) it would be meaningless to interpret the curves as showing social value. The value to the marginal chooser is arbitrary. What counts is only the difference ($\Delta$) between the FR and C curves. Ordinarily indeed, as the fraction cooperating grows, value to each chooser also grows (the more cooperation, the better off for everyone). But that is not necessarily the case. Though we are starting here from a positive case, cooperation with a corrupt regime might be making (almost) everybody worse off.

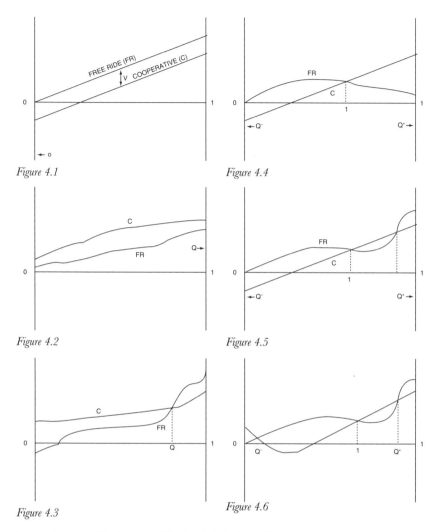

*Figure 4.1*

*Figure 4.2*

*Figure 4.3*

*Figure 4.4*

*Figure 4.5*

*Figure 4.6*

*Figures 4.1 to 4.6* Variations of the basic Schelling diagram.

The context could be one of seeking voluntary donations of money to some public function (say to a July 4 fireworks display or a political campaign), or seeking donations of time (say, to clean up a neighborhood), or sometimes the costs could be something subtler and in a dimension that involves neither time nor money, like offending old friends. The activity (taken to be beneficial, but contrary cases are also important) could be anything that provides benefits to everyone in a group, whether or not they have helped provide the benefits. The relevant community (conspicuously so in a political campaign) might be only a segment of what in another context the chooser would see as his community. On almost any such matter there will be some temptation to go along for the ride, letting other people handle the costs. But if we all do that, nothing gets done, and we are all worse off.

If the group is small, and everyone pretty well knows what everyone else is doing, then the free-rider temptation may be small even if choice is strictly voluntary and self-interested. But as numbers grow large, anonymity and other advantages to self-interest make free-riding an increasingly tempting option.

As with markets, the analytics are simplest for cases with large numbers of actors, no single one of whom alone has a perceptible effect on the social outcome. But whatever the size of population, if there are N choosers, each chooser represents a length 1/N of the total space between 0 and 1 on the horizontal axis of Figure 4.1. For large N, this width occupied by a single chooser would lie inside the thickness of any line we could draw. You can think of the lines in the figure as actually steps, but with the individual steps so tiny that it looks like just a smooth line.

Moving left to right in the Schelling diagrams as we will use them, we are always considering the person most easily tempted to change his or her choice (switch from cooperation to free-riding, or the reverse), given any particular level of cooperation by others. The propensity to cooperate = C – FR = $\Delta$ is a *net* value. If there are risks that go with free-riding or rewards to cooperation, that would shift the FR curve down or the C curve up. The advantage a chooser would gain by free-riding is worth less if free-riding entails a risk of punishment or forgoing a reward. So $\Delta$, if originally negative (favoring free-riding), may eventually reach 0 or change sign, prompting cooperation. We want to think about conditions under which that can happen, starting from the simplest possible case (Figure 4.1), where the FR curve is everywhere above the C curve, so $\Delta$ is everywhere negative.

In this large-N setting, individual choosers cannot see the individual social effect of their choice, as the same individuals cannot see the effect of their individual choices about private consumption on the prices and quantities of goods in the market. But an individual can extrapolate what that effect might be from a judgment of the aggregate effect of "people like me" making the choice. And the effect on self-interest will be directly perceptible to the marginal chooser (if he should choose to contribute), namely the cost of his contribution, though perhaps adjusted because he gained some reward available to contributors or avoided some risk of punishment for not cooperating. But for the strictly voluntary case of Figure 4.1, there is no prospect of reward or risk of punishment, so that the cooperate curve C is just the free-ride curve FR net of the cost of cooperating.

The only equilibrium in Figure 4.1 is at the extreme left. As we move across the horizontal axis, the marginal chooser is changing. But whatever we might assume about the prevailing level of cooperation, that marginal chooser always does better to free-ride. Wherever we started, consequently, the prevailing level would move a bit to the left, where another person is the marginal chooser: and that person also will choose to free-ride. So wherever we are when the process starts, unraveling continues until we reach the long-familiar result (Samuelson 1954; Olson 1965) that although everyone would be better off if the social choice were at 1 (100 percent cooperation), the only equilibrium outcome for strictly voluntary self-interested choice would be at the extreme left, where no one is cooperating.

But since actual communities commonly manage to avoid this dismal result, it follows that somehow there are commonly incentives present (beyond what can be accounted for in terms of strictly voluntary self-interest) whose aggregate effect is sufficient to offset the cost of cooperating.

## Tipping points and equilibria

So next consider the simplest conceptually possible ways in which the curves of Figure 4.1 might be shifted to allow a non-zero level of cooperation. Figures 4.2 to 4.6 show various possibilities, starting with the complete reversal of Figure 4.2. This complete reversal could reflect, for example, some coercive threat sufficient to make every chooser see her self-interest as best served by cooperating. Now the *cooperate* curve (C) dominates the free-rider curve. The unique equilibrium is at the far right, with 100 percent cooperation. But in realistic situations, what needs to be done to obtain increasing levels of cooperation almost always eventually becomes prohibitively difficult, so that the complete reversal (as in Figure 4.2) will rarely be seen. But it is a logical possibility, and if the marginal cost of contributing is low it can even be observed, or at least closely approximated. Think of applause after a good concert performance. The applause is satisfying to the audience as well as the performer. It is a public good. You get to enjoy it even if you don't bother to applaud yourself. But although it is strictly voluntary, essentially everyone chooses to contribute, though not absolutely everyone, since there is a cost (getting caught in the crowd) unless you start to leave immediately.

Figure 4.3 shows a far more prevalent case in which the offsetting incentives are most effective when cooperation is low, with diminishing marginal effectiveness with increasing cooperation. The net advantage favors cooperation at the left of Figure 4.3, but the advantage falls and eventually free-riding does better as the fraction induced to cooperate increases. Beyond the intersection, the net incentives become increasingly negative (adverse to cooperation). Or, in terms of the relative advantage of cooperating rather than free-riding, $\Delta$ is positive at the left of the diagram but decreasing so that the C and FR curves intersect. Since choosers are ordered by decreasing propensity to cooperate, this situation easily emerges even if the cost of incentives favoring cooperation to the marginal chooser is constant.

Figure 4.4 shows the opposite case, in which the offsetting incentives are most effective when cooperation is high, so that the strong free-rider advantage when cooperation is low decreases as we move to the right, reaches 0 at the intersection, and thereafter the net advantage increasingly favors cooperation. This situation is not typical but also not terribly uncommon even when the cost of contributing is not trivial. For as fewer and fewer choose to free-ride, it becomes easier to identify severe shirkers, and more feasible to punish them. If N is not very large, this is a common situation, and it is approximately right even for many large-N situations where the cost of cooperating is not very large but more than trivial.

The structure in Figure 4.3 most easily arises when free-riding is not at issue. Using one of Schelling's examples, if there are two roads (A and B) connecting a pair of locations, drivers will distribute themselves to make travel time approximately equal either way, since as more and more drivers choose one road (increasing congestion) it becomes increasingly attractive to choose the other. Draw the situation as a Schelling diagram, with the declining line showing values for choices of road B and the increasing line showing choices of road A. With the horizontal axis showing the fraction choosing road B, we get a version of Figure 4.3, with an equilibrium near the middle. Here self-interest and socially effective choice are aligned, so there is no problem of how to reach a reasonable social outcome. What we want to understand is what happens, or might happen, to reach a reasonably good social outcome when they are not.

Figures 4.3 and 4.4 illustrate starkly different contexts for the evolution of the social result. In Figure 4.3, where the cooperate curve (C) crosses the free-ride curve (FR) from above, the crossover identifies an equilibrium (Q). In Figure 4.4, where the cooperate curve crosses the free-ride curve from below, the crossover identifies a *tipping point* (t) with two equilibria: one with zero cooperation, the other at 100 percent cooperation. To follow the balance of the argument, it is essential to be completely clear about why in Figure 4.3 the crossover is an equilibrium, but in Figure 4.4 it is a tipping point.

In Figure 4.3, starting from any point along the horizontal axis, the social process would always move toward Q. For a chooser anywhere to the left of Q, the net advantage is always to cooperate. The C curve lies above the FR curve. The chooser would make herself better off if she chose to cooperate. So by construction, the marginal individual would always choose C, which moves the level of cooperation to the right in the figure (fraction cooperating is a bit larger than if this marginal chooser chose to free-ride) until we get to Q. But starting from any point to the right of Q, the opposite net advantage prevails, and again we would always move toward, never away from, the equilibrium at Q.

But for Figure 4.4, the opposite holds. We would always move away from the crossover at *t* until we reached equilibrium, which here would be at the extremes. The only stable points are either 0 cooperation or 100 percent cooperation. In contrast to Figure 4.3, where social evolution is always moving toward a unique equilibrium no matter where we start, the result for Figure 4.4 would be fully contingent on events leading to the eventual equilibrium. Path-dependence would determine whether we ended up with no cooperation or full cooperation, though underlying individual preferences are identical for both Figure 4.4 outcomes. Conceivably we could be exactly at the tipping point (*t*), like a pole balanced exactly on its end. That could happen, but the pole would not stay put very long, because the slightest perturbation would set things moving away from perfect balance, and the same would hold for the social analoge.

A simple example that approximates the Figure 4.4 situation is driving on the left versus driving on the right. It is socially best if everyone would adopt the same practice. But which possibility emerged would be path-dependent. If either way would work just as well there would be no social dilemma. But suppose that (as in Britain once the Channel Tunnel made it much more common for British drivers to be on the continent and the reverse) it would really be better if the community switched from driving on the left to driving on the right. How to get there would be a policy puzzle whose resolution (whether to try, how to do it) would be contingent on how to manage what would necessarily be a path-dependent route to the alternative equilibrium. And devising a feasible path would be a puzzle with a free-rider component, which would come especially at the stage of enlisting political support for getting the change made, since a proposal to move would not be immediately popular even if it was certain that within a few years essentially everyone would agree it was the smart thing to do. In the short run, it would be unpopular, and ambitious politicians might not be willing to expend political capital on it, and especially so if they could not be sure their rivals also would. I will return to this simple example in Chapter 5.

But until the change was made, a more exact diagram would be that in Figure 4.5, where a considerable number of accidents occur because visitors to Britain sometimes forget the local practice until an oncoming car reminds them, sometimes too late. In Figure 4.5, a visible fraction of people are not cooperating with the local practice (in the figure, on the far right) even though it is in their own interest to do so. And of course there are always some people not conforming to local practice for nastier reasons. Although I am using the label "free-riding" for non-cooperation, that is to be understood (as the driving example requires) as just a label for not cooperating in some way, only sometimes, not necessarily, with the invidious connotation of free-riding.

Finally, we could get more than one crossover, and in particular (for the balance of the discussion) under conditions where cooperating or not cooperating with prevailing practice turns on conflicting motivation between self-interested and group-interested choice. A combination of decreasing marginal effectiveness for some incentives and increasing marginal effectiveness (up to some high level) for others could yield situations like that of Figure 4.6, where there is a tipping point and two equilibria (as in Figures 4.4 and 4.5) but now with neither equilibrium at the extreme of complete free-riding or complete cooperation. We can notice that this is an important configuration. For we can easily point to situations in which a practice that had been rarely favored rather abruptly (relative to some usual timescale) turns into the dominant practice in the community. But in real situations, there are still usually some people making a choice when almost no one else is, and some who are not making that choice even when almost everyone else is. The high ($Q^+$) and low ($Q^-$) equilibria look like those in Figure 4.6, not like those in Figures 4.4 or 4.5.

## Rewards and punishment

So now consider characteristics of the requisite incentives to yield social coordination with respect to some choice if the *ex ante* situation was that of Figure 4.1. What might shift the curves of Figure 4.1 to yield a high level of cooperation? Consider at first only incentives to individual choosers with given beliefs and strictly self-interested preferences. Assume there is no disagreement that the coordination at issue would benefit everyone, but the cost of participating is such that no one finds it worthwhile to bother in terms of their private self-interest. The possibilities for shifting the free-rider advantage then could come only from either imposing a risk of punishment on those who fail to cooperate or offering a promise of reward for those who do (Olson's "selective incentives"). We want to consider how the effectiveness of such negative or positive incentives might vary as we move from low toward high compliance. Or put another way, we want to consider typical variations in returns to scale of incentives.

Either rewards or penalties could work to push down the net advantage of free-riding. But workable incentives must yield more value than they cost to provide. Incentives to cooperate must provide something analogous to gains from trade. Some entity interested in influencing the result (call this entity the agent: it might be the government, or an issue-oriented foundation, for example) will look for incentives which cost less to provide than the value to the agent of the effect on cooperation they can secure. There are now three distinct "values" in play. The *value to the chooser* of the reward must be enough to offset the cost of cooperating. But this value has no necessary connection with either the *value to the agent* of securing this chooser's cooperation or the cost to the agent of providing the incentive. The value to the agent must be enough to offset the *cost to the agent* of providing the reward. But whatever that cost might be, we can expect to see typical patterns in how cost of incentives would usually scale with the level of cooperation they could be expected to achieve.

The outstanding example of something which costs agent very little but might be of high value to a chooser is the honorary award. Honorary rewards – an invitation to a White House reception, a knighthood – which cost essentially nothing to give may be highly valued by individuals, and indeed may have substantial economic as well as psychic value to some set of potential cooperators. But (conspicuously for honorary awards) the value of an incentive that costs little to give is tied to how rarely it is awarded. Positive incentives typically encounter either increasing costs to the agent (since rewards whose values are contingent on their rarity are soon exhausted) or decreasing value to marginal compliers, or both. Awards with significant value to choosers even though widely distributed would rarely cost nothing to give. So marginal effectiveness in eliciting cooperation (the gain from the incremental cooperation versus the cost of providing that incentive) for rewards will ordinarily decline as we move toward higher levels of cooperation: perhaps because the value of the incentive is contingent on its rarity, or because it is not cheap at all, hence can be provided only to some subset of potential cooperators judged to be of particularly high value, or because only a limited subset of potential cooperators are particularly enticed by this reward. Across the whole society, positive individual incentives with increasing or even constant net marginal effectiveness must be rare.

The more general situation is certainly that net value to an agent of positive incentives diminishes as the needed level of cooperation increases. This implies that, considering positive incentives only, free-rider temptations overcome by positive incentives would have the general shape of Figure 4.3, where the cooperate curve (C) is above the free-rider curve (FR) when cooperation is low, but eventually falls below it. And for many contexts the limited opportunities for positive incentives to be workable will mean that the crossover point (Q) will be far to the left of the intersection shown in Figure 4.3.

The situation is more complicated for negative incentives. With exceptions (such as honorary awards), which can be effective only if awarded to a few, providing positive incentives is costly, but the administrative costs are low. People who have earned a reward will not ordinarily conceal their behavior or evade attempts to supply the promised consequences. But of course the opposite applies for penalties. It is possible and it sometimes actually happens that negative incentives are profitable for an agent. This is at least sometimes the case for fines, or denying ordinarily available benefits, even taking administrative costs into account. But that is not the usual situation. Indeed, when negative incentives are cheap, or even profitable, something quite different from what is under discussion here is likely to be going on. What we would be seeing would mostly not be a matter akin to organizing efficient incentives to correct a market failure, but of predatory exploitation of vulnerable targets.

Much more usually, the various components of policing – what it costs to detect non-compliance, identify non-compliers, and bring them to the point at which penalties have been imposed – make negative incentives costly. But an effective negative incentive requires only some risk (not certainty) that not complying in any particular case will be detected and punished. Even if it looks like you could completely safely run a red light, so you see neither social nor private value in waiting, you are unlikely to do it. Sufficient risk to elicit compliance might be small enough that it could be reasonably cheap to create, but almost always only with the proviso that it does not need to be enforced very often. In the extreme case, if detection is easy and punishment reliable, the negative incentive can be very cheap to provide, since it almost never actually needs to be imposed.

Just where negative incentives can be efficient (from the perspective of the agent) depends on options that might be available and on penalties that can then be feasible. The agent can start by choosing particularly favorable targets (for example, people who are particularly easy to watch, or particularly risk-averse, particularly likely to be bound by habit if a habit of compliance can be established). But plainly a high level of cooperation cannot be gotten that way. Marginal costs then must rise as less and less vulnerable individuals must be covered. But negative incentives might work very well to maintain a high level of cooperation already in place, since now there would be few candidates for application of the punishment, and the costs of enforcement averaged across all cooperators might be very low. This would yield the Figure 4.4 mirror-image analog of the Figure 4.3 situation. Now it is at high levels of cooperation, not at low levels, that free-riding no longer looks tempting relative to cooperating. In Figure 4.3, rewards to the most easily tempted cooperators push up the cooperate curve from the left. In Figure 4.4, threats which become cost-effective only if compliance is high push down the free-rider curve on the right. But that opportunity comes into play only if somehow the situation has moved to the right of the tipping point. A high level of cooperation is sustainable, but only if the agent has somehow already gotten there.

Suppose the agent has invested in a fence, but many people take to scrambling over the fence. Unless the agent can start shooting – there are cases in which draconian measures are taken but more often that would be suicidal (politically and sometimes physically) – the incentives cannot be enforced. But when only a few people are trying to scale the fence – when most people are cooperating (in the diagram when the status quo is well to the right) deterrence of all but the hardest cases might become cheap, given the initial investment in the fence.

And allowing for a fraction of especially hard cases at the right of the diagram, and starting from mainly easy to reward cases at the left, we could get a curve like Figure 4.6, which exhibits the multiple crossovers mentioned at the end of the previous section. Mainly positive incentives elicit some modest level of cooperation, but decreasing marginal effectiveness limits what can be elicited. Then there is a range of cooperation over which it is too expensive to provide adequate positive incentives and impractical to impose effective negative incentives. But eventually, if participation were sufficiently high, negative incentives can become effective. So if we could somehow get beyond a tipping point, we would be in a region where potential free-riders are successfully deterred, where coordination could move up to a point where increasingly intense efforts to apprehend and punish increasingly reluctant non-cooperators exhausts what is practical.

Yet so long as we are dealing with strictly self-interested choice, this logical possibility is inadequate for the level of cooperation with social goals we see in actual societies. When there is an emphatic alignment of self-interest and social value (as, using one of Schelling's examples, with everyone driving on the same side of the road), a satisfactory social outcome is likely to spontaneously emerge. But if the result is path-dependent, there are possibly (recalling the earlier driving example) different outcomes, which at a later stage become conflicting outcomes. But even setting that complication aside, societies that work rely on more than self-interest. In many contexts self-interested choice would be dominated by free-rider temptations (absent further incentives the situation would look like Figure 4.1), or there is a positive equilibrium, as in Figure 4.3, but dangerously far to the left, or comfortably far to the right as in Figure 4.4 or 4.5, but there is no way to get there. Then feasible strictly self-interested rewards and punishments might be catastrophically insufficient.

All that is so even though, as mentioned at the outset, there is a familiar class of cases where self-interest alone is sufficient to get past a tipping point. For fads and fashion (and not entirely differently, for the far more fundamental case of the evolution of language), all that is needed to get a version of Figure 4.6 is that people vary in how far they are moved to do what nearly everyone else seems to be doing. Everyone has a tendency in that direction (most of the time even a determined non-conformist is in fact conforming), but with variation across issues and persons. For matters of mere fashion, the basic story requires only that there be some segment of the community that wants (on this matter) to be "ahead of the crowd," a much larger segment that wants to keep up with the crowd, and a segment that wants to stay with what they liked in the past. We can then see the influence of the social contagion that is the focus of Gladwell's book, where the formal dynamics resemble those of epidemiology. A novelty gradually spreads but eventually dissipates as the conditions for contagion weaken (for fad or fashion, its novelty appeal ages with those most likely to be motivated to be ahead of the crowd).

But if the novelty grows sufficiently before starting to fade, and in particular if by chance or design (usually needing some help from chance) new centers of contagion are ignited, it may reach a critical mass or tipping point where the number of new cases accelerates and the novelty quickly spreads across a large fraction of the whole community. That happens when it is no longer just specially sensitive or specially located people who are exposed but essentially everyone in the community. Then all face multiple exposures and all but the most resistant become likely recruits. Gladwell is very good on this.

Sometimes ideas and passions, not just fads and diseases, can take hold in that way. We are interested in the contagion of ideas and passions, but especially in cases where the process in fact requires more than self-interested motivation, such as adopting or complying with social norms even when you could get away with not bothering, or joining a demonstration defying your government, even when you might get shot. Suppose an agent sees how to sustain a high equilibrium if he could somehow reach it. What might the agent seek to do by way of getting over the hump and past the tipping point? Even when tactics tied only to self-interest are not enough, an essential contribution is likely to come through the contagion process just described. The tendency to want to be like other people, or merely to feel uncomfortable not being like other people, might be widespread enough on the issue at hand that if a tipping point were crossed the punishment for not cooperating might need to be only the embarrassment that deviants feel on being seen as deviants (for once cooperation is high, non-cooperators become deviants).

So we can give an account of how social equilibrium can shift where for a few people the spontaneous rewards of being ahead of the crowd generate the incentive to produce a seed for social change at $Q^-$, and then occasionally a sufficient number of ignitions to reach a critical mass might occur in some chancy way, so that once beyond the tipping point the spontaneous punishment of being left behind the crowd is sufficient to maintain a high equilibrium at $Q^+$ until a gradual erosion of conformity opens the way for another cycle to displace the current fashion. And (conspicuously in the case of the fashion industry) that can be speeded up and even routinized when agents with a serious interest in promoting the cycles come on the scene and resources become available to sweeten the bare incentive to be ahead of the crowd, or at least not behind the crowd. When what is needed is only coordination that no more than mildly conflicts with self-interest, that may be as much of a story as is needed. But by itself this becomes increasingly inadequate to account for large-scale cooperation when there is at least a phase where self-interest puts a substantial barrier in place. Nor would it always be adequate to explain how cooperation is sustained past the tipping point in the face of inevitable transient shocks that can erode it.

We can see that societies can sometimes get there, and stay there. Indeed, societies that survive somehow do get there on numerous aspects of social life, and even revolutions and other social movements facing strong opposition (so there are incentives, perhaps severe, to discourage participation) sometimes get there. To capture that possibility we need to consider motivation beyond self-interest. A second tier of what I will now call the S-diagram (because it is like a Schelling diagram and derived from it, but different enough to need a different label) comes into play. This arises from the possibility that people motivated to be "neither selfish nor exploited" might see sufficient social value in the cooperation at issue, or (contrariwise) might see that cooperation as sufficiently socially perverse, that in addition to the social contagion effects that can generate a Schelling diagram like Figure 4.6, a second set of factors come into play which also generate that structure.

## Social motivation

Rewrite the NSNX equilibrium defined in Chapter 1 ($W = G'/S'$) as $WS' = G'$. We can then reinterpret the C and FR curves of Figure 4.6 as reporting $G'$ and $WS'$ for the marginal chooser. Call this the *S-diagram*. See the enlarged copy is printed as Figure 5.1 at the start of the next chapter. The marginal chooser will now contribute to whatever cause is at issue (donate to the fireworks, spend time on the neighborhood clean-up, join the protest march) if G′ > WS′, and won't if G′ < WS′. As before, the height of the curves are arbitrary. What is relevant is the vertical distance (Δ) between the lines, which scale with how much change in incentives would be needed to change choices, and sometimes the slopes. The discussion of Schelling diagrams to this point can be straightforwardly applied, with rewards and punishments (positive and negative incentives) still affecting choice directly by altering the S′ factor as already described. But now we are also interested in possibly altering W and G′.

Even prior to this section we were already concerned with more complicated situations than Schelling had occasion to explore. In creating the diagrams, Schelling dealt only with average or typical choosers. But for the fad-and-fashion models to yield striking effects, heterogeneity across choosers is essential. There have to be some people who care about being ahead of the crowd, some people who can afford to be different, many people who mainly do not want to be left behind. Allowing for that gives up some features of Schelling's original. And extending the discussion to social choice shaped by NSNX motivation sharpens the departures.

We need to allow for preferences about the choice at issue that not only vary from one chooser to another but often conflict. Even with adjustments for possibly transient side-payment (rewards and punishments), WS′ and G′ are not entities which can be the basis for showing aggregated social or private values even of the marginal chooser. I show the curves with an upward trend, suggesting that more cooperation is better, as is usually the case. But the absolute positions of the two curves carries no information. What is significant is just the way Δ changes in relation to participation, which yields group-interested choice from the marginal chooser when G′ > WS′ and self-interested choice when G′ < WS′. It is contention over social values and competition between social and private values that can be analyzed in terms of the S-diagram, not social value itself. Unsurprisingly, the S-diagram does not capture everything.

Contention over social value has played no role until now. For a self-interested chooser could not be significantly motivated by the effect of her individual contribution on the cooperative endeavor. She might strongly believe one outcome over another (in an election, for example) would have great social value, but in a large-numbers context, the marginal value for herself of her own choice, even in terms of some notion of enlightened or enlarged self-interest, will still be inconsequential.

What makes the difference between the discussion here and a discussion in a more standard framework is not that for a self-interested chooser G′ would be zero. Even narrow self-interest is not inconsistent with having a perception of the social importance of a policy or electoral choice. And as mentioned at the outset, current versions of maximizing a utility function often go beyond narrow self-interest. But as discussed in Chapter 2, what makes G′ inconsequential in a standard model of even broadened self-interest is that in terms of what the chooser would be willing to pay to have their preference included in an overall social weighting, G′ might as well be zero. It is not zero, but in a large-number setting it is too small to make a difference big enough to motivate an individual to participate. But if NSNX holds, that would no longer be so, again for reasons spelled out in Chapter 2. And we can observe that actual choosers who understand the rational choice argument that it cannot be rational to vote nevertheless may find themselves voting. Even if NSNX does not hold, people nevertheless seem to behave *as if* it held. So perhaps it does hold. But even if NSNX holds, that does not mean that choosers have any conscious access to the NSNX equilibrium condition. Feeling selfish or feeling exploited is accessible. Coming closer to $W = G′/S′$ is not, any more than in a Darwinian world agents are consciously maximizing fitness.

In the S-diagram, as before, we are lining up choosers such that the person most easily tempted (or coerced) into cooperating is at each position on the horizontal axis. So the very first person ready to join in some effort is at the extreme left and the very last holdout is at the extreme right. With $\Delta = G′ - WS′$ as the incentive to cooperate, as we move from left to right along the horizontal axis, the marginal chooser is always the person for whom the absolute value of $\Delta$ is the smallest. If a free-rider, it is the free-rider who can most easily be moved to cooperate; if a cooperator ($\Delta$ will now be $> 0$), it is the cooperator most easily tempted to defect.

If all choosers were identical, or the curves represented the values of the average chooser, then the aggregate value of a particular level of cooperation to the whole community could be calculated by multiplying the value to a cooperating chooser by the fraction of cooperating choosers, and adding to that the value to a free-rider multiplied by the fraction of non-cooperators. But here the values are increments as judged by the marginal individual at each point along the curve. The summation just described would be meaningless. I show the curves with an upward trend, suggesting that more cooperation is better, as is usually the case. But the slopes are really arbitrary. All that is meaningful is the way $\Delta$ changes.

Could the same individual turn up as the marginal chooser more than once? That will sometimes happen. The most obvious case would be a contrarian who wants to do whatever is the opposite of what most people are doing. And although I will not explicitly deal with the point (and the diagram as drawn makes no attempt to show it), choosers near each other, and with nearly the same $\Delta$'s, might be responding to very different combinations of G′ and S′ and in subtler ways even W. It is convenient and harmless for the discussion here to keep the diagram simple. But it is only $\Delta$ that should be thought of as changing by small enough increments (across marginal choosers) to look continuous in the diagram. For equal values of $\Delta$ might come from adjacent choosers, one of whom has a higher value of G′ but also a higher value of S′. But dealing explicitly with these and various other complications I will set aside would not change anything substantial in the discussion here.

An S-diagram could even look like Figure 4.1, where $\Delta$ is always negative. There now is no seed visible. Whatever motivation beyond self-interest is in play is everywhere too small to noticeably overcome the temptation to free-ride. This in fact is common: endless possibilities for social coordination that at least a few people favor never get off the ground. Or the situation might be like that of Figure 4.4, where until others are cooperating even those most ready to cooperate require a large incentive beyond what is at hand. But if the individual most easily moved to cooperate was indeed moved by some new incentive (a bribe or threat or maybe even a revelation) or by a change in circumstances, the next most ready person would (by construction) require a milder bribe or threat or revelation. But in Figure 4.4 until one of those possibilities arises, even the most easily moved chooser never in fact moves.

The $\Delta$ for a particular chooser will depend on that chooser's own sense of the marginal social value of the marginal choice at issue ($G'$) and on the cost to that chooser of cooperating ($S'$), both net of adjustments already described. $S'$ for the chooser would respond to both the direct cost of contributing and to the chooser's individual vulnerability to any risk from free-riding and to this individual's valuation of any rewards from cooperating. $G'$ would respond to the chooser's sense of the social value of his own increment to cooperation on the matter at hand, allowing for any costs to the group in reaching that cooperation and for favorable or unfavorable effects on future cooperation. With or without adjustments, $G'$ would be a very tiny increment on the scale of social value, but the individual cost to the chooser would also be very tiny on that scale. The relevant ratio, $G'/S'$, need not be small at all. See the discussion here in Chapter 2 and the more detailed discussion in Chapter 6 of SA&R. And $\Delta$ would depend also on the weight (W) given to self-interest in this choice, as governed by the NSNX equity rule. An agent who wants to discourage, or an opposing agent who wants to encourage, the cooperation at issue will look for opportunities to shift the curves through effects on $G'$, or on $S'$, or on W, and usually on all three together.

For the fireworks example, as with many others, there may be no significant contest about what would be socially valuable. Essentially everyone agrees on what would be good, and rewards and punishments are only relevant when purely voluntary action will not produce enough of that good thing. But many choices are contested, which means that some actors are interested in encouraging cooperation and reducing free-riding, but others have an opposing interest in discouraging cooperation on just that matter. So actors on both sides will be interested in how to encourage potential supporters and discourage potential opponents.

Conflicting preferences among agents can then yield competing promises of rewards and threats of punishment, possibly including threats or promises affecting $G'$ rather than $S'$. Sometimes incentive effects on $G'$ will have large consequences. A threat, after all, may target a group or a community not just an individual chooser contingent on just her choice. Or if the cooperation at issue is to pursue some reform, then an agent opposed to that kind of cooperation might try to reduce $G'$ by some gesture that seems to favor the reform. So the propensity to cooperation might be reduced by individual rewards to non-cooperators or punishment for cooperation (either, if effective, increasing net S', hence reducing Δ). But Δ might also be reduced by punishment that targets the group, hence reduces G' indirectly by adding a component of loss to the group, or reduces G' directly by some partial reform that makes the object of cooperation seem less urgent. When we come to discuss concrete cases, examples will readily arise.

With that framework, start again from the case of purely voluntary action, considering what we might treat as the typical shape of a diagram reflecting the NSNX social effects when *no* private incentives due to an active agent are in play. As in the earlier discussion of purely self-interested social contagion, but now setting aside effects of social contagion, we are again led to the S-diagram.

What we are looking for is some "in general," or usual, way in which the W, S', and G' would vary with respect to an interesting issue, conditional on the level of participation by other people. We would like to define a base case that will work across a wide range of contexts, and from which occasional departures from the "normal" configuration could be assessed. Within standard analysis of markets, the basic supply/demand diagram (with downward-sloping demand curve and upward-sloping supply curve) provides a base case which continues to be useful as a point of departure for interpreting special contexts where the usual interactions are violated (by snob or bandwagon effects, for example). We want to establish a parallel to that.

Start from the situation of "most people," as distinguished from the small fraction of people who are joiners when virtually everyone else is a free-rider – or not even a free-rider, since perhaps they are not yet even conscious of anything they might be free-riding on. At the other pole, there are always at least a few people who do not go along even when everyone else is. In this respect, we are running parallel to the fads-and-fashions context, but here what makes the distinction is not that some want to be ahead of the crowd and others (on this matter) want to just conform with the crowd, but that some are aroused to a social opportunity or risk while others are not.

Near the poles we have some ordinarily small fraction easily aroused and some also ordinarily small fraction irrevocably opposed, tautologically, are most people. In Figure 5.1 this is the range along the horizontal axis some distance to the right of $Q^-$ and across to some distance to the left of $Q^+$. And for "most people," the W, G', and S' functions can ordinarily be expected to follow a usual pattern. Weight to self-interest (W) must go down as participation by others increases, and must go up when a chooser's own participation increases. Define $g$ as the current ratio of group-interested to total use of resources for a chooser. And define $g^*$ as the typical value of $g$ for what that individual, in this context, recognizes as "people like me." For any given $g^*$, NSNX equity (from NSNX Rule 2) requires that W increase as the chooser's own group-interested spending fraction, $g$, increases. But for any given individual, W becomes smaller as $g^*$ grows larger. So for most people, as what "people like me" are doing grows more social, a chooser becomes less easily concerned with being exploited by contributing, and more easily concerned about being selfish by not contributing. Although NSNX mechanics are out of sight to a chooser (NSNX does not assume conscious calculations of the state of the equilibrium condition any more than standard modeling assumes conscious calculation of marginal utilities), these affective responses are not always tacit, and I doubt that any reader is unfamiliar with them.

So directly from Rule 2, weight to self-interest, W, will slope down as we move left to right across the "most people" range in the S-diagram, since exactly what that means is that more people "like me" are contributing. Recalling the remarks of Chapter 1, it is an affective, not a rational, choice issue to say what governs what a person treats as "people like me" in a particular context. But for this general discussion, we can just say that for "most people" the reference group in a situation is just about everyone facing the choice, or at least everyone who is not conspicuously *not* "like me." To the degree that most are cooperating, weight to self-interest declines, and the converse.

Direct S', setting aside individual incentives or a conformity effect, can be taken as constant across the range of participation that covers "most people." But in more detail a chooser's sense of S' must reflect three kinds of effect on private interests. There will be the direct (out-of-pocket) costs of contributing and there will also be conformity effects. Conformity effects are apparent across the entire taxonomy of choice (fashion, language, and anything else that might be mentioned). Allowing for conformity effects, S' would be higher when the prevalence of cooperation is low, since there is some discomfort in behaving differently from others, and S' would be lower when prevalence is high, so that a person is not only comfortably choosing in what is the usual way, but also has minimal decision costs since he can see that "everyone knows" what to do, so he does not have to think about it. How steep an allowance for mere conformity ought to be must depend on how costly cooperation is on the matter at hand. But on overwhelming evidence, it will rarely be inconsequential. S' will then tend to decline across the range of "most people."

And participation often has private costs or benefits beyond these, most conspicuously so in violent situations where there are determined partisans with respect to the social cooperation at issue. A person taking part might be shot or otherwise harmed (his house destroyed, his job lost). Hence, aside from conserving the direct value of resources that would be needed to participate, a chooser who free-rides will also gain whatever there is to be gained by avoiding the risks of participation, but lose whatever might be gained by rewards for that participation or by avoiding penalties that might be inflicted for not participating. Net S' might be complicated by competing incentives from opposed interests.

But Δ for "most people" must ordinarily decrease as participation by others increases even aside from the conformity effect. If tens of thousands of people are in the streets, the government will have to be more cautious about ordering that demonstrators be shot than if there are hundreds. And even if the order is given, and obeyed, the probability that any particular demonstrator is shot will be far less when there are tens of thousands than when there are a few hundred. And the risk that friends and neighbors will notice and resent or otherwise behave in ways that might prove costly accordingly grows larger when more are participating and you are not. Net S', even aside from any conformity effects, will almost always grow smaller when larger numbers are participating.

When incentives conflict (the government is discouraging participation, the opposition is encouraging it), there may be penalties for not participating from one side and rewards from the other. Both affect choice, but unless an agent who wants to discourage participation is in a position to apply and willing to apply ruthless force, the net of these side-payments will usually favor doing what most others are doing. And indeed, if participation becomes very prevalent, a different kind of reward component appears, as participation becomes something of a consumption good: not only would the mere conformity effect be high, but out there with the demonstrators can become "the place to be."

And since W, by Rule 2, slopes down, WS' for "most people" will be compounded of two downward-sloping factors, and so certainly must ordinarily slope down.

G', on the other hand, can be expected to increase for "most people" as participation by others increases. For as others join in, a typical individual will feel increasingly reassured that there is real social value to this effort, that social cooperation is succeeding, that "everyone knows" it is important that people support it. The combination of a downward slope for WS' and an upward slope for G' yields a *potential* tipping point in the central zone of Figure 5.1, where "most people" are. To the left of $t$ in the figure, cooperation will unravel towards the low equilibrium at $Q^-$, to the right it will cumulate toward the high equilibrium at $Q^+$. And that there will be an actual not merely potential tipping point in a situation becomes more likely when we next consider incentive effects (rewards and punishments).

In sum, then, with respect to "most people" S' net of side-effects must ordinarily be declining between $Q^-$ and $Q^+$. And, as already noticed, directly from the NSNX equity Rule 2, W must decline. Hence odd cases aside, WS' must certainly tend to decline. But as discussed, G' will tend to rise with increasing participation and ordinarily be at least stable. Hence for most people, as participation increases $\Delta = G' - WS'$ must ordinarily be increasing (for free-riders, $\Delta$ is becoming less negative, for cooperators it is becoming more solidly positive). We get the geometry of the S-diagram.

## Movers and shakers

So now turn to the choosers who are not like "most people." In Figure 5.1 they are near or to the left of $Q^-$ and also sometimes of particular interest, near or to the right of $Q^+$. Consider first the situation on the left of "most people" in the figure, where participation is very low. To elicit participation, people near this pole must have (relative to most people when participation is low) some combination of low weight to self-interest (W), high G' and low S'. But there need be – indeed, since they must be atypical in some significant way, there could only be – only relatively few such people providing what I label the *seed*. Positive Δ (WS' < G'), favoring cooperation, could result from many different combinations of sufficiently high G' and sufficiently low W and S'. So it is the existence of a region near 0 participation where there are choosers with positive Δ that creates the seed, not some particular combination. Indeed, as will play an important role when we consider some exemplary applications in Chapter 11, similar contexts might have contrasting seeds, and even within a given situation there may be important heterogeneity within the seed. But all should be characterized by some combination of plausible values of W, G', and S' that distinguish them from "most people."

High G' could reflect special knowledge, or special ability to influence outcomes, or longer than typical time horizons, or special experience. A person with special expertise who knows (or at least believes he knows) what is of special importance can have a strong sense of social value (high G') for some project that "most people" would never think about, as could a person with powerful religious or political or social commitments: all these provide examples of individuals who might see G' for some social activity as very much larger than a typical person. These are also people who would be more inclined to act in terms of where an initial commitment might eventually lead even if in the short run there is no visible social effect.

On the other hand, S' can be small for many of these same people. If you are rich, the private sacrifice in contributing money to help get something going may be not merely tiny but zero: a matter of allocating among social causes not of sacrificing anything that would otherwise be used for private needs. If you are a celebrity, even if not rich, all you may be contributing is your name, not involving any private sacrifice. A person with a sense of a calling – a religious or political revolutionary – may put very little value on what would seem enormous sacrifices of private value to another person, especially when there is a prospect of life chances if the effort succeeds that seem entirely out of scale with ordinary lives. (The counterpart in terms of self-interested motivation might be found, for example, among the 100 or so people a year who pay about $70,000 to spend some days in severe discomfort climbing Mount Everest, and do so knowing that almost every year some of them will die miserably along the way.) And sometimes there will be an interaction between S' and G'. A celebrity who can command media attention, or a rich person who can not only do a lot with her own resources but who is well connected to other well-endowed people, can sense a high G' for what (for them) is only a minimal cost. For they might see a multiplier effect of their own effort on engaging the efforts of others.

Or on a much less grand scale, there are a great many "local" cases of social action, where S′ may be low because a person can do as well, or almost as well, for their private interest by the social commitment as they could by attending only to private interests. If you are an insurance agent in a small town, the private cost of working on town concerns, organizing a boy scout troop, and so on are plainly diminished by the obvious point that such activity can hardly be anything but good for business. So although the commitment will ordinarily be real, and go substantially beyond what would be warranted merely by being good for business, the effect on diminishing the opportunity cost of social behavior need not be trivial.

Further, for some people near the zero participation pole, even W can be atypically favorable (low weight to self-interest). W responds to how "people like me" are choosing, which for people at the extremes of the social distribution may be quite different from how most people see that. Aristocrats, revolutionaries, or (more commonplace in our own society) leading professionals in any field commonly see themselves as special, hence come to see as a proper reference group how other special people – people like themselves – are behaving. How ordinary people are choosing must have a constraining effect on this, since the elite group as a whole must not have a shared sense of being exploited or (on the NSNX argument) they would shrink back from what would then come to seem an excessive commitment. But we can expect to see a constrained but still substantial special "people like me" effect on W near the low participation pole. Most people, for these people, are not "people like me."

Members of an elite group will see other members of that elite as "people like me," and participation will be easier to organize within such a grouping of people, who often know each other and almost always know of each other, and if not, easily find mutual connections. And (not always crucial but rarely negligible) there will also be opportunities to lighten the burden by providing special benefits ("perks") to members of that elite, and special costs to someone who would not want to be ill-thought-of within that elite, all of which reduce the opportunity cost of joining the effort (S′). So across the whole range of situations that turn on promoting social cooperation, from revolutions to small town civic improvement, it is not hard to see how a small core of initial support might arise, where some sufficient combination of G′, S′, and W are atypically favorable to participation, yielding the region of early cooperation (the seed) at the left in Figure 4.6. In a variety of ways, varying hugely across individuals and contexts, NSNX conditions can arise sufficient for the small number of people needed to "get something going" when almost no one else is attending to the matter.

Of course, on many matters of conceivable social cooperation, there is essentially no seed. Nothing is going on, and until a seed grows to noticeable size, nothing is likely to happen. The S-diagram, we can say, is often degenerate. But when a seed is apparent, by construction as we move away from the left pole in Figure 5.1, we encounter choosers for whom some combination of W increasing (marginal choosers more readily see themselves as like those not yet active than like those who are active), S′ increasing (the cost to self-interest is not so readily borne) or G′ decreasing (the marginal chooser is less likely to see effort on this issue as far more important than most people realize) yields a declining value of Δ. Eventually we must reach a point where the WS′ and G′ curves cross, beyond which the incentive to free-ride becomes stronger. Δ continues to decline even after it has already turned negative until the general tendency for Δ for "most people" to shrink in the opposite direction takes hold. This yields the low equilibrium at Q⁻, and to the right increasingly reluctant marginal choosers until that tendency is overcome, once we are clearly into the region of "most people," by the characteristic decline in W and S′ and increase in G′ as participation increases.

And when conditions are sufficiently favorable, though there is no guarantee, eventually this may yield a tipping point at *t*, where the curves again cross. But sufficiently further to the right, we begin to encounter marginal choosers who are now no longer like "most people," so that again there is a shrinking of Δ, to creating the high equilibrium at Q⁺ as we increasingly encounter people who unlike "most people" exceptionally resist cooperation on this issue. To the right of Q⁺, we then have the *holdouts*, forming a mirror-image of the *seed*. Here are people who will not be won over to cooperation even if almost everyone else has already joined in.

These holdouts might be people alienated from the community, for whom G′ is negligible, or even negative, even when almost everyone else is going the other way. And (partly the same people), there will be choosers in desperate positions (for whom S′ is exceptionally high), and choosers who have opportunities to escape social sanctions that are not available to other people, because they have access to mountains or borders, or have criminal connections, or in some other way can more easily evade risks imposed on those who avoid what almost everyone else accepts (so although negative incentives can be intensely targeted, they are hard to reach). And at that right-hand pole there will also sometimes be a group of special interest for us: people who are in fact the counterparts of the social activists at the opposite pole but with contrary views of what would be good for society. Individual choosers – and more significantly, on some occasions, a substantial fraction of all individuals – may see social value in defying a policy, hence a social loss in compliance. We then see the atypical but familiar and important case of principled civil disobedience. Then treating non-compliance as just another form of free-riding would miss the point. But the analytics are just those already sketched. For theses non-compliers, G′ for the cooperation with established authority is negative, so of course they would want to avoid cooperating: a point which came up in Chapter 1.

The prospects for getting beyond the tipping point will be contingent on how far to the right participation must grow to reach a tipping point and by how large deficit Δ is over the interval from Q⁻ to *t*. Jointly these two elements determine the size of the *hump* that must be gotten over. But once beyond *t*, participation will spontaneously expand as far as Q⁺, providing a *cushion* that now protects the new status quo against reversal. But the process is reversible in principle and sometimes in practice, with the former Soviet Union providing a spectacular example.

Reviewing the labeling of features in the generic S-diagram: the WS′ and G′ curves typically cross at the three points already defined, $Q^- > 0$ and $Q^+ < 1$, with a tipping point ($t$) between. On the left, a low participation equilibrium at $Q^-$ marks the participation level currently achieved by a group of early activists. Between the left pole and $Q^-$, the G′ curve is above the WS′ curve. Participation will grow (the marginal chooser will join in rather than stand aside) up to $Q^-$. But to the right of $Q^-$ up to $t$, the reverse holds. As things stand, participation will not grow beyond $Q^-$. If some temporary shock shifts the curves – for example, something prominent in the news shifts the G′ curve upward for a few days – that would move participation to the right. But unless it moves things so far right as to get beyond the tipping point, the increase in participation may be only temporary and participation may return to the equilibrium at $Q^-$. On the right, there is a high participation equilibrium at $Q^+$, with the characteristic downward tendency of the WS′ curve I have described between $Q^-$ and $Q^+$. If the status quo is at $Q^+$, then again, unless something changes sufficiently to push participation below $t$, we will stay there. High cooperation can be sustained even though in terms of self-interest free-riding temptations should erode it away.

But this means there is an intrinsic potential for instability built into the S-diagram. As things stand, the equilibrium will stay low, or stay high. But if things change, a radical shift can occur. That is appropriate, since we can observe that potential instability as a feature of the world. Even for quite mundane sorts of emergent social cooperation, we routinely talk – and talk from experience in the world – of reaching a "critical mass," "getting the ball rolling," and so on. And for more dramatic situations, such as revolutions and outbreaks of ethnic violence, instability is even more strikingly observed – not routinely, which it certainly is not – but often enough to be a major feature of human sociality.

Specifically, if the curves go as in Figure 5.1, and participation is high (the equilibrium is at $Q^+$), a disturbance that pushes compliance down to the left of $t$ will lead to unraveling. Unless some further consideration intervenes (for example, effective imposition of martial law) compliance would fall all the way back to the inferior equilibrium at $Q^-$. So we want to think about the social processes that could affect the shape of the S-diagram, and in particular yield movement in either direction across the tipping point. If the social equilibrium is at $Q^-$, we want to see how a society might reach the high compliance equilibrium at $Q^+$, since we can observe that sometimes happens. And, if $Q^+$ is reached, we can observe that that favorable (or at least favorable for those in power) equilibrium could still be vulnerable to some shock, with potentially radical consequences for the society. For sometimes there is a collapse of established authority.

And indeed, although compliance with the social order is ordinarily high, we do occasionally see striking shifts. Apparently something like the unraveling implicit in the existence of tipping points actually occurs. Sometimes (as in Iran at the time of the fall of the Shah, or more recently throughout Eastern Europe) these shifts in compliance with the social order develop suddenly enough to surprise knowledgeable observers inside and outside the country (Kuran 1989). Thus certain features of observed social processes suggest that diagrams for real social situations often take the form of the S-diagram. A theory whose logic generates a structure which exhibits these features might yield insight into real cases.

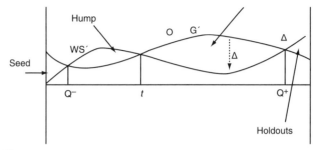

*Figure 5.1*

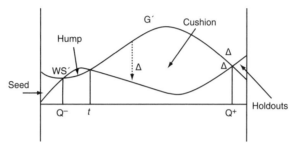

*Figure 5.2*

*Figures 5.1 and 5.2* Examples of S-diagrams.

In these S-diagrams, the shape mirrors the situation. The *seed* may be so small as to be invisible, or so large that there is no need to get over a hump, though enlarging the seed (moving the equilibrium still further to the right) may seem important. Or the hump may be larger (wider, deeper) than here. And so on. Agents will seek to change the shape in the various ways developed in the chapter. In Figure 5.1, there is a sizeable hump, but a large cushion if the hump could be gotten over. But many holdouts would still remain on the far right and it would be difficult to change that. That G′ starts to decline near full cooperation would reflect a context where the costs of trying to move Q$^+$ make that a declining prospect. For example, declining G′ here might be due to a reaction from constituents to what they see as inordinately intrusive enforcement. Or it might be that this is an environmental issue where the value of yet stricter compliance is declining.

In Figure 5.2, the situation has become much more favorable for shifting the equilibrium. The WS′ curve has shifted down, which enlarges the seed, shrinks the hump, moves the tipping point closer to Q$^-$, enlarges the cushion, and moves Q$^+$ closer to complete cooperation. We will be considering the tactics which are implicit in the S-diagram for agents to push the social situation towards a new equilibrium and to opposing agents for defending the status quo.

# 5 Using the S-diagram

Figures 5.1 and 5.2 are versions of the S-diagram developed from the basic Schelling diagram in Chapter 4. The prospect for shifting the status quo will vary with the size of the adverse region (the hump) between Q⁻ and the tipping point (*t*). Recall that the diagram lines up choosers in order of readiness to cooperate. So at each point along the x-axis to the left of the tipping point, the depth of the hump indicates how big a gap in motivation must be bridged to move the marginal individual at that point to participate. The span of the hump indicates how large a fraction of the community must be moved to enlarge participation enough to get from Q⁻ to the tipping point. The bigger (in depth and span) the hump, the harder it will be for circumstances, or activists, or (usually) interaction between that pair to yield emergence of a high level of cooperation. And when the situation starts from the high equilibrium at Q⁺, the bigger (similarly defined) the cushion, then the more stable a high level of cooperation will be.

But the S-diagram is a snapshot of some moment in time, as pointed out in the caption for Figures 5.1 and 5.2. An opportunity can open, or opportunities arise for forcing a window open. Or a reservoir of potential support for change, or to suppress change, may be close at hand but not yet visible. I comment first on the general prospects, then consider some characteristic particulars.

As I write, at the end of 2006, the Democrats have just won control of both Houses of the US Congress. This looks like a consequence of a gradual erosion of support for Republican control of Congress, not a tipping point result. We do have tipping-point effects within the Houses of Congress, where a switch of one vote can yield a huge shift in power across the two parties. In the Senate a fractionally tiny shift in the voting in either of two states (Virginia or Montana) would have left the Republicans in control. But the tipping point here is governed by the legislative rules and has nothing to do with the tipping point in the S-diagram. So not all shifts in social equilibrium involve tipping points, nor do all shifts in social equilibrium that do involve tipping points involve the dynamics captured by the S-diagram. But as I will be trying to show, the range of cases that do is large.

Tipping-point phenomena of another kind arise through the social contagion treated in Gladwell's *Tipping Point* (building on academic work by writers like Granevetter, Kuran, and Schelling). As described in Chapter 4, in the context of fads and fashions, this yields a version of the S-diagram. Parallel effects on ideas and passions would reinforce the NSNX effects as discussed in Chapter 4. But the explicit concern here will be with the intrinsically NSNX tension between social and self-interested motivation, which can generate tipping points in the S-diagram entirely aside from social contagion.

What we see will always be generated at least partly by quirks of circumstance. Things happen which no one controlled, and in particular things happen not within the control of some agent seeking that result. But ordinarily what is fortuitous will be pushed along or exploited by activists seeking to move from $Q^-$, or by opponents of an existing mode of cooperation pushing the situation back from $Q^+$. Shocks to any system are bound to occur, so that agents seeking to upset the status quo, and agents committed to defending the status quo, will seek to exploit whatever circumstances provide to them.

We might want to ask (if we see the high equilibrium) how the seed was established, how cooperation got over the hump, whether its cushion could collapse, and various more detailed questions that concrete situations will prompt. Or, seeing only some modest seed, or even seeing no seed but noticing that conditions in this context look favorable for the emergence of a seed, we can ask what deters its development, and what might reverse that.

Consider what would happen if the curves in Figure 5.1 shift. Movement *down* by the G′ curve, or movement *up* by the WS′ curve, would shift both equilibria (low at $Q^-$ and high at $Q^+$) to the left. But the tipping point at $t$ would move in the opposite direction, to the right. So you can see that a change in the situation that would shift the G′ curve down all across the diagram, or shift the WS′ curve up, would shrink the seed, expand the hump that needs to be gotten over to get from $Q^-$ to $t$, and it would deflate the cushion that could protect the high equilibrium were that to be managed anyway. With sufficient movement down of the G′ curve, the diagram would lose the tipping point entirely, hence also lose the $Q^+$ high equilibrium, and eventually lose the explicit low equilibrium at $Q^-$ as it becomes an invisible equilibrium too close to the vertical axis to be seen. And converse possibilities would arise from a shift up in the G′ curve or down in the WS′ curve.

But since the chooser at any particular point along the horizontal axis is the marginal chooser at that point, there is no reason to expect a uniform shift across the diagram. An action or event that increases G′ for choosers just beyond the seed might decrease G′ for potential choosers further out on the x-axis. What is a call to action that might engage a chooser just beyond the seed might seem reckless and perverse to another chooser far from being ready to join in.

So there is much room for complications and subtleties to arise beyond the simple story of shifting G′ or WS′ curves I've sketched to this point. The S-diagram nevertheless implies quite a bit which does not depend on explicit attention to the always-present heterogeneity across choosers. I run through what seem to be the salient points about the tactics and possibilities that an agent seeking change, or seeking to block that change, might be able to exploit. Most of this can be seen in a first-cut discussion neglecting complications. I start with a particularly important type of situation which requires only the general discussion already in hand.

Suppose the equilibrium were at $Q^+$. What sort of developments could lead to collapse of the status quo? For this context (overthrowing an existing high level of cooperation), we need to read the diagram from the right. And although this kind of case does not arise only in the context of political revolutions, that does provide the most striking cases. In this context of political revolutions, people to the right of $Q^+$ are not last holdouts against the social order but the seed of an effort to overthrow the social order. Those to the left of $Q^-$ would be those who would be the last holdouts to a successful attempt to overthrow the existing order. But for that to occur, some combination of shifts in the situation must deflate the cushion sufficiently to allow some final push to move the situation back to the left of $t$. That has been seen repeatedly in recent decades.

Sometimes it has been a conservative regime that falls (Batista in Cuba, the Shah in Iran). From the other side of the political spectrum, an avalanche of collapse spread across the communist regimes in Eastern Europe, climaxing with the shattering of the Soviet Union itself. But the classic case came much earlier, with the fall of the *ancien régime* in France, memorably analyzed by De Tocqueville. It was Tocqueville who first pointed to what has turned out to be a characteristic feature of abrupt revolutionary shifts. Think of the threatened regime as being at $Q^+$ (an unpopular but functioning regime is in place). For this context, as mentioned earlier, the seed is on the right of the S-diagram. Opponents here hope to push cooperation with the regime back to the point where the regime will collapse. In terms of the S-diagram, opponents hope to push cooperation with the regime back from $Q^+$ to $t$.

But an explicit S-diagram is not something that either activists or the regime can see. They cannot know where $t$ is located, even if they have an intuitive sense of something like the S-diagram, nor can they see the size of the cushion between $Q^+$ and $t$, though inferences can be made about how things are changing (in the formalism, comparative statics inferences can be drawn). But it is the existing prevalence of compliance that is salient. That can be directly seen. This invites an interpretation of a repeatedly noticed odd feature of the collapse of regimes, which is that it is commonly the case that not only the regime but its opponents are taken by surprise by the suddenness of the collapse.

For right up to the moment of collapse the regime will have possibilities both for offering rewards and for tightening coercion. For an indefinite (but not infinite) period, drawing on those possibilities can keep compliance from visibly deteriorating. So the situation can be kept looking no worse or at least not much worse than it has for some time. Yet moves which may indeed serve to keep the location of $Q^+$ from visibly deteriorating will usually compete with moves that might halt the deeper deterioration of support for the regime. In terms of the S-diagram, minimizing any visible adverse shift of $Q^+$ (to the left in the S-diagram) might entail a harder to notice adverse shift of the G′ and WS′ curves which enlarges the seed, shrinks the hump, thins the cushion, and moves the tipping point to the left, even though the location of $Q^+$ does not visibly change.

Reforms may be instituted that at one time would have significantly reduced G′ (here, social value of ending the regime) but now are seen as much as evidence of weakness that raises hope the regime can be supplanted entirely. Or the regime may become ever more focused on its most immediate concern – the level of visible compliance – to the disadvantage of changes needed to reverse the less easily noticed inframarginal deflation of the cushion between $t$ and $Q^+$. In particular, the regime may be cautious about reforms that might offend its dwindling base of active support, such as disciplining the police or army.

As a regime comes to rely more heavily on coercion to keep compliance high, or on rewards to active supporters which in fact aggravate underlying resentment outside that core of support, cooperation is becoming increasingly dependent on coercion. And recalling the discussion of negative incentives in Chapter 4, the effectiveness of coercion depends on a high level of success to remain potent. But relying on coercion to maintain at least *pro forma* cooperation with the regime will almost always aggravate the regime's unpopularity. The cushion will be getting thinner, and the tipping point will be sliding closer to $Q^+$. With no immediately apparent loss of control by the regime, a shock no worse than others that have repeatedly been weathered turns out to be fatal – and unexpected, since compliance can be observed, but thinning of the cushion and a shift in the tipping point cannot.

At the moment of actual collapse the curves in the diagram over the range of the cushion are likely to be inverted, with G′ for cooperation with the government negative. Then, as shown in the discussion of negative G′ in Chapter 1, cooperation with the regime could be sustained only if S′ was also negative (the "cost" of cooperation is actually a gain). Cooperators in that critical range would increasingly be those for whom coercive threats for failure to cooperate are so severe or rewards for continued cooperation so generous that the cooperation leaves the individual chooser sufficiently privately better off to at least stave of defection. But then we are dealing with people ready to revolt, even if for the moment kept at bay.

But the opposite sort of situation may follow the collapse of a regime. What had been a beneath-the-surface simmering of resentment against the old regime might then be replaced by enthusiasm for the new regime among most of the public which allows, without prompting resentment, severe measures against opponents or even potential opponents. A regime lacking confidence that it has a robust cushion might then seek to entrench its position by harsh measures that intimidate or destroy its potential enemies. But success with such measures is most likely for a new regime which has some prospect for credibly claiming that what is being done is justified by the need to preserve the social gains so recently achieved, not by a faltering corrupt regime long in power.

From the point where a seed is substantial enough to be easily seen, it certainly does not follow that it will triumph. More often an incipient movement dies out, though often with some remnant which may later re-emerge. If we were trying to trace a major shift in social equilibrium, we would need a series of S-diagrams where $Q^+$ of one context (for example, a particular faction wins control of a revolutionary movement) becomes $Q^-$ for a new phase. For a successful case, at each phase a further segment of the community joins in, becoming part of the enlarged seed for the next phase. I am not proposing to push use of the S-diagram to anything like that degree. I am interested here only in extracting what is available from thinking about the S-diagram without a huge amount of elaboration, which could turn what seems to me a useful heuristic device into a burdensome contraption.

Establishing and expanding the seed is a matter of "retail" promotion. The initial steps turn on a very small cluster of activists; at the very beginning perhaps a single idiosyncratic individual, but more likely a coalescing across a few individuals or small groups with similar ideas. But to become socially significant, this must arouse the sympathy and interest of, and eventually a commitment from, enough of these particular individuals or small groups of individuals to provide resources (of varying kinds, not just money) for reaching a much wider public. But at the very beginning that initial cluster must recruit, one by one, others who look especially promising, through some combination of how easy they might be to recruit and how valuable they would be if recruited. The recruitment device might be broadcast (a speech, an article, today very possibly a blog), but the recruits come one at a time, and then perhaps a few at a time. But we would still be dealing with the specially accessible segment of a much larger public discussed in Chapter 4 as likely members of the seed. And they would be conscious of that. They can see they are taking up something that very few others are, and they would see their role as agents for promoting change not as part of a general movement towards effecting change.

These "retail" conversions are analogous to the first discoverer and early converts to a radical idea in science (Kuhn's initiators of a revolutionary paradigm shift). The analogy with science is limited but worth pursuing for a few lines. In that context (of a scientific revolution), the curves in the S-diagram would need a different interpretation. Instead of a tension between group-interest and self-interest, there would be tension between "economy" (favoring a new idea that in fact works better) and "comfort" (favoring what is familiar). So in a diagram for such an episode, the equivalent of the WS' curve here would be a curve for discomfort with the novel idea and the G' curve would capture the economy of a new idea that can explain a lot. The tipping point now occurs where enough converts are on board that anyone active in the field becomes repeatedly exposed to the main arguments, which will also mean that the mere tendency to social conformity will make all but firmly committed opponents open to the possibility that the new idea may in fact be right. So an advantage in economy becomes easier for a new convert to grasp, and the discomfort wanes as the idea becomes familiar and widely held. The Copernican case, about which I happen to have written for reasons tangential to the NSNX argument, may have some extra relevance here, beyond the sheer contagion parallel available with the tipping point cases of fashions and epidemics. I provide a bit of detail in the note.[1]

General points about earliest recruits were taken up in Chapter 4. I continue the story here, assuming a seed has been established. From the low equilibrium at $Q^-$, we want to consider how activists might seek to move the situation in ways favorable to reaching $Q^+$. The diagram suggests why the set of tactics sketched next can be recognized across a wide range of empirical examples of activists seeking social change, from evolution of novel social norms to political revolutions.

*Vertical* tactics aim to shift the curves up or down, with the effects considered earlier in this chapter – shrinking or enlarging the hump, and so on. Shifts in the curves might come by way of (1) changing *beliefs* (persuasion) or (2) changing *incentives* (rewards and punishments, as discussed in Chapter 4), or (3) changing the *salience* of various issues at stake, so that evaluations of a situation may change a great deal even if beliefs about the issues have not changed at all. And (4) what can be interpreted as a larger-scale version of a change in the salience of issues when there is a change in *identification*, so that a person who responds as, for example, a Canadian is somehow nudged over to respond as a member of a particular Canadian political faction or region or religion, or the reverse, so that larger concerns dominate more parochial ones. A change in the salient identity guiding a person's responses would not necessarily involve any change in beliefs but nevertheless can easily yield a wholesale change in issue salience, and through that a radical change in response. In NSNX terms, this involves a shift in the group to which, in the choice at issue, a person's sense of group loyalty is directed.

But another set of tactics – what I will call *horizontal* tactics – might shift the prospects of reaching a tipping point even if there were no change at all in the categories I have just introduced as vertical tactics. In practice, the two kinds of tactics are never entirely separate. And there will always be some interplay with serendipitous events (*shocks*) which in one way or another affect the plans and opportunities of active agents.

## Horizontal tactics

I will label three ways that an agent might deal with the problem of shifting participation beyond the tipping point (getting over the hump): (1) top-down, (2) segment and coalesce, and (3) intensity/prevalence tradeoffs.

## *Top-down*

The most common form of successful promotion of a new form of cooperation occurs in so routine a manner that nothing worth noticing is apparent. A functioning authority simply asserts what is to happen with respect to some matter. Everyone knows that overwhelmingly people already in the habit of obeying this authority can be expected to comply with a new regulation. The situation can go immediately from a seed consisting of a few well-placed experts and officials to high compliance where even people unhappy with the novelty judge it prudent to go along. Ordinarily, when a source of authoritative decisions exists whose choices are routinely obeyed, there is no "getting over the hump" problem. Cooperation, backed at least potentially by what is seen as the legitimate coercive powers of established authority, is what is taken for granted, so of course cooperation is what ordinarily occurs.

But top-down effects are sometimes far more interesting. Sometimes there is resistance. A seed forms which opposes what authority prescribes. Sometimes even established authority, confident that it will be obeyed, follows a more cautious route, since leaders are commonly constrained by considerations of maintaining morale and conserving political capital even when they have no doubts that people will follow the leadership's move. This prudential behavior makes it uncommon to see cases where an authoritative policy decision is widely resisted. But of course in the aggregate many cases of resistance occur, and sometimes with severe consequences for the authoritative agent, since successful resistance prompts the thought that further residence might also succeed. And general resistance can sometimes be seen, sometimes immediate, sometimes through a gradual erosion of compliance (as with prohibition in the 1920s).

But top-down effects commonly play a role in cases where the seed does not (yet) include people in a position of authority. For the most obvious tactic for getting over the hump would be to seek to win sufficient support among those who already enjoy authority in the society, to enable top-down tactics. Except where there is simply no prospect of top-down support, a salient focus of promotion will be winning support, or at least softening opposition, among those who can ordinarily determine what will be accepted as legitimate social choices. A spectacular exemplar is provided by the conversion of Constantine to Christianity, and a millennium later by the choices of sovereigns in northern Europe about whether the populations under their control would be Protestant or Catholic.

A memorable example was the remarkably uneventful and rapid (on the scale of major social change) collapse of segregation in public accommodations in the Old South after the Civil Rights Act of 1964 mandated it. But top-down effects are routinely crucial at some stage even when that is in opposition to established authority. For at some stage leaders within the seed are likely to call on sympathizers to act. If action in concert by sympathizers is sufficient to get past a tipping point and if the call is obeyed (neither guaranteed), large consequences follow.

A major episode on the way to the Civil Rights Act was the Montgomery bus boycott. A boycott sharply exhibits the incentive features discussed in Chapter 4. Participation by only a few accomplishes very little at a substantial cost to the boycotters. In Montgomery it invited the antagonistic attention of the city police, which could be focused on the few "troublemakers." But overwhelming participation makes selective punishment ineffective, imposes large costs on the target of the boycott, and subjects people who break the boycott to humiliation and shunning by the participating majority. The woman whose act sparked the boycott, though, seems to have had no such ambition. Rosa Parks was actively involved in the civil rights movement, which surely contributed to her on-the-spot decision to refuse to give up her seat to a white man who demanded it, but at that moment (as she reported when people complimented her for heroism) she was just thinking how tired her feet were. But the leadership of her community sensed the depth of outrage on news of her arrest and correctly judged the moment right to call for the boycott which had been long discussed, with memorable results. This was a top-down move: the mass refusal to ride the segregated buses any longer was not spontaneous.[2]

### Segment and coalesce

Within a small vanguard group that fosters identification as a special group NSNX equilibrium will be higher relative to the mass of potential cooperators, nearly all of whom are still passive. Within that small group (where everyone knows everyone else), social pressure will be especially effect-ive and social cohesion especially strong. So there will be conspicuous private costs for a free-rider. From the first point (as discussed in more detail in Chapter 4) W is smaller. The salient reference group consists just of people likely to be actively engaged, so a person contributing does not feel exploited relative to "people like me." From the second point $S'$ will be smaller (for the multiple reasons noticed in the *seed* discussion of Chapter 4). And I have already mentioned (again in Chapter 4) some reasons why $G'$ will tend to be larger as well. So the equilibrium commitment (where $W = G'/S'$) may be large enough to allow a substantial seed to emerge.

Often these effects will be most striking when that initial effort is not focused on a special subgroup spread across a large population, but on a subgroup which is a localized subgroup of people who live or work together, often with significant kin relations as well. All this favors solidarity among otherwise typical choosers. Then a local effort may succeed when an immedi-ate effort at large-scale (what I will call "global" as opposed to "local") cooperation would be hopeless. But if the activity is global in its aims, or in its consequences, or even merely in its potential, then local successes can coalesce into a global movement. That might have been intended from the start, but even if not it will occur as similar local movements, partly inspired by the existence of local success elsewhere, perhaps with material support, and routinely with moral support and advice, recognize in each other both common elements and potential gains from mutual support.

Exemplars of this process are easily noticed. For activities as diverse as the origins of national labor unions, to the recent spread of recycling and of smoking restrictions, many activities can be found where *segment & coalesce* effects are an essential part of the story. Sometimes this will be spontaneous (global ambitions were not an element at first). But often it reflects a tactical judgment that it would be best to segment the effort. Both strands can be seen especially clearly in the origin (always intrinsically local) and contagion (often local as a tactic) of what have come to be vast religious movements, most strikingly Christianity and Islam.

### Intensity/prevalence

One dimension of participation is prevalence. How large a fraction of potential cooperators are in fact cooperating? But another dimension is intensity. Among cooperators, how much is each contributing? This offers a third tactic for getting beyond a tipping point, since ordinarily reducing the contribution required will reduce $S'$ proportionately more than it will reduce $G'$.

As noticed in passing in Chapter 1, $G'$ and $S'$ are each defined as finite quantities, so $G'/S'$ is not the ratio of infinitesimals. $S'$ is the finite private cost of participating, $G'$ the finite social value of the contribution, each as seen by the chooser, and each net of side-effects as discussed in Chapter 4. Suppose that cooperation at a high level of intensity risks provoking a costly reaction that would harm the individual cooperator or that would harm the group, but the more modest level of intensity does not. Then unless there were increasing returns to scale for spending on $G$, $G'$ at the lower level of intensity would be higher relative to $S'$ at that level, since the individual cost would not be augmented by the adverse response. Even if that were not so, $S'$ ordinarily diminishes more than proportionately.

So in general, with a reduction in how much is asked of cooperators, the $WS'$ curve shifts down relative to the $G'$ curve, favorably affecting the prospect that participation will get beyond a tipping point. But once prevalence is high, activists can try to increase intensity, but now starting from a status quo which is at $Q^+$ (beyond the tipping point) rather than starting on the wrong side of the hump, at $Q^-$.

Here is another, slightly different, way to look at the *intensity/prevalence* tradeoff. Suppose that at a certain stage, the challenge for promoters of some social change is not to persuade people that cooperation on what is at issue would be good if achieved. A substantial value for $G'$ (for cooperation on the matter at issue and relative to cost) is widespread. But widespread actual cooperation does not follow from that. $G'$ may be large, but with participation still low, since beyond the seed $W$ will be high. If cooperation entails a substantial private cost, people feel closer to equilibrium by waiting to see when others will act. So almost nobody acts. We are at $Q^-$ in the diagram, facing the problem of getting over the hump.

But if the costs of cooperation are substantial, so that few people can be moved to cooperate unless they believe that almost everyone else will, then a possible tactic is to ask less of cooperators. Lowering the cost of participation will ordinarily shift the WS′ curve down more than it shifts the G′ curve down. The private cost of cooperation, by definition, is now less; and although the social gain from cooperation is also less, the social gain per unit of resources committed is not likely to be less. That effect will be magnified by effects on expectations. A person's expectation of how far others in fact will cooperate will increase (when cooperation seems cheap). Risk-averse concerns about the costs of cooperation if others turn out not to join in will be less.

So the propensity to contribute increases across the community. In the S-diagram, WS′ shifts down proportionately more than G′ does, increasing $\Delta$, moving $Q^-$ and $Q^+$ to the right (higher participation) and moving the tipping point to the left, shrinking the hump and enlarging the cushion, as illustrated in the contrast between Figure 5.2 and Figure 5.1. Contingent on elasticity, the total amount of contributions from all choosers might either decrease or increase. But since every chooser's individual equilibrium condition shifts to favor participation, participation necessarily increases whether aggregate contribution immediately does so or not.

This has a paradoxical character that warrants a little thought to get straight. You learn it costs only \$5 to join (rather than \$10). This increases your willingness to join. Your NSNX individual equilibrium has shifted to the right (higher social spending) relative to the \$10 cost which exceeds your equilibrium by enough to prompt you to free-ride when prevalence is low. But increasing prevalence will reinforce the propensity to cooperation (from Rule 2, by decreasing W). If high prevalence is established (if the prevalence grows sufficiently to get over the hump), what had before (at low prevalence) seemed more than a chooser was ready to spend might now be acceptable. You might now be willing to contribute \$10 after all. This is aside from a second effect likely to be important. For seeing what look like social gains from the more modest level of participation might enlarge G′ as well as shrink W. A modestly credible conjectured social gain from cooperation might be turned into a convincing visible social gain.

Kuran (1997), from another perspective, draws on this possibility in pointing to ethnic solidarity of individuals at first promoted by increasing commitments to mere tokens of ethnic identification (dress, and so on), only later escalating to overtly political commitments.

Top-down tactics by definition always involve overt agency. But *intensity/ prevalence* effects, and also *segment & coalesce* effects, can occur spontaneously, not as conscious tactics promoted from a seed. But it is often hard to distinguish active agency from spontaneous cases, since what begins spontaneously is almost always sooner or later promoted as well, as agents notice something they would want to encourage. An activity (like recycling) might begin in a particularly favorable locality, which is only after-the-fact noticed by agents interested in promoting the novelty on a wide scale. But activists then consciously choose *segment & coalesce* tactics, focusing initial effort on other particularly promising localities.

Similarly, even when visibly promoted, it will ordinarily be hard to judge how far an active agent actually played an essential role or was merely imagining he was controlling a bandwagon on which he was really only another passenger. Often it will be clear that agency appears only after the bandwagon had gathered momentum (but then may be crucial in shaping the climax). The collapse of regimes – most spectacularly, the collapse of the Soviet Union – commonly begins with spontaneous *intensity/prevalence* effects. People begin to just barely grumble about the regime, make slightly sarcastic remarks, and if (in contrast to earlier times) this does not generate looks of concern or disapproval, such comments spread so widely that there is no way for the regime to crack down since everyone is guilty. And the grumbles become bolder, the jokes less good-natured. A process of this kind led eventually to the collapse of the Soviet Union, extending over a long period before overt agency played any visible role, gradually growing into a general reluctance to cooperate with the regime even among many inside the regime.

## Vertical tactics

The horizontal tactics already reviewed deal with how agents might seek to reach a tipping point even taking preferences as given. Vertical tactics seek to shift the preferences, hence directly changing the vertical relation between them.

The discussion in Chapter 4 noticed that the curves can be shifted without challenging underlying beliefs and commitments by changing *incentives* (rewards and punishments). Or beliefs themselves might be changed by *persuasion*. Or $G'$ might be changed aside from either incentives or persuasion by shifting the *salience* of a particular component of belief, which is easier and often more important. And changes in $G'$ can also occur wholesale, by shifting the salience not of beliefs but of *identities*, which when successful can create large shifts in both the $WS'$ and $G'$ curves. For that would shift both the reference group for "people like me" (affecting $W$), and the group to which group-interested commitments might be made (affecting, possibly very radically, $G'$). Each is the concern of a large body of work in psychology and the social sciences. I will comment just briefly on each.

*Incentives* (positive and negative: rewards and punishments) were reviewed in Chapter 4. This noticed, in particular, that individual rewards (positive incentives, reducing $S'$) will usually exhibit decreasing marginal returns as the level of cooperation increases, but negative incentives (penalties, increasing $S'$) will usually increase marginal returns (at least up to some very high level of cooperation). These are essentially the "selective incentives" of Olson (1965).

NSNX adds the possibility of group rewards and punishments to Olson's selective incentives to individuals. In Olson's analysis, where only self-interested motivation is in play, extension from individual to group incentives would not be consequential. If self-interest alone governs choice, a chooser would care about reward or punishment of a group only to the extent that his individual incentive would be altered (his own reward enhanced, his own punishment mitigated). The effect of a group incentive on an individual might be large. If every member of the group is threatened by a severe fine unless cooperation within the group is high, there is a strong incentive to each individual to hope cooperation is high. But discounted by the ordinarily microscopic effect of an individual choice on group-level effects, no marginal incentive of consequence may remain. But in a NSNX world group reward or punishment sometimes will be crucially relevant, on an argument that does not need to be spelled out here, since (as mentioned in Chapter 4) it exactly parallels the discussion of voting in Chapter 2.

But how that will be judged also is subject to tactical effects. *Rewards or punishments* shift the curves by adding (or changing) the side-effects of choice, so that net G′ and net S′ may yield a value ratio very different from what they would otherwise be. *Persuasion, salience*, and *identity* tactics each shift the G′ curves directly (and less often for the concerns here, S′), but in entirely different ways. Arguments are always important, but good arguments (arguments that people not caught up in the passion of the moment would on reflection judge to be good arguments) are almost never as important as rational creatures would want them to be. Good arguments are often hard to sell and bad arguments hard to put down.

Outside settings that make careful, detached attention to arguments a strong norm, and indeed if situations are examined closely, even within them, persuasion is never simply by argument (uninfluenced by slogans, analogies, symbols, authority, loyalty, social pressure, all mediating visceral feelings). And persuasion is always slow unless powerfully encouraged by the extra-logical elements. Zajonc (1980) appears to be correct in his claim that "emotions come first": our response to whatever comes to attention is colored by an automatic, subjectively immediate affective response which establishes a presumption leaning one way or another, which sometimes can be overcome but not easily or quickly. In the long run, careful argument is enormously powerful. Every theorem established in Euclid by careful argument almost 2,500 years ago is unchallenged today. But in the short run, good arguments alone are never sufficient to do more (referring now back to the brief earlier discussion of paradigm shifts in science) than establish a seed which over time might win out.

When the circumstances are right, persuasion by the various extra-logical means noted parenthetically (aided by slogans, analogies, symbols, authority, loyalty, social pressure) can be fast, but persuasion by argument itself is always a process, and a slow process typically requiring many iterations before a novel claim takes hold. A window of opportunity (see *shocks*, below) may open the door to the means of rapid persuasion, but since persuasion by argument is slow, it needs to be well in place among some key members of the community before a window of opportunity opens, at which point potential sympathizers may quickly see a point that did not at all reach them before.

But *salience* and *identity* shifts, relative to persuasion (changing beliefs) can be rapid. An effective argument (here including the effects of slogans and so on which may facilitate or even pre-empt argument) needs to be focused on some particular point of belief. The starkest case is a mathematical argument, focused on a particular proposition. Sometimes a particular point casts a wide shadow. If the point is that your current leadership is incompetent or cannot be trusted, or has betrayed you, then that particular point of persuasion will make you ready to believe many other arguments adverse to that leadership. So persuasion on one point has contagion effects on other points. Nevertheless, changing belief (persuasion) does not have the immediate wholesale effects of a shift in *salience* which immediately crowds out rival beliefs without needing the slow process of directly changing beliefs. And shifts in *identity* can have even more powerful effects, since here the shift may immediately prompt wholesale shifts not only on priorities (salience effects) but on a person's entire sense of what would be socially valuable, since the sense of which group my loyalty concerns can be radically changed. A person does not abruptly shift from conservative to liberal. But he may quite abruptly shift from salient high level, usually national concerns to salient local concerns, or sometimes the reverse, as conspicuously in the US for some time after 9/11.

Identity effects turn on how an individual's sense of loyalty is governed in contexts where there are competing cues to what is "my group." Sometimes sharp gestalt-like shifts occur. The most famous case is still that of ardent international socialists who, after many passionate discussions of the need for socialists to stand aloof from imperialist wars, discovered themselves in August 1914 to be patriots. On this, and on many less discussed cases, we can see sudden shifts in G′ for some sort of social action that reflects a gestalt-like shift in the focus of group loyalties.

## Shocks

"Stuff happens" as Mr Rumsfeld remarked: sometimes unanticipatable, sometimes only unanticipated, and often enough actually foreseen but neglected nevertheless. Even the last come as shocks because the targets of tactics that the shock brings into play did not recognize what would happen (even if an agent considering what to do could), or hoped that what seemed likely to happen would somehow not happen after all, or because it is so hard to make even the foreseeable effects of a foreseeable shock sufficiently vivid to move people. The "emotions come first" point of the discussion of persuasion tactics is especially important here. If appeals to logic are rarely effective unless there is an emotional anchor, and in particular when they require displacing an adverse emotional anchor, then until a potential shock is actually shockingly evident it will rarely be playing a prominent role. But with more qualifications the same holds for the other aspects of vertical tactics (persuasion, salience, identity), and then the point becomes relevant indirectly for the horizontal tactics (*top-down, intensity/prevalence, segment & coalesce*) since what might look promising to agents as horizontal tactics will be contingent on their sense of the vertical situation and its stability.

But the S-diagram, returning now to recall the discussion in Chapter 4, is a special case of the general social phenomena captured by such now familiar language as "tipping points," "cascades," "critical mass." The S-diagram captures one especially important class of tipping point situation, where the issue is the success or failure in organizing cooperation for some social end, hence activating NSNX motivation. But then a component entering the dynamics of an S-diagram will be multiplier effects from social contagion, which become a source of unforeseeable shocks to the system.

I will return to that in the concluding chapter.

# 6    Adverse defaults

This chapter is about cognitive illusions in the form of simple logical questions that overwhelmingly prompt answers that are not smart from subjects who are. It has nothing immediately to do with NSNX. But the argument developed here is essential for the analysis of cooperation experiments that will take up the following four chapters. I begin by explaining the diversion.

Half of the 2003 Nobel Prize in economics went to Vernon Smith for his pioneering work in establishing *experimental economics* as a major subfield within economics. The other half went to a psychologist, Daniel Kahneman, for his work (mostly with his late collaborator Amos Tversky and with economists, especially Richard Thaler) in exploring departures from the narrowly rational choice accounts that had for a long time been almost unchallenged among economists and game theorists. That cognitive work has created another major subfield, *behavioral economics*. The two are intimately linked. For exploring or even clearly exposing cognitive anomalies is almost impossible outside the controlled realm of a laboratory. So experimental economics is an essential complement of behavioral economics. But the converse is also true.

The experimental economics work of course has been much concerned with simulations of auctions and markets. But almost from the start it has also been concerned with choices that are intrinsically social: with public as well as private goods. And sometimes the results have been anomalous, in the sense that we see choices, which are hard to make sense of in terms of any plausible model of rational choice. Further, anomalies are especially conspicuous in the context of *social* choices, where players who somehow manage to cooperate do better than players who don't. And it is easy to understand why that might be so. If I am making a choice for myself alone, even a choice that interacts with others (as in an auction), but where I have no doubts about what others are trying to do – like me, they just want to buy cheap and sell dear, maximizing their profit – then I may still be subject to some cognitive illusion, giving rise to anomalies with labels like "winner's curse," "probability neglect," and many others. But a further and severe layer of difficulty comes with extension of the work to social choices. For then behavior of one person may be contingent on the motivation of others, and what that motivation may be will no longer be unproblematical. If the game is a cooperation game, I may want to cooperate if I could be confident you want to cooperate also, but definitely not so (I do not want to be a sucker) if you are likely to be choosing selfishly. In particular, on the NSNX conjecture of this study that must be so.

But since laboratory games are not real-world situations but simplified and highly artificial analogs of real situations, there is always a question of how far what is seen in the lab reveals insight into actual cooperation and failures of cooperation, as against how far what is revealed is only an artifact of the artificial situation (Harrison and List 2004). An essential step in dealing with that difficult topic turns on understanding how far and where choices in the artificial and impoverished environment of an experiment reveal some misperception or misunderstanding of the game that is being played, as opposed to choices that reveal how players would choose if they had the kind of understanding of the game that corresponds to their behavior in normal social situations. Even when misperceptions seem to be in play, further steps are needed to identify situations in the world that might give rise to similar misperceptions and judge where (and whether) such circumstances are of much empirical significance. In the final chapters here, I will try to say something about such questions. But as background I need an account of cognitive anomalies in social experiments. And as the basis for that, I need the account in this chapter of certain cognitive anomalies in the far simpler contexts of individual choice.

From a Darwinian perspective, there surely must be default responses available to handle commonly encountered situations when familiar cues are sparse or weak or conflicting. Creatures who survive must come equipped with defaults for what to do when they would otherwise be unsure what to do. A conspicuous example would be the fight-or-flee situation. This is pervasive in nature. Indefinite hesitation is not a viable option. And even an elephant would probably do best if equipped with a *flee* default when in doubt, though presumably an elephant would not often be in doubt.

The defaults must be usually *benign* (or they would not be selected for as defaults), but sometimes these usually benign defaults must turn out to be *adverse*. That should not be in the least controversial. But the particular role of defaults discussed here seems to have gone essentially unnoticed. That in itself is an interesting cognitive point, but perhaps not surprising. The bare existence of what I will call *neglect* defaults could be expected. But their strength in some contexts is very surprising, and it is perhaps not surprising that it is hard to believe in something so surprising.

What makes sense of cognitive shortcuts in general is that they conserve attention when the delay otherwise required would be too costly to tolerate (as with the default for fight-or-flee situations), or simply useless, or inefficient, or something else easily interpreted as a reasonable response to the circumstances at hand. But what defines the *neglect* defaults is not the economy of using them on particular occasions (which is usually slight), but that the occasions for the default responses are so very common. Without neglecting almost all such occasions by default, a person would be overwhelmed by hesitations. These are hesitate/*proceed* defaults. As long as the default is in place, we rely on what Gladwell (2005) popularized as our "blink" intuition and proceed, not hesitate. The hesitations avoided are usually individually negligible, but in the aggregate they would be an intolerable burden.

We constantly make choices, mostly trivial, mostly in fact not reaching the level of conscious attention. We also constantly encounter opportunities to hesitate and reconsider whatever choice is on the table at the moment. So if we had to adopt a default rule about whether to stop and reconsider a choice when we have no sufficient indication one way or the other, we would be crippled unless that rule made us unlikely to stop. If I am walking across a minefield, it will not take much to get my attention, but in an ordinary field I will not stop to consider how to maneuver around every bush I encounter. I know it is possible that if I looked more carefully I would see a rusty nail or maybe even a rattlesnake. But I move on, disregarding such possibilities unless some cue is salient enough to displace the *proceed* default. Random choices will be almost always be good enough, while spending time mulling every choice would be a disaster. But inevitably cases will arise in which proceeding rather than hesitating will turn out to be a mistake.

Noticing an *adverse* neglect default at work, however, need not be easy even when a chooser is ignoring information immediately at hand which could surely improve a choice. Suppose that indeed I have an opportunity to improve a choice. There might nevertheless be enough difficulty or complexity to the problem to make it hard or unprofitable to actually use that opportunity. That provides a tempting route to denial that *neglect* defaulting might have serious consequences. Even if there isn't actually much difficulty or complexity to the problem, it might be tempting to suppose there is. For even inferences that we make routinely and easily, can sound complicated and difficult if we try to spell out every detail of how to reach the inference. I can assure you that it is no trouble at all for me to sneeze. But if someone could write out all the nerve signals and muscle movements required for that, you might wonder how I can possibly manage it all. I will make an effort to pre-empt that line of denial of the role of neglect defaults.

## Three neglect defaults

Three defaults come into the discussion here. Each is some functional equivalent of a hesitate/*proceed* neural switch whose default position is "proceed," so that the effect of the default is to neglect some possible occasion for stopping to think about how an incremental piece of information might be relevant to a choice at hand – in the context of a puzzle, for seeing how to answer the puzzle. Each allows a person to proceed rather than hesitate unless a sufficient jolt pushes the default switch to hesitate.

Escape from the default might operate by cuing escape from a primary hesitate/*proceed* default. Alternatively, the primary default might itself not be a neurally embedded mechanism, but only the union of all the secondaries, which operate independently, or at least on the same level. How the neurophysiology works is not needed for the argument here.

### Incremental information

Suppose that I stop to consider a piece of incremental information which has come to my attention. I might then judge the effect of that information as significant enough to warrant taking more time to think about it. Call that the *interactive* case. There seems likely to be some consequential interaction between the novel item and a choice I face. But perhaps what I do, or might do, does not look like it interacts significantly with that incremental information. In that case, I would have done better to have just neglected the issue and proceeded. Of course, I cannot know how I would judge that interaction possibility unless I hesitate long enough to consider it. But if I stopped to consider whether a choice is *interactive* or *passive* with respect to anything that came to attention while facing a choice, I could hardly get through the day. We are facing choices all day long. And whenever we consider a choice we will be aware of other things in the vicinity of the choice that conceivably might be affected by the choice, or which perhaps ought to influence the choice. If I go on a picnic, that does not make it more likely to rain (a passive case). I would not gain anything by stopping to think about the difference in the probability it will rain, contingent on the picnic. But if I bet the limit in a poker game that does make it more likely other players will fold (an interactive case), and I better think about who might fold and how likely that would be. If another player seems to be studying how many chips I have on the table, that might well be relevant to what I should do, and I ought to consider that. So there are many contexts in which I would do better to hesitate. But to get through the day I will have to almost always just proceed. As between interactive or passive, *passive* will have to be the default. So this is a quite transparent application of the notion of a default favoring *proceed* over *hesitate*.

The interactive/*passive* default is about how readily an agent can be prompted to look ahead or look around and think about the effects of some item at least momentarily in sight. An example of that would be when inferences from recent or local experience might be improved by adjusting in light of some item of long-term or global experience. And the particular context of that sort that has gotten special attention concerns statistical base rates. For attention to or neglect of base rates, being quantitative, lend themselves to formal discussion (Bayes' theorem) and tightly designed experiments. But quantitative cues which logically should but cognitively do not prompt affective or causal or otherwise sensitive alerts would be especially vulnerable to adverse neglect.

In an extensive review, Koehler (1996) showed that even naïve choosers sometimes act as proper Bayesians, adequately taking into account base rates. But at other times even sophisticated choosers are likely to ignore base rates entirely and might do so even in a context where it is hard to make rational sense of that. And indeed, it often does make sense to ignore base rates, or give them only modest weight, because the conditions that make their full use logically compelling are often lacking in real-world contexts, as Koehler stressed. But even when that is not so, absent cognitively effective cues, the default would be to tacitly neglect possible correlations between the local context and whatever is in the global background. So *if* (I am not claiming to have shown it yet) neglect defaults might be much harder to dislodge than we would consciously see as sensible, then base rates might often be ignored by default, even when logically it is clear that they shouldn't be.

And the point relevant to this entire topic of defaults is that what is needed to cue departure from neglect of base rates is apparently something more than verbal guidance in a problem statement that logically entails giving attention to what might be neglected. Merely specifying a base rate often has close to zero effect.[1] But a clue to what might govern stubborn neglect is the very large difference it can make whether a logically relevant base rate is stated as a fraction (0.34) or as a frequency (34 out of 100) even when the subject is someone who knows very well that what 0.34 means is that he can expect 34 out of 100 cases to go that way. What appears to be a logically inconsequential gap (between 0.34 and 34/100) often turns out to make a cognitively large difference. Sometimes it seems to take a very direct jolt indeed to nudge the switch from proceed to hesitate.

### Modus tollens neglect

As with "base rate" neglect, *modus tollens* is academic talk for something routinely encountered without any such label. When one thing entails another, if that second thing is absent the first thing ought to be also absent. You need no formal study of logic to know that "if it's raining it will be cloudy" lets a person suppose (*modus tollens*) that if there are no clouds it is not about to rain. But opportunities to notice totally useless *modus tollens* inferences are ubiquitous. Overwhelmingly, we just ignore those opportunities. Using an example much discussed among philosophers (Hempel's paradox), suppose I assure you that "all ravens are black." And I am wearing a green tie. Noticing something green, and observing that it is my tie, should you not gain an extra mite of confidence that indeed all ravens are black? For no one doubts that "all ravens are black" implies (you will follow even if you have never studied formal logic) that "non-black things are non-ravens." And my green tie, which is not black, is also not a raven, just as predicted by a theory that all ravens are black. So here is a bit of evidence supporting that theory. Philosophers debate how to handle this silly but logically impeccable inference.

But unless provoked by an academic discussion, we do not notice this silly inference at all. Rather, we are protected from wasting time noticing it only to have to waste more time concluding it was not worth noticing. It takes a raven to provide us with an occasion when we might check for a case where a raven is not black. But it only takes an object which is not black to provide an occasion when we might check for a case where (*modus tollens*) a non-black thing is a raven. We could spend the day gathering such evidence at a pro-digious rate and be no more confident than we were at the start that indeed all ravens are black.

Nor is the burden of inferring what might be implied *modus tollens* limited to the very occasional cases of sweeping generalizations like "all ravens are black." Mom says, "Dinner will be ready by the time you get hungry." So the kid expects that if dinner is ready, he will be getting hungry. But he is not burdened every few seconds over the next several hours with thoughts of "I'm not getting hungry, so dinner isn't ready."

So in addition to the looking ahead (interactive/*passive*) or looking around (what we could label global/*local*) categories of the general hesitate/*proceed* pairs, we can identify at least one logical category (*modus tollens*) that ought to be subject to mostly benign but potentially adverse defaulting.

As with base rates, it is not that people untrained in formal logic are incap-able of noticing and using everyday versions of *modus tollens* (I will give some further examples in a moment). Rather, a tacit default blocks such inferences unless there are sufficient cognitively effective cues in the context to displace that default. And we can observe, and not just in artificial puzzles, that bare logic does not easily offset beliefs supported by interests, emotions, physical experience, or social pressures, so that perhaps we should not be surprised to find that bare logic unsupported by interests, emotions, physical experience, or social pressures also does not easily offset defaults likely to have been entrenched long before our ancestors had any capacity for explicit logic, and presumably to some substantial extent before our ancestors had language to reason with.

### Ordinary language

And the most readily understood of this set concerns how we pragmatically respond to language. An entire academic movement (deconstruction) was built around the inevitability of multiple meanings for anything we might say or anything an author might write. Language is intrinsically *polysemous*. The hesitate/*proceed* default is to rely on what Gladwell has popularized as "blink" intuitions. We do not think about what is intended. Ordinarily, we take it to be immediately transparent, though if you try to parse it out in an exact way it often proves difficult to say why it should be seen as transparent. This is so utterly commonplace that no detailed argument is likely to be needed to persuade a reader that our understanding of language relies heavily on a default that it takes a jolt to displace. The pragmatics that tacitly guide our understanding of language have been quite elegantly discussed in Grice's set of William James lectures at Harvard in 1967. Deconstructionists, logicians, and lawyers in one way or another develop very refined techniques for picking apart the multiplicity of meanings of ordinary language. But outside of very specialized contexts, even deconstructionists, logicians, and lawyers use and comprehend language in the pragmatic, taking-it-for-granted, tacit way that everyone else does. Outside of specialized professional contexts they *hesitate* to mull the multiplicity of possible meanings in every remark no more than you do. Overwhelmingly, they just *proceed*.

## Wason

Each of the three examples of hesitate/*proceed* defaults now in place (inter-active/*passive*, *modus tollens* neglect, ordinary language) will next be illus-trated with the help of some striking cognitive illusion, starting with the Wason selection task, which is by some wide measure the most exhaustively studied of all cognitive illusions:

---

Four cards are labeled "A" or "D" on one side and "2" or "3" on the other. A rule says: "If the letter is A the number must be 2."
  You see two of the cards letter side up, the other two number side up. Which need to be turned over to find any violation of the rule?

---

A majority of people, offered the array [A, D, 2, 3], respond by choosing "A&2" or only "A". Few give the correct response of "A&3". Understanding *ex post* that turning the "2" is beside the point (a D on the other side of 2 would not violate the rule) is easy, and so is understanding that you must turn the "3" (an A on the other side of 3 would violate the rule). But usually upward of 90 percent of subjects miss that logically almost trivial inference. Professors do not do much better than their students. The "if/then" rule can be pragmatically read either as a conditional (as in "if it's raining, it is cloudy") or biconditional (as in "if it's nice we'll go on a picnic"). Context that ordinarily would suggest an intended meaning is absent in this abstract puzzle. That the most common response is "A&2" not "A" shows that the reading is more likely to be biconditional, though as a sentence in formal logic it would not be read that way. The deeper question is why smart people are so likely to get this simple problem wrong even if the verbal ambiguity is explicitly resolved.

The usual explanations turn in one way or another on a claimed limited capacity of human beings to handle the *modus tollens* inference: "if p then q, & not-q, therefore not-p." For some (e.g. Cosimedes 1989) the intrinsic difficulty of *modus tollens* outside of special contexts is the heart of the matter. For others, the difficulty of *modus tollens* is a component interacting with other difficulties. So Sperber *et al.* (1995: 52), tying the argument to Sperber and Wilson (1986), argue that "the artificiality of the task is so overwhelming as to discourage any but the lowest expectations of relevance, and anything except the most superficial interpretation processes."[2]

On a *"modus tollens* is difficult" account, outside of specialized contexts (cases of moral or legal obligation, for example), it is burdensome to try to use *modus tollens*, so that subjects either usually can't do it, or at least are discouraged from making the effort. But do people really have any difficulty noticing that "if he's coming, you'll have a message on your phone" implies that "if the message light is not blinking, apparently he isn't coming"? More generally, how could incompetence handling *modus tollens* be plausible in evolutionary terms, since although we couldn't get through a day if we noticed every available *modus tollens* inference, we also couldn't get through the day effectively without informally responding to many such inferences.

We use *modus tollens* so readily we do not ordinary notice when we do it. And it would be a puzzle if our brain has not evolved in a way that ordinarily made that easy.

In terms of the *neglect* defaulting proposed here, the Wason illusion does not turn on *modus tollens* being difficult to handle, so choosers miss it, but on the ubiquity of occasions when *modus tollens* is at hand but pragmatically pointless, so we do best to ignore it.

When I first had occasion to write on Wason (Margolis 1987), I encountered an advertisement for an anti-dandruff shampoo using the slogan: "If you use it, no one will know. They'll only know if you don't use it." The ad-men choosing this did not expect that 90 percent of the audience would have to consult a logician to make sense of the slogan. But to see the point, a person has to see the connection (*modus tollens*) between the first sentence and the second sentence. A person also needs the pragmatic inference that the reason they know is that they will see dandruff on your clothes. But if the shampoo works, there would not be any dandruff to see. So if you do use it, then (*modus tollens* again) indeed people won't know you use it. Hence parsing out this advertising slogan is by a considerable measure logically more complex than the bare *modus tollens* inference required for the Wason problem. But people get the point immediately.

In general, people can do what you almost certainly did several times in the previous few sentences. We see the point of a *modus tollens* inference in a subjectively immediate way, with no sense of effort. That fluent competence is in our brains. But the point of the account here is that access to conscious attention is by default turned off in the absence of cognitively effective cues to a context where it is likely to be useful rather than a diversion. The default is that *modus tollens* is neglected. The switch is off. And on that view, the key to understanding Wason is to notice that the basic Wason puzzle, lacking anything to arouse an affective response or any tie to experience in the world, apparently provides only a very weak bump – a surprisingly weak bump, but we will see the same thing with later examples – that does not move the *modus tollens* switch even when as simple logic the occasion is clear.

Successful remedial versions of Wason most often use language that invokes a sense of obligation or a concern about being cheated, or that invokes a familiar situation in which explicit use of *modus tollens* is common. There is no puzzle about how these versions provide sufficient affect or recognition to displace a *modus tollens* neglect default. In an exhaustive analysis, Sperber *et al.* (1995) show that more general conditions are sufficient. It is enough to provoke surprise or curiosity. The simplest maneuver yielding a big improvement (Evans 1989) is just to change the rule to a negative (here, from "A → 2" to "A → not-3"), which not only makes the *not* card salient, but invokes an element of experimenter demand ("if I'm not expected to suspect the '3', why is the rule framed in this roundabout way?"). Nudged to consider the card, the *modus tollens* connection is far more easily available.

In my 1987 book, I showed another very simple manipulation, about equally effective, which is to reduce the array of choices from [A, D, 2, 3] to just [2, 3]. The two easy cards ("A," which is rarely missed, and "D," which is rarely chosen) are removed, leaving only the two hard cards: "2" and "3", which supply nearly all the errors. One might suppose, since essentially all errors are in relation to the hard cards, that subjects will continue to do badly. But they don't. Subjects shown an array reduced to [2, 3] will return a majority of correct responses. The defaulting account offers an explanation. Unless *modus tollens* is switched on, *no* card violates (since "A" is no longer available). But a puzzle normally has a positive correct answer, so that as Evans's negative framing of the rule draws attention to the "3," seeing no card to turn prompts a "look closer" response and a person may notice the *modus tollens* violation after all.[3]

Another curious effect reported in *Patterns* (with a replication in Griggs 1989) first frames the question as: "Circle two cards to turn over to check whether the rule has been violated." This unsurprisingly maximizes "A & 2" responses. But when the instruction is turned around to read: "Figure out which two cards could violate the rule, and circle them," the predominant response switches to the otherwise rarely seen "D & 3." The categories/ instances conjecture of my account in *Patterns* yields what still seems to me an elegant account of that. But it becomes redundant in the light of the broader neglect defaulting account here. What seems to be happening is this. With only the four combinations the problem statement allows, logically it must be the case that "if A then 2" is true so is "if 3 then D." But *modus tollens* neglect would miss that. Rather, a set of implications that are often pragmatically appropriate would come into play for "two cards that could violate." Pragmatically "if A then 2" might be intended to also carry "and if D then 3," or "and if 2 then A," or "and if 3 then D" or any combination among these. I provided a survey of the possibilities in *Patterns* (pp. 148–51). So if *modus tollens* is *not* neglected, the salient response would be the same "A & 3" that is correct without specifying "two cards." But if *modus tollens* is neglected, and with looking for "could violate" candidates more salient in the instruction than "circling two," a person might sense a lot of possibilities.

Then Kahneman and Frederick's (2005) "attribute substitution" could prompt subjects to slip from the complex task of choosing among the various "could violate" possibilities, over to the simpler task of picking the two cards that "can't obey" the rule.

A final variation, but one that requires more qualification, uses a slight variation of the rule which logically should make the problem easier:

---

RULE: If the letter is D, the number can be either 2 or 3. But if the letter is A, then the number must be 2.

Here are the cards, showing the top then the bottom of each card.

---

But now *both* sides are shown. Subjects do not need to infer anything. The array is:

A/3        D/2        2/A        3/A

And the task is merely to identify any cards that violate the rule.

There is now nothing in the task that requires use of *modus tollens*. The A/3, 2/A, and 3/A cards each has an "A" on the letter side. And of them 2/A conforms to the rule but A/3 and 3/A violate it. A person can hardly get this version of Wason *wrong* unless she tacitly sees the A/3 card as "looking like" *modus ponens* ("if p then q") while the same left-to-right habit of reading prompts the 3/A card to be seen as the *modus tollens* cognate of the rule, which (by default) a person would easily neglect. So contrary to supposing that choosers miss *modus tollens* because of its difficulty, here a person has to fluently recognize *modus tollens* to get the problem *wrong*. We will see another "in your face" case of neglect shortly.

Given the stark triviality of this both-sides version of Wason, it is not a devastating criticism that if the circumstances are such that subjects are motivated to take care, they will get this version right. But an *abstract modus tollens* inference, where nothing is there to tacitly nudge the defaulting switch, feels harder than a *modus ponens* inference. The situation is analogous to what happens if you want to switch a TV channel but have forgotten that the TV/VCR toggle is on "VCR." You need an extra step. The step is trivial, as is the actual channel switch that follows. But there is a perceptible bit of delay. Here it is easy to notice that facing this both-sides Wason, respondents visibly have some difficulty with the 3/A card and sometimes miss it.

### Three cards puzzle[4]

But if a *neglect* reading of Wason is sound, then we should be able to find parallels in other cognitive illusions. Here is a favorite brain-teaser from books on probability (Bertrand's box puzzle).

Three cards are in a box. One is white on each side, and another is red on each side. The third card is white on one side and red on the other. So there is one white/white card, one red/red card, and one white/red card. Without looking, you take out one card, and lay it on the table.
1.   Suppose the up-side turns out to be white? What is the chance that the down-side will also be white?
2.   What if the up-side is red? What is the chance that the down-side will also be red?
3.   Before you see the card, what is the chance that it has the same color on both sides?
4.   Suppose you answered 1/2 in response to Questions 1 and 2. That would mean that whichever the up color of the card, the chance is 50/50 that you have picked a same-color card. But if at Question 3 you said that chance is 2/3, aren't you contradicting yourself?

As implied by Q4, the usual response to (1) and (2) is 1/2 and the almost universal response to Q3 is 2/3. The response to Q4 from the large majority who report 1/2 for Q1 and Q2 but 2/3 for Q3 is then invariably that there must be some mistake in the reasoning which claims to show a contradiction. Indeed, this is often a most emphatic response, which is hard to overcome, and especially so for people (like economists and engineers) whose experience in the world gives them confidence that they could not have *mistaken* clear intuitions about such simple probability questions. Yet no *reasoning* is required to see the "1/2" intuition for Q1 and Q2 can't possibly be correct if the "2/3" intuition for Q3 is right. If you can read English, how could you doubt that for a moment? In this symmetric context (no one gives different responses to Q1 and Q2), what else could it mean to say that the chances are 2 in 3 that a card has the same color on both sides other than the chances are 2 in 3 that if it is red on top it is red on the bottom, and ditto for white? But it ordinarily takes a while to get free of the illusory conviction that the chance in Q1 and Q2 is 1/2, and there is a stubbornness of the faulty intuition here very much more severe than can be seen in any of the Wason variants.

For this three-cards puzzle, another simple argument notices that:

*Ex ante*, any of the sides are equally likely to turn up. If the side you see is red, you know it is one of three equally likely red sides. Two are on the red/red card, and only one on the white/red card. So the chance is 2/3 that the red side you are looking at is on the red/red card.

And yet another argument comes from noticing that:

Ex ante the red/red and red/white cards are equally likely. But when it's red/red the color on top is always red, while when it's red/white, the color on top is red only half the time. So when you've picked on a card with a red side showing, it is twice as often on the red/red card.

But the immediate, and often far more extended than immediate, intuition of even sophisticated subjects commonly defies the simple logic. The red/red and red/white continue to seem equally likely no matter which color is showing, as if seeing the color on top tells you nothing. But exactly what the inter-active/*passive* default describes is this kind of situation. Anyone starts with a sense that each of the three cards is equally likely to be drawn. But a further bit of information is provided, but neglected. The color on top is red. This trivially eliminates the white/white card, and on any of the three simple bits of reasoning already given makes the chance 2/3 that the red/red card has been drawn. But few people see that. And parallel to the both-sides variant that concluded the Wason discussion, a strong piece of evidence that indeed this is another case of adverse neglect defaulting is that even an in-your-face inference requiring no argument, just attention to what the language in Q3 must mean at all, is sometimes missed.

A variant reported by Fox and Levav (2004) tried to help choosers by using the default propensity to treat a set of alternatives as equally likely. Asked for the chance that Sunday would be the warmest day of an arbitrary week, subjects reliably respond "1/7" only if attention was specifically cued to the days in a week. Fox and Rottenstreich (2003) showed that without explicit cuing to "days," subjects seem to anchor on "Sunday" or "not Sunday," as if each was equally likely, with an adjustment well short of what every subject knows is the correct number of days in a week.

Fox and Levav sought to meliorate the downright terrible performance of their Duke students on the three-cards puzzle by pushing them to focus on the colored sides (red/red, white/white, and red/white) not on the cards themselves. That seems promising, since if a person is focused on the sides, which by a (here benign) default would be correctly seen as equally likely, then (as in the second bit of reasoning just given) no calculation is needed to see that when the side you see is red, two of the three equally likely red sides are on the red/red card, only one on the red/white card. But having been initially set to think about the card picked, apparently subjects often answered in terms of the chance they picked the red/red card even though pushed to think about the sides.

For the basic problem, the Fox and Levav results were: 1/2 (59%), 1/3 (13%), 2/3 (2.6%), and others (26%). So barely more than 1 in 40 Duke students (2.6%) got the problem right, leaving a great deal of room for improvement.[5]

The remedial variant told subjects the sides were labeled red1-red2, white1-white2, and red3-white3. The question was no longer about the card picked but about the sides: "Given that the side showing is red, what is the probability that it is side red1 or red2?" So the manipulation explicitly numbers the sides, and asks specifically about the numbered sides. If the focus stays where the manipulation tries to push it, on the sides, the natural inclination demonstrated by the *days in the week* experiment is to treat the three sides you might see (red1, red2, or red3) as equally likely. Asked for the chance that the side on view is 1 or 2, would any sensible subject fail to see that the chance is 2 out of 3?

And this quite emphatic manipulation indeed changed responses. In fact, it increased correct responses ten-fold. But the news was not overall very good. The ten-fold increase still only moves the fraction of correct responses from 2.6% to 27%. Almost 3 of 4 (73%) were still getting the problem wrong, even though the question is now about sides of the cards and requires only seeing that the chance of picking "1" or "2" out of the set [1, 2, 3] is 2/3. Even worse, the modal response changed in a perverse way, revealing a tendency for subjects to revert to thinking about the setup of the problem (a card has been picked) and to then often see the "red1 or red2" question in terms of whether they picked the red/red card. And then they very often get that totally wrong. The illusory but usually modal "1/2" declined from 59% to 24%. But a large share of that decline shifted to "1/3," which now increased its share from 13% to 35%.[6] So for some subjects changing the problem to focus attention on particular, numbered sides (red1, white1, etc.) corrected an illusion, but for about as many others it made things worse.

A person who responded "1/2" at least had noticed that one of the three cards was eliminated absolutely (the white1/white2 card). The new modal response (1/3) did not even get that far. Like the both-sides variant of Wason, looking at information that with no non-trivial reasoning at all shows that the card cannot be white1/white1, the modal choice does not notice that the only two cards in play are red1/red1 and red1/white1. The largest fraction neglect the signal entirely, and see the chance that the card is red/red as only 1/3. Of those who don't, most neglect to look carefully enough to notice the correct response (2/3), though with the strong manipulation focusing on sides not cards, that appears to require no reasoning more difficult than counting to three. So it appears that neglect defaulting can vary in strength. A person might completely neglect what he sees (here yielding the 1/3 response), but he also might hesitate long enough to notice a gross implication (here that there is 0 probability he picked the white1/white1 card), but not long enough to notice the modestly subtler implication needed to reach the logical result. Either way, it is hard to see how students at an elite university could do this badly unless somehow they were simply blind to the signal they were given. But that is what the neglect defaulting argument says could happen. And if we now turn to another intensively discussed puzzle, we find a very similar story.

## Monty Hall

As I write (early 2007) Google reports 275,000 hits for "Monty Hall," overwhelmingly for the puzzle, not for the once television quizmaster who used a version on his show. But the puzzle in other versions had been notorious among statisticians long before the television-show version.[7] Here is a variant which avoids some ambiguity in the version tied to the quiz.

[MH] An Ace and two 5s from a deck of playing cards lay face-down. You must point to one. **I then will check the two remaining cards and turn one over to reveal a 5.** You win $10 if you end up with the Ace. You can keep your original card, or switch it for the remaining unchosen card. Is there an advantage to switching?

The usual response is a very confident intuition that there is no advantage to switching. But in fact switching doubles the chance to win. A reader not already familiar with the problem is likely to find this claim incredible. And as anyone who has tried the puzzle on colleagues will know, it can be hard to persuade even extremely sophisticated victims of this illusion that the immediately and powerfully intuitive response is wrong. Yet the only reasoning required is:

[MH*] Since it is 100 percent certain that at least one of the unchosen cards is a 5, checking them to reveal a 5 doesn't change the 2/3 chance that one of them is the Ace. It just tells which of those cards must be the Ace if either is. So unless you picked the Ace initially (a 1/3 chance), switching wins.

This reasoning is short, simple, and correct. But until a person is thoroughly familiar with Monty Hall, it is likely to seem like a trick proof that 2 = 3. Even if you can't see what is wrong with it, your intuition can assure you it must be wrong.

Parallel to the cards problem, a reader starts from the intuition that any of the three cards is equally likely to be the winning Ace. Once only two cards are left in play that equally likely intuition yields an illusion unless you adjust that initial sense of the situation for the new information that someone who knows the winning card has been required to reveal a losing not-chosen card. But if the interactive/*passive* default is hard to escape in this arbitrary context, you don't make any such adjustment. You see your initial pick and the remaining unchosen card as still equally likely to be the Ace.

But if that neglect defaulting is what yields the illusion, then this variant on Monty Hall, which differs only in the italicized sentence, should be easy to get right:

[XMH] An Ace and two 5s from a deck of playing cards lay face-down. You must point to one. **Without looking, you must turn over one of the two remaining cards. Suppose the card you turn reveals a 5.** You win $10 if you end up with the Ace. You can keep your original card, or switch it for the remaining unchosen card. Is there an advantage to switching?

And the reasoning for this problem would be:

[XMH*] When you pick a card to turn (without looking), but before you've turned it, the chances are certainly equal that any one of the three cards is the Ace. And so the chance is 2/3 that one of the other two cards (your first pick and the one you did not choose to turn) is the Ace. Once you turn over the card (blindly, not looking) that changes. If the turned card is the Ace, the other two cards each now has 0 probability of winning. If it is a 5, each now has a 0.5 chance. Either way, there is nothing to be gained by switching.

The reasoning is about as simple as the MH* reasoning for Monty Hall, but certainly not simpler. Nevertheless, subjects indeed find it as easy to get XMH right as it is hard to get MH right. That XMH is as easy for subjects as MH is hard is not at all a small point, since analyses of Monty Hall typically explain the trouble subjects have as growing out of its intrinsic difficulty, and explain the problem for readers with reasoning far more complicated than the simple but entirely adequate remarks in MH*. This parallels the propensity to explain Wason in terms of the difficulty of *modus tollens*, or to explain the three-cards puzzle in terms of a Bayesian argument a good deal less simple than any of the three short arguments given here. That probability intuitions are sometimes faulty, even for experts, must contribute to the notorious stubbornness of Monty Hall intuitions. It is trivial to point out the contradiction in ignoring the *not-2* card in Wason, since once attention is explicitly drawn to it, anyone can see that a card with A on the letter side but 3 on the number side violates the rule. But looking at a single play of Monty Hall (or parallel to that, of the three-cards puzzle), there is no *error* to be seen. Not switching in Monty Hall might in fact be the winning choice. The trickiness of probability intuitions is itself tied to inability to directly see an error in intuition in any single case.

But that does not account for why MH should generate overwhelmingly wrong responses, while XMH generates overwhelmingly correct responses. On the defaulting account, however, there is a very simple explanation. The interactive/*passive* default which is adverse for MH, leaving in place the intuition that the remaining cards are equally likely, is benign in XMH, since now the remaining cards indeed are equally likely. The default efficiently prompts a person to the correct intuition in XMH, even though the explicit reasoning might be judged a bit more complicated in XMH than in MH. But since the default-governed response happens to be correct, there is no cognitive illusion to be seen. Nor does the problem feel subjectively difficult. Here the default is benign, not adverse. XMH "feels" easy, since to get it right you just ride along with your intuition. But MH "feels" hard. To see why it pays to switch, you have to jolt the neglect default switch.

We can notice the same two elements which jointly make the three-cards problem notoriously hard. By default we favor treating the alternatives in sight as equally likely. And by default we tend to neglect incremental information that might interact with our immediate intuition. So the equally likely default plays a role here, but so does the interactive/*passive* neglect default. Relaxing even one of the defaults may be enough to make the puzzle much more manageable. And indeed this variant usually works.

---

[MHdeck] A deck of cards is spread out face-down. You must point to one. **I will then turn over 50 of the remaining 51 cards, but checking first to be sure I don't turn over the Ace of Spades.** You win $10 if you end up with that Ace. You can keep your original card, or switch it for the remaining unchosen card. Is there an advantage to switching?

---

The reasoning for MHdeck is the same as that people typically have severe difficulty grasping for MH, but just a bit more complicated, since 50 cards are turned not just one. So why would MHdeck be much easier than MH? Apparently, picking one card out of 50 is stark enough to jolt a person away from the equally likely default. In that many-cards context, far beyond what can be managed with iconic perception, the salient intuition is not that the card you picked is as likely as any other card (though you would have no doubt of that if asked) but that your pick is not at all likely to be the winning Ace. And now, as with MHX, the neglect default is benign. As before, there is actually no connection between the chance you already have the Ace and the signal. But now the intuition that is left in place happens to prompt you to the right choice. For the intuition in place is now that it is unlikely you have the Ace, hence you'd better switch.

Alternatively, try:

---

[XMHdeck]: A deck of cards is spread out face-down. You must point to one. **You then turn over (not looking) 50 of the remaining 51 cards, and you never turn over the Ace of Spades.** So the Ace is either your pick or the remaining unturned card. You win $10 if you end up with that Ace. You can keep your original card, or switch it for the remaining unchosen card. Is there an advantage to switching?

---

People now are often sure they should switch, though in fact in this case there is no advantage in switching. Think of exactly the same situation framed another way. You pick one card with your left hand. This is "your pick." You now pick another card as the "remaining unchosen card" with your right hand, and then turn over the other 50 cards. If you do this enough times, eventually none of the up-cards will be the Ace. Then either your left-hand or right-hand pick is the Ace. But why would you think your right-hand pick is any more likely to be the Ace than your left-hand pick?

But in the basic version (MH) why not start from the also logically imme- diate intuition that your pick has 1/3 chance of being the Ace? On the argu- ment here, the neglect default should benignly leave that in place instead of adversely leaving the equally likely intuition in place. But the history of probability answers that. The equally likely intuition is primordial. That is why it is a well-marked default. No one discovered "equally likely" as a default for a context in which you have no basis for supposing one possibility more likely than any other, since everyone always felt they knew it. But the notion of probability as a number (here 1/3) emerged only around 1660 in the wake of the Scientific Revolution that began half a century earlier. I give a detailed discussion in my 2002 book. Consequently although no one would doubt either intuition (it is equally likely that any of the cards is the Ace of three cards, the chance is 1/3 you picked the Ace), they are not at all on equal footing cognitively. Even the 52-card variant does not make it likely that the primordial (equally likely) intuition can be readily displaced by a quantitative probability, only that one primordial qualitative intuition (equally likely) can be replaced by its complement (highly *un*likely), prompted by an aggressive change in context (from 3 to 52 cards).

And turn now to a very different example of a hesitate/*proceed* default, this time involving professors rather than student subjects.

## An opportunity cost puzzle

Ferraro and Taylor (2005) asked economists encountered in the hotel lobby at the 2005 meeting of the American Economics Association to answer a question adapted from Chapter 1 of an introductory text by two particularly well-known economists (Ben Bernanke, as I write chairman of the Federal Reserve Board, and Robert Frank of Cornell and a columnist for the *New York Times*). The question should have been trivially easy for any professor of economics. But catching people as they stroll through a hotel lobby is hardly favorable to extended thought. So here was a context of the sort where even the both-sides-showing version of Wason fools choosers. Nevertheless, the result was remarkable. Almost four out of five of this sampling of professional economists got it wrong. Ferraro and Taylor argued that what that showed was a need for more attention to fundamental concepts in training economists. In a reply, I argued that, on the contrary, what it showed was that economists are human, hence that economists, like all other human beings, are vulnerable to cognitive illusions when presented with a question outside of the sort of context in which they are familiar with that sort of question (Margolis 2007).

On the defaulting account, the difficulty comes from the normal pragmatics of language discussed earlier as the *ordinary language* default. By default we treat language as "ordinary" language unless the context pushes us away from that. We know the Earth goes round the Sun, but it does not bother us in the least to talk about the Sun as "setting" not the horizon as rising, nor does it bother an astronomer. Unless the context triggers him away from the ordinary usage default, the astronomer no more senses anything odd about the Sun moving than anyone else.

Here is Ferraro and Taylor's survey question for economists:

> You won a free ticket to see an Eric Clapton concert (which has no resale value). Bob Dylan is performing on the same night and is your next-best alternative activity. Tickets to see Dylan cost $40. On any given day, you would be willing to pay up to $50 to see Dylan. Assume there are no other costs of seeing either performer. Based on this information, what is the opportunity cost of seeing Eric?

And offered a multiple choice of [$0, $10, $40, $50], only 43 of a sample of 199 (21.6%) saw that $10 is the correct response. The number of correct responses from professors of economics, consequently, was somewhat less than the expected number if the respondents had been chickens pecking randomly.

The nearly 80+ percent who missed the correct response scattered their answers about equally among the three incorrect responses. Subjects relying on their "blink" intuition give what they suppose is a correct response to what was obviously (to a professional) a really elementary question. This turns out to yield what are essentially random responses, but slightly biased *against* the correct ($10) response because it is the only choice not mentioned in the question, hence the least salient to a "blink" guesser. But this does not really show that professors of economics have a grossly inadequate grasp of a routine technical term in their discipline, only that Ferraro and Taylor's rather odd question happens to trigger the sort of cognitive mechanism that accounts for illusory responses elsewhere. The phrase "opportunity cost" rings a bell for economists. They *know* they know what that means. But in ordinary language it doesn't mean anything. If you combine economists' confidence their intuition would not let them down with a hesitate/*proceed* default, there is the makings of a cognitive illusion here.

In Ferraro and Taylor's simple problem, you can't go to both the Clapton concert and its alternative because you can't be in two places at the same time, not because (the usual context for economists thinking about "opportunity cost") money to pay for Dylan isn't available for Clapton. What is needed is the opportunity cost of using time in one leisure activity rather than another. And this is also not the value of time issue ordinarily encountered in an economic analysis, which usually trades off value of work versus value of leisure. Finally, since the out-of-pocket cost for the Clapton concert is zero, nothing prompts a subject to think about the price of the concert, though of course $0 is indeed technically a price, though in ordinary language no one would refer to zero as a price. This combination of odd features makes the problem just a bit "translucent" relative to a question where a person doesn't have to switch dimensions to get to the opportunity cost. The value of the time used to attend the free Clapton concert is the consumer surplus forgone by not going to the Dylan concert, for which you have a willingness-to-pay of $50 but need to pay only $40. And although consumer surplus is another perfectly familiar notion to any economist, outside a professional context no one thinks about the consumer surplus you could have gotten from the next-best thing you did not choose to deduce the opportunity cost of whatever you did choose, though indeed that is correct.

The textbook question is a really good one for students. It provokes them to see what at first sight is a weird connection and see why, though weird, it is correct. But as a question outside that tutorial context, it is only weird. The cognitive connection needed to make the correct response readily intuitive is not difficult but it is certainly unusual, so that even though the concepts engaged (opportunity cost, value of time, consumer surplus) are familiar to any economist, the connections among them do not just "click" into place.

Indeed, just as with the various other "neglect" defaults introduced early in this discussion, if an economist were easily prompted to thinking about the opportunity cost of the use of time implications of everyday choices, she could scarcely get through the day. You are almost constantly making choices of what to do next. At each choice, there is something else you might have chosen (or it wouldn't be a choice). Even if a next-best alternative is salient, all you need to know is that you prefer A to B, though every time you choose A there is an opportunity cost from not choosing B. It makes sense that our brains are organized in a way that inhibits being distracted by contemplation of such questions. It is only under special conditions (here indeed is where training comes in) that focusing on such things as opportunity cost is fruitful.

On Ferraro and Taylor's problem a usually efficient hesitate/*proceed* default pre-empts really simple logic that any economist would know very well. It is logic that most respondents would have had occasion many times to explain to students. But they do not notice what they know very well. This startling result ought to sharpen alertness to the possibility that more serious situations must arise where cognitive effects yield bad choices by people who certainly know better.[8]

But in a real situation that turns on opportunity costs, competent economists will not reveal gross ignorance of what they must in fact know, and if there were real consequences of the technical error for experts described in note 15, it certainly would have been caught very early, not survived for 400 years. Adverse defaulting can prompt cognitive illusions. But the defaults are usually only sticky, not locked in place. Sooner or later everyone comes to see the right answer to three-cards or Monty Hall. But in the realm of judgments beyond the scale of artificial puzzles, more serious consequences can arise, for there contexts are not so simple as to allow a flat, no qualifications, verdict of "error," and other aspects of social contexts add further difficulty. We have reason to consider the possibility that cognitive illusions of the individual choice sort we have been examining in this chapter might have counterparts at the level of social judgment.

And, pointing to the sequel to the argument here, a reader might not be surprised that this source of cognitive difficulty turns out to play a large role when the discussion of defaulting is extended from puzzles put to individuals to the more complex contexts of choice among interacting actors.

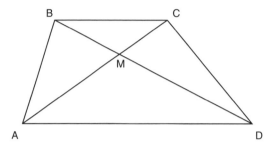

*Figure 6.1* Within trapezoid ABCD, prove whether ΔABM = ΔCDM.

### Geometry (8th grade level)

Finally, lest non-economists feel too smug, consider this quite trivial geometry puzzle. Within the trapezoid (Fig. 6.1), is ΔABM the same area as ΔCDM? Prove your answer is right. Hint: the proof is trivial, though few people solve it without considerable effort. See note[9] for the proof and a comment on how the quite astonishing difficulty of this simple puzzle relates to neglect defaulting.

# 7 Anomalies in experimental economics

Table 7.1 shows how a person might understand a social context, or the judgment a person might reach about how someone else is understanding that context. When I write about social perceptions and misperceptions in this chapter, I mean the subjective framing of social context within the tax-onomy of the box. On the evidence of Chapter 6, it makes sense to consider the possibility that social intuitions, not just individual intuitions, might sometimes be governed by what turn out to be adverse defaults. Parallel to what was seen in the context of responses to logically simple but cognitively difficult puzzles, misunderstandings as well as accurate understandings of social situations might occur. That would open the door to difficulties in reaching or sustaining cooperation which are invisible to the parties involved, as in Chapter 6 neglect defaults invisible to choosers can sometimes yield choices that the chooser herself, on reflection, comes to see as transparently unsound.

In the individual choice context, choosers whose only motivation is to get a simple logical puzzle right get it wrong. In the social context, both motiv-ations and situations are far more complicated. NSNX choosers would want to be "neither selfish nor exploited." But choice within a natural setting, not a set-piece puzzle, usually can't be reduced to simple logic, even in a simple context like choosing among alternatives on a routine trip to the grocery store. But the situations that concern us here are where choices affect other people as well as the chooser, and where how others are choosing, or might be choosing, can change what our chooser would want to do.

We are interested, in particular, in cases where parties to a social inter-action in which everyone could gain from cooperation, and in which everyone would prefer cooperation, might nevertheless act in ways that lead to failures of cooperation. The source of the difficulty might lie in misperceptions that, parallel to the neglect defaults of Chapter 6, could be entirely out of sight of the parties involved. And what I want to show in this chapter is evidence that adverse defaulting parallel to what was seen in Chapter 6, but here among social contexts in the taxonomy of the box, indeed can be a source of serious difficulties, and where the cognitive difficulties here turn out to be usually linked to the neglect defaulting which was the concern in Chapter 6.

*Table 7.1*

---

**1a.  competition (games)**
**1b.  competition (markets)**
**2a.  cooperation (weak): free-riding temptation**
**2b.  cooperation (strong): coordination**

---

Response contexts that might guide an individual's intuition in a social interaction.

Market competition (1b) is a situation where each agent is concerned only about own payoff. Games competition (1a) is the quite different context in which a person is motivated by how well he is doing relative to other players. In a market context, 10 for me is better than 9 for me, no matter how that interacts with your payoff. But in a games context, 10 for me and 10 for you is only a tie: I prefer 1 for me, 0 for you, which is a win. In either context, specifically NSNX effects are not involved: an agent is concerned only with own payoff, either absolutely (1a) or relative to other agents (1b), as will occur in many real situations even if motivation is NSNX.

And for the second pair: weak cooperation (2a) is where an agent sees the context as an opportunity for mutually advantageous choices, but subject to free-rider concerns, so that even an agent who would want to cooperate might not, since he does not want to be exploited should too many others free-ride. Strong (but not always easy) cooperation (2b) is where the player sees the problem as coordinating choices to get a good result with free-riding either not even an available option or where it seems so unlikely in the context that it is not a complication for the chooser (as in a transaction with a known party and a well-established pattern of cooperation). Even for context 2b, sometimes cooperation might still be risky, as when communication is difficult and finding a mutually preferred choice seems unlikely. But the difficulty is not due to a conflict of interest across players.

I will use the label *frame* to refer to the subjective perception, in distinction from *context*, which refers to the objective situation. The heart of the discussion here will concern the possibility that the *frame* governing a choice may not match the context even when in hindsight there is a puzzle about how the chooser could have missed that.

Mixed cases (e.g., a context where a common interest in coordination but conflicting interests in the coordination point) are common. A buyer and seller have a common interest in making a deal but a conflicting interest in the price to agree on. But for the situations discussed in this chapter, the mixed cases can be set aside, though they will obviously be prominent in applications.

Even without this possibility of covert difficulties, cooperation might be harmed by noisy communications, unreliable feedback, lack of commitment mechanisms, and so on. I might misunderstand your actions or your intentions even if there is no misunderstanding the social context. All of these possibilities have been much discussed. But if covert difficulties are involved, I might even misunderstand my own actions. It is that more surprising possibility that is the special concern of this chapter.

For in the puzzles of Chapter 6, almost everyone eventually comes to see the usual responses as illusory. We then have very good reason to look for some covert process that could account for how people who are certainly not stupid are prompted to form intuitions that are certainly not smart. I want to find a counterpart to that stark situation, where responses from intelligent subjects seem to make no sense given the situation they are actually in. In particular, we are interested in experiments where we could expect subjects to be able to do well by cooperating but instead they do badly. And to make the problem clearly visible we need to start with a special subset of such experiments in which managing cooperation should be *very* easy.

Cooperation experiments usually involve games in which, if players could communicate freely and make binding agreements, cooperation would be trivially easy. But cooperation is then made harder (since otherwise the results are likely to be uninteresting). Typically, players have never met, and are not allowed to communicate. Each will receive her payoff privately, so that a player need not be concerned with being confronted by others in the game, and everyone knows that. No side-payments or binding agreements of any kind are allowed.

Despite all this, in a context where cooperative choice would benefit everyone, a NSNX agent should still respond to some measure of other-regarding concern. Given the condition that is likely to be cautious and partial, and perhaps even invisibly small. But what we see should be choices that could look reasonable to an agent concerned with being "neither selfish nor exploited." In the taxonomy of Table 7.1, the context is usually that of weak cooperation (2a). Since NSNX actors respond to social values as well as to self-interest, if NSNX is right there is something to be explained if that is missing.

Accounting for such puzzles will come up very prominently in later chapters. But for the argument of this chapter, I want to set aside any commitment to social motivation. We want to identify a special category of experiment which provides puzzling results that do not depend on whether or how far subjects respond to NSNX motivation or any other notion of other-regarding motivation. This requires experiments where self-interest coincides with, rather than competes with, any tendency to social motivation. Then whatever motivation is plausibly in play, a cognitive puzzle needs to be resolved.

The qualifier "plausible" is needed since some sort of rationale can be concocted for any choice whatever. Perhaps the players are really stupid, or masochists, or sadists, or neurotic, or just trying to confuse the experimenter. Perhaps they think it would be nice to deliberately keep their payoffs down to save the experimenter money. Such things might happen, conceivably even the last, but not often enough to be plausible explanations when a large fraction of responses have to be explained that way. If we can find experiments in which self-interest, or group-interest, or any compromise in between would all, on any plausible account, yield the same result, but the result observed is far from that, then we will have what we need. We can use such results to explore whether, and if so how, adverse defaulting might extend beyond the individual choices considered in Chapter 6 to the social contexts that are our real concern. And, perhaps surprisingly, it is not hard to find experiments of the special sort we are looking for.

In a standard Public Goods experiment, players choose how much of an endowment to contribute to a common pool. The tokens in the pool are then multiplied and divided among the players equally. In a standard game, the multiplier is >1 but less than the number of players, so what an individual gets back from his own contribution is less than he gave, but the amount shared across the group is more than the sum of what everyone gave. So the group does best when all contribute fully, though each individual can profit by free-riding on the contributions of others. But starting with Andreoni (1995), a line of Public Goods experiments have been manipulated to eliminate any rational basis for contributing. The robust result has been that what Andreoni labeled "confusion" plays a large role in player choices, since in the degenerate variants contributions remain about half of what they are in an otherwise identical actual Public Goods game. Andreoni's alteration was to add a paragraph to his instructions which explained that tokens earned in the game were used only to rank players. Actual cash payoff then depended solely on rank. This converts what looks like an experiment about cooperation into a strictly zero-sum game. With payment strictly by rank, contributions have no effect other than to lower a player's rank relative to others in his group.

Since payoff depends only on rank, there is no point at all to concern about how many tokens are earned. So unless you are the sort of person (assuming there actually is that sort of person) who likes to lose in order to make his opponents better off, it makes no sense whatever to contribute. In terms of the taxonomy of Table 7.1, Andreoni changed the context of weak cooperation (2a) to strong (zero-sum) competition (1a). A player can improve her own payoff only by reducing other players' payoffs. And players should not feel uncomfortable about that. After all, that is the way games are usually played.

Later experiments (Houser and Kurzban 2005; Ferraro and Vossler 2005) were even more stark, since there were not even other players. Rather, subjects were explicitly told, with quite elaborate precautions to make sure this was understood, that others in their group did not actually exist. Responses from others in their group would be generated by a computer which mechanically reports pseudo-contributions. A player would receive his own payoff from the pool (from his own contribution plus the pseudo-contributions). But there were no other earnings, no other actual players, and no connection between the mechanical pseudo-contributions and the actual contributions by the human subject. If the return was half a token per token in the pool, the only consequence to a player of contributing a token was just to throw away half a token from his payoff.

In these games with "robot" partners, the more a player contributes, the less he earns and no social value of any kind exists to qualify that stark situation. A post-game survey confirmed that players indeed understood that robot earnings did not actually exist. Nevertheless, as in Andreoni's game, contributions in this degenerate game were around half of what they were in a parallel actual Public Goods game. Again, these excess contributions were interpreted as due to confusion.

But the responses to the puzzles of Chapter 6 could also in some sense be ascribed to "confusion," which I put in scare quotes since for the puzzles no one is likely to doubt that something more systematic than mere confusion is involved. In the puzzles, subjects have confident, widely shared intuitions about the right answer, and those confident, widely shared intuitions are demonstrably wrong. For it is simple to set up physical situations where choices for the three-cards or Monty Hall problems can be run through many iterations in a few minutes. So we can easily generate data sufficient to satisfy any reasonable demand for a statistically significant demonstration. A skeptic does not need to grasp the logic; he can see what in fact happens. But if there is something systematically misleading going on in a degenerate Public Goods game, it will be harder to see. There is no *particular* inappropriate response that attracts predominant but unsound support. Given n tokens, there are n+1 choices available (from 0 to *n*), and usually with multiple rounds of play. So while non-zero responses in the degenerate games are always unsound, player choices vary across rounds and individual choices vary within each round, so things indeed look confused, as if subjects just try out various choices to see what happens, or just blindly imitate what they see from other players.

Yet if the odd results of Public Goods games with a degenerate twist indeed revealed that choices in Public Goods games were in large part *merely* confused, some robust characteristics of Public Goods data would be very mysterious. One that will play a role in some data we will consider in Chapter 8 is the "restart" effect. The games typically run ten rounds. And it was Andreoni who found that contrary to clearing up confusion if the players were then invited to play the game over, they would behave much the same way as in the original ten rounds. This has proved to be a very robust feature of Public Goods games. On the "confusion" hypothesis, we would have to say (among other implausible things) there is a very reliable renewal of "confusion" if players are given the opportunity to play again, this time immediately following ten rounds of experience. But if what accounts for choices that make no sense when the game is degenerate is not confusion, then what is it?

The degenerate Public Goods experiments provide a starting point for considering such puzzles. We especially want data in which the "confusion," or whatever else is at work, yields failures of cooperation where cooperation should be easy. And as explained earlier, these must come in contexts where even a strictly self-interested player should find it sensible to cooperate. It turns out this special requirement is not hard to meet. Here are three examples.

## The convertible Prisoner's Dilemma

Neugebauer (2007) recruited students to play a version of the Prisoner's Dilemma with an option that made it easy to almost guarantee that both players cooperate. So the key factor for the Prisoner's Dilemma (PD) is missing here. The dilemma is ordinarily that players have no way to commit themselves to cooperation, hence easily end up jointly defecting, to their mutual disadvantage. In Neugebauer's game, players are offered a very simple way to escape the dilemma. Yet overwhelmingly, they failed to take advantage of it, with very bad consequences for their payoffs.

Neugebauer's PD payoff matrix (Figure 7.1) was inverted relative to the usual display. And the choices were neutrally labeled "A" and "B," not Defect and Cooperate. Players within a group of eight (four groups in all) were randomly and anonymously matched for 50 rounds. At the start of each round, a player lets his partner for that round know whether he accepts a 20 point penalty if he chooses A. So a player who accepts the penalty but then defects (chooses A) can never end up with a positive payoff, whatever his partner does. For a player who intends to cooperate, accepting the penalty for defecting is just a no-cost way of signaling to his partner that indeed he intends to cooperate. He will never incur the penalty. Then, knowing whether the other player has accepted the penalty, each player decides whether to pass this round or play it. And if both decide to play, each decides whether to play A or B.

The only strategy that makes sense in this game is: (1) accept the penalty for defecting; (2) continue only with another player who also has accepted the penalty; (3) cooperate. Call this Strategy X. This is plainly socially best, maximizing group payoff, but also plainly best simply for self-interest. For wouldn't a person have to be stupid to enter this game against a player who refused to commit himself to playing B? Refusing to commit is likely to mean you either won't get to play this round (which yields zero payoff) or will get to play it only against someone who has refused to commit, hence presumably

| −1 | | 20 | |
|---|---|---|---|
| | 1 | | −10 |
| −10 | | 10 | |
| | 20 | | 10 |

*Figure 7.1* Neugebauer's convertible Prisoner's Dilemma game.

intends to play A, giving you a negative payoff. Risk aversion would make Strategy X even more attractive. Forward induction, considering that you are playing 50 rounds with only seven possible partners, would make it still more attractive. But neither refinement is needed to make blindness to the advantage of accepting a penalty that will never be incurred puzzling for subjects smart enough to be university students.

This is so even though it does not formally dominate a competitive rather than cooperative alternative (call it Strategy Y). Strategy Y would not commit, offer to play only if partner does commit, then defect. When this works, it earns 20 rather than the 10 available from mutual cooperation. But it is hardly surprising that it did not work very often.

If players chose Strategy X all the time, everyone would have earned 500 British pence in Neugebauer's game. But most players earned less than 150. Not one of the 32 players was 100 percent consistent in following Strategy X. Only four players were as much as 90 percent consistent with Strategy X. But these four earned on average nearly three times as much as the far larger number (13) who, despite plenty of opportunity to learn over 50 rounds, followed Strategy X less than 50 percent of the time.

Why was such a large majority of these players (English university students) so incompetent?

## Inverted Public Goods games

A few "Public Goods" experiments have reversed the usual incentive to free-ride by making the return to each player from contribution to the pool larger than the contribution. So these games are degenerate, like the Andreoni and other games described earlier, but in the opposite direction. Instead of removing any rational reason to contribute, in these games it is any incentive to free-ride that is removed. In the inverted games if you give a token it is not just the group return that exceeds 1, but each player, including the donor, gets more than 1 token in return. In the standard Public Goods game, other-regarding motivation is required to make giving generously to the pool seem reasonable. In the inverted game, pure self-interest is enough. It pays to send all your tokens to the pool.

This inverted experiment has been run in both Japan (Saijo and Nakamura, 1995) and Canada (Brunton *et al.* 2001). In both experiments contributions were not much larger in the inverted game than in a standard game with the same subjects. Figure 7.2 shows the result of the Japanese trials in which players played ten rounds with (above) a return to each player per token of 7/10 token, then ten rounds with the super-return of 10/7 (about 1.43). The reverse order is below. Closed circles are for the 7/10 return (free-rider incentive), open circles are for the inverted 10/7 (easy-rider) incentive. You can see that the average contribution was about half of endowment in all rounds for the "easy-rider" game (where the more a player gives the more he earns), and also about half in most rounds of the actual free-rider game (where the less a

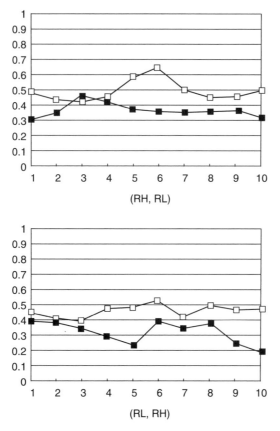

*Figure 7.2* Standard vs. inverted contribution in a Public Goods game.

player gives the more he earns). Offered a risk-free opportunity to choose a higher payoff, these players were not moved very far.[1]

Saijo and Nakamura labeled the behavior "spite." Giving a token nets 0.43 tokens to the donor, but it gives 1.43 tokens to the other players. So a player focused on how well he is doing relative to other players might hold back on giving. That damages the player's own payoff but damages other players' payoffs even more. So "spite" has become an item in the repertoire of candidates for amending the basic utility function to account for other-regarding behavior, now allowing other-regarding choices to include wanting to make others worse off, or at least worse off relative to the donor.

But when the experiment was later repeated with Canadian students, a preliminary test was run to identify spiteful subjects. The Canadians offered their players a clear opportunity to exhibit spite, as by letting them choose in the preliminary game between the equivalent of a payoff of [10, 5] and [10, 15], where the first number is what they get and the second number is the payoff that an anonymously matched partner will get. Very few players made the spiteful choice of [10, 5]. And the players most prone to spiteful choice in the Public Goods game were not the players who made especially spiteful choices in the preliminary game.

Indeed, even within the main Japanese and Canadian trials, choices are incoherent if what motivated holding back on donations was spite. It is not that some players are spiteful, giving zero, while most maximize their payoff, yielding the average results in Figure 7.2. Rather, almost everyone is spiteful. Even without the negative evidence of the Canadian preliminary test, would it be plausible that almost all players are spiteful? And if inclined to be spiteful, shouldn't they be markedly more inclined to be spiteful when that is reinforced by an increase in their own payoff (when "spite" is also profitable)? But response to the inverted incentive was so inconsequential that some players actually gave more when giving was costly than when it was profitable. Or shouldn't spiteful players give least in the final round, when there is no chance that others will retaliate? But there is no decline in late rounds. On the other hand, perhaps players are unwilling to be cooperative if others aren't, even if it costs them to do that. But how could that account for withholding contributions in round 1, when there is as yet neither evidence nor any reason to expect that others will be less than fully cooperative?

So as with Neugebauer's game, the question arises: what makes these students choose so perversely? And again the issue does not turn on how far, or if at all, they are inclined to compromise self-interest by other-regarding concerns. Whatever their motivation, the choices appear to make no sense.

## The Minimum game

Table 7.2 shows the payoffs for the "Minimum" game studied by Van Huyck *et al.* (1990) using rather large groups (around 15), but more recently and repeatedly replicated with smaller groups. When there are only two players, they are generally able to coordinate on their mutual best outcome (choose 7).

*Table 7.2* Payoff table for the Minimum game (Van Huyck *et al.* 1990).

| Own choice | Smallest number chosen by anyone | | | | | | |
|---|---|---|---|---|---|---|---|
| | *7* | *6* | *5* | *4* | *3* | *2* | *1* |
| 7 | 1.30 | 1.10 | 0.90 | 0.70 | 0.50 | 0.30 | 0.10 |
| 6 | – | 1.20 | 1.00 | 0.80 | 0.60 | 0.40 | 0.20 |
| 5 | – | – | 1.10 | 0.90 | 0.70 | 0.50 | 0.30 |
| 4 | – | – | – | 1.00 | 0.80 | 0.60 | 0.40 |
| 3 | – | – | – | – | 0.90 | 0.70 | 0.50 |
| 2 | – | – | – | – | – | 0.80 | 0.60 |
| 1 | – | – | – | – | – | – | 0.70 |

But the situation deteriorates as more players are added, and for groups of six or more, the results become terrible.

Players must each choose a number between "1" and "7". The lowest number picked within a round determines the column in the table that governs payoffs in that round. A player's own choice (possibly itself the minimum) then determines which of the payoffs within that column he will get. Hence, as you can see in Table 7.1, those who chose the low number get the highest payoff available for that round; and everyone else is penalized by a dime for each notch her choice is above what turns out to be the minimum.

But the lower the minimum number chosen, the lower the payoff to everyone, including the player who chose what turned out to be the minimum. In the extreme case, if someone chooses "1" in each round, he guarantees himself a payoff of $8 \times 70¢ = \$5.60$ over the eight rounds. Anyone who fails to match this earns less. But if everyone picks "7" in each round, each player gets almost double ($10.40). If players could communicate, they could quickly agree to pick "7", and this would be self-enforcing since each individual profits from complying. It is best for the group, and in a way that a player cannot improve on by being anything less than fully cooperative. But the players are not allowed to communicate. And they do very badly.

The very robust result of Minimum game experiments is that groups quickly converge to coordination on their worst outcome ("1"). This is a puzzling result from the NSNX + cognition perspective here, but elsewhere has been seen as easily explained. Players are correctly foreseeing that others will choose a number less than 7, so that choosing a number less than 7 indeed increases their payoff. A player who reports "7" even in round 1 always loses some payoff. So how could it be a puzzle that players anticipate that and act accordingly?

But I will argue that indeed a cognitive illusion is needed to account for what happens in this game. That will, however, not come until Chapter 10. Here we are only going to be concerned with a degenerate version of the game, where everyone will agree that the players must be vulnerable to some cognitive illusion, since most choices make no sense at all.

The data come from a game framed as a variation on the standard Public Goods game which will be introduced in a more detailed way in Chapter 8. In the variant (Fatas *et al.* 2006), players choose a number of tokens to offer to a common pool, with the balance kept for a player's private account. This looks different from Van Huyck's game in which players choose a number guided by the payoff Table 7.2. But although the games at a glance look different, in fact the incentives are essentially identical. In the variant, a pool is generated by doubling the minimum contribution within a group, then multiplying that by the size of the group. The pool that results is then divided equally across the group, adding to whatever each player kept in his private account. This creates the same incentive to avoid giving more than the minimum that drives the Van Huyck results (see note 8.11).

But in the degenerate version (which is what concerns us here) only the smallest offer is taken. Any higher offers are reduced to match that smallest offer. It is impossible to waste a token. A marginal token is either needed to increase the minimum, or if not it goes back into the choosing player's private account. So the game is degenerate in the stark sense that the best choice in terms of either self-interest or group-interest is trivially obvious (offer all your tokens). No one could possibly lose by offering to give all his tokens, nor gain any advantage over other players by offering less. What of any possible interest could be learned from such a trivial game? But it turns out to yield a strange and striking result.

In this Spanish experiment players were all university students studying economics. They were given instruction in how the contingent offer arrangement works. They then passed a test to show they understood how it works. So players who have demonstrated they know enough to make it logically trivial to see that offering all their tokens is the only sensible choice now get to choose. This might seem a pretty easy task even for players who were not university students studying economics.

But in round 1 of the game only 5 of 24 players chose to assure they would take all the payoff they could get. Since 5 of 24 players choosing the maximum level of cooperation would not be at all unusual even in either a Public Goods game or in the standard Minimum game, it is not clear that *any* of the 24 players responded to the game they were playing.

In one of the six groups of four, over 20 rounds no one *ever* chose 50 (Table 7.3), and in another of the groups no one offered a full donation earlier than round 18. In only one of six groups did everyone catch on to how to make the most money until very close to the twentieth round. So we are not looking at an occasional lapse of attention or some other sort of odd choice that can be dismissed as just the inevitable quirks in experimental data. This is highly systematic but quite transparently inane behavior, governing the great majority of choices. Outside the laboratory, we see many stupid things, but not *this* stupid.

## The cascade conjecture

So we now have a sample of results which meet the criterion set out earlier. In each of these three games, choices that would maximize gain for everyone also maximize strictly self-interested gain for the chooser. There is no need to decide how to model other-regarding choice, and indeed no need to decide whether to allow for any other-regarding motivation at all. It makes no difference at all. On very simple reasoning, in each game there is only one sensible line of play, and in each of these games the players mostly miss it.

Here is a NSNX account of how that might happen, which extends the defaulting discussion of Chapter 6 to the context of social choice.

In Chapter 6, adverse neglect defaulting appeared as an inappropriate response in the unfamiliar and impoverished environment of a puzzle. The

Table 7.3 Degenerate Weakest Link game (from Fatas et al.). In this poorest-performing group, no one ever made the risk-free dominant choice (50) over 20 rounds. But only one of five further groups did much better.

|     | 1 | 2 | 3 | 4 | 5 | 6 | 7 | 8 | 9 | 10 | 11 | 12 | 13 | 14 | 15 | 16 | 17 | 18 | 19 | 20 |
|-----|---|---|---|---|---|---|---|---|---|----|----|----|----|----|----|----|----|----|----|----|
| Max | 25 | 30 | 25 | 33 | 35 | 39 | 40 | 42 | 45 | 45 | 35 | 30 | 35 | 39 | 25 | 38 | 39 | 39 | 41 | 49 |
|     | 20 | 18 | 25 | 28 | 35 | 38 | 40 | 41 | 44 | 45 | 30 | 22 | 27 | 35 | 25 | 30 | 35 | 38 | 40 | 45 |
|     | 20 | 12 | 15 | 23 | 19 | 33 | 30 | 39 | 40 | 37 | 12 | 15 | 15 | 21 | 25 | 22 | 34 | 37 | 40 | 45 |
| Min | 4 | 10 | 11 | 15 | 19 | 25 | 27 | 35 | 20 | 35 | 5 | 10 | 10 | 18 | 14 | 19 | 30 | 32 | 39 | 41 |

default still made sense as what might be entrenched as what to do when cues at hand do not confidently point to what to do. But as a response to a simple puzzle at hand, where there was no logical ambiguity, it did not make sense. Nevertheless, in the unfamiliar and impoverished environment of a puzzle, verbal cues that logically pointed away from that default were not strong enough to overcome it.

So consider a parallel to those effects in the more complex context of social interactions. I want to specify how defaulting could be expected to work in terms of the basic contexts set out in Table 7.1, which a reader should review before proceeding. The sketch that follows is only a "just-so" story, tentative in its details. But it gives us enough to consider what we might make of the sampling of strange results we now have at hand.

Figure 7.3 shows what I will call the cascade.

Consider an encounter with another agent, who might or might not turn out to be cooperative. Over Darwinian time, some default response would evolve for ambiguous encounters – what to do when at first it is not clear what to do. And the default response to an unfamiliar encounter could hardly be anything but caution. At the first level of the cascade the default would be the competitive branch. And within that branch, it is the zero-sum games-competitive frame (1a) that would be at least a tentative default, since there certainly appears to be much less chance of bad (for life in the jungle, possibly fatal) consequences in treating a context as at least possibly zero-sum until you see evidence for a more benign sense of the situation.

But although caution would favor starting from the zero-sum frame, that should be in some tentative way. It would be dangerous to be too easily moved to dovish behavior. But to be uncontrollably hawkish would also not be good. An agent would be alert for cues that would move away from the zero-sum frame (1a) over to the payoff-maximizing frame (1b), where it feels prudent to go about your business, rather than be constantly on alert for a fight-or-flee choice.

More positive cues that the situation is one that engages social motivation would prompt a shift across to the cooperative branch. The cautious default there would be the risky cooperation frame (2a), where intuition would be

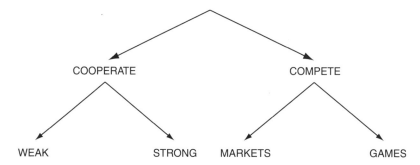

*Figure 7.3* The NSNX cascade.

guided by "neither selfish nor exploited" propensity to favor what is socially useful, but alert to free-rider concerns. But if a social context appears to involve no free-rider risk, that would prompt a move to the strong cooperation (coordination) frame (2b). If cues are sufficiently favorable (for example, you have had successful dealings with this individual in the past, or there is an opportunity for social gain with no risk of harm or exploitation to self), a NSNX agent could be expected to go immediately to the strong cooperation (coordination) frame (2b).

Facing an opportunity for cooperation subject to free-rider temptation (you are not sure that even if you do your part of the deal, he will do his), a NSNX agent would be in the weak cooperation frame (2a). He must decide whether or not to chance complying (or chance not complying). But as an agent in the zero-sum frame would be alert for cues that warrant shifting across to payoff-maximizing (if it is safe to be there, it is better to be there), so an agent in the risky cooperation frame (2a) would be alert for cues that make it prudent to be in the coordination frame (2b). The argument of Chapter 1 which underpins the NSNX balance between social and self-interested motivation would favor alertness to the possibility of a context where cooperation need not be compromised by concern that others have an interest that conflicts with cooperation.

On the competitive branch, NSNX is irrelevant. Motivation beyond self-interest could be in play, but the motivating group-interest would not involve the people you are interacting with. On the cooperative branch, the "neither selfish nor exploited" concerns with free-riders that characterize NSNX become prominent (making the weak cooperation frame 2a the default) but so does concern with social consequences (making the coordination frame 2b a possibility).

So consider how these cascade effects, possibly interacting with the neglect defaulting effects of Chapter 6, might give an account of the three examples of challenging results now at hand: the convertible Prisoner's Dilemma, the inverted Public Goods game, and the "money back guarantee" version of the Minimum game.

### The convertible Prisoner's Dilemma

Since even pigeons will learn something over 50 rounds, it is scarcely surprising that human subjects did better as play proceeded through the 50 rounds of Neugebauer's game. Nevertheless, as noticed earlier, across all 50 rounds only 4 of 32 players followed the only sensible strategy in this game as much as 90 percent of the time (accept the penalty, play only if partner has also accepted the penalty, then cooperate), compared to 13 who followed it less than half the time. The 4 quick learners averaged triple the payoff of the 13 slow learners.

But we saw examples in Chapter 6 where subjects sometimes neglect what seems too obvious to miss. In the three-cards problem, no subject could be so stupid as to find it hard to understand that if the side showing is red, the chance that the card you picked is one with a red side has increased. But in the Fox and Levav "sides" variant, more than a third of their Duke University subjects missed that. Information is staring them in the face, but they neglect it. Since outright neglect can be seen, it cannot be too surprising that incremental cognitive "distance" that is logically trivial can have large effects, as with presentation of a base rate as "34 out of 100" rather than 0.34. Relative to these completely trivial examples, Neugebauer's English university students faced a considerably more difficult task.

People often do not easily recognize the perimeter of their own country if it is shown upside down. Here the payoff matrix (Figure 7.1) is upside down relative to the way the Prisoner's Dilemma is always presented in classrooms and textbooks. The "cooperate" and "defect" choices were neutrally labeled "A" and "B." And unless a person is comfortable with the game theory notation, seeing incentives in the form of a payoff matrix may be intrinsically cryptic. Combining all these effects, what to the experimenter is transparent might easily be translucent bordering on opaque to a typical subject. On the record, apparently that was so. In a game where it is hard to do anything but badly by playing competitively, players failed to recognize the context as cooperative.

On the cascade conjecture a player would by default start from the competitive branch of the cascade. Within that competitive branch, the default would be the zero-sum strongly competitive frame (1a), looking to "win" the round, where the scare quotes are needed because there is no payoff for winning a round. Subjects appear to treat the game as too complicated to figure out. With two players, each potentially facing three decisions per round, players missing the cooperative structure built into the game (which makes Strategy X the single best line of play) would see a complicated set of many possibilities. For as many rounds as that persisted, the way to do well would seem to turn on somehow outwitting or at least outlucking another player seen as an opponent, not on seeing how to cooperate with a potential partner. Players seem to experiment with whatever happened to come to mind.

That makes no logical sense, given the incentives actually at hand. But it serves well enough as a description of what we see most players doing. Especially in the earlier rounds it was even common for a player to commit himself to cooperation, then play (rather than pass) the round against another player who declined to commit himself. This happened 82 times, and a reader will not be surprised, but apparently players were, that overwhelmingly (70 times) this yielded the severely negative "sucker" payoff.

The most telling situation is that of a player who accepts the penalty for defecting, seeming to assure cooperation, but who then defects against a partner who also has accepted the penalty. Call that a betrayal. To a player in the zero-sum frame (1a) this would not at all feel like a betrayal, but rather like a poker player managing a successful bluff. He "wins" the round, netting nothing from a payoff of 20 dissipated by the 20-point penalty, but the other player loses 10. On the cascade conjecture, however, it is not hard to slip across frames within a branch. Given a strong and direct cue (betrayal reduces payoff from 10 to 0), at the moment of choice even players who indeed started from the zero-sum frame would seem unlikely to remain caught on that default. Then a player who was not seeing his choice at all as a choice to cooperate, but merely doing what makes sense for himself, would make the payoff-maximizing choice (from frame 1b). That happens to be the cooperative choice but with the penalty in force it need not be motivated by any inclination beyond strict self-interest.

So although even players whose opening choice is to accept the penalty might be starting from the zero-sum frame, at the moment of choice they are likely to be nudged over to payoff maximizing (frame 1b). Their choices, in this round, are the same that a player starting from the cooperative branch would make.[2] So can we see evidence in the data that will test the cascade conjecture that starting from the zero-sum frame, though illogical, should nevertheless be common? That turns out to be possible because, in addition to the game with a 20-point penalty, Neugebauer ran an experiment with a 10-point penalty, which allows us to draw some comparative inferences.

For a player who accepts the penalty facing a partner who also accepted the penalty, but with the penalty reduced to 10, either choice ("A" or "B") gives an identical short-run payoff (+10). But for a zero-sum player choosing "A" (defect) yields both the 10 tokens and a win [me +10, him −10], while "B" yields only a tie [me +10, him +10]. So in the 10-point game, we might be able to actually see players who apparently did start from the zero-sum frame, because they record final choices that make no sense other than if they are still in that zero-sum frame. There might not be many such choices. Even in the 10-point game, forward induction would alert a player that there is likely to be a payoff cost. But (on the cascade conjectures) we have reason to look for betrayals in the 10-point game.

And a second inference might discriminate intrinsic zero-sum behavior (players explicitly prefer reducing payoff to the other player even when yields no gain for themselves) from tactical zero-sum players (who are responding intuitively to a misperception of what kind of game they are in). On the NSNX + cognition argument, we should expect to see the latter not the former. But if intrinsic motivation is zero-sum, then since betrayal must reduce the prospects of cooperation from the betrayed player in a future round, betrayal ought to be more restrained in round 1 (where the forward induction motive against betrayal is strongest) relative to round 50, where that motive has disappeared. On the other hand, if zero-sum responses are prompted by adverse defaulting (on reflection a player would regret what she had done), the opposite should hold. As players come to know the game better, vulnerability to that adverse default should decline. It becomes more likely in later rounds, and in particular by round 50, that a player has come to understand the game she is in, and she would no longer be starting from the zero-sum frame. So for intrinsic zero-sum choice, betrayal is more likely in round 50 than in round 1, and the reverse for defaulting zero-sum choice.

Fifty rounds of play among 32 players generate $32 \times 50 = 1,600$ individual choices (800 pairwise interactions). For a player who saw the actual structure of the game, deciding whether to accept the penalty is easy. There is no need to guess, since accepting is best every time (Strategy X). But declining the penalty was sufficiently common in the 20-point game that at least one of the partners refused the penalty more than half the time.

So in that 20-point game, among the 800 interactions there were only 345 that were played out between players who had both accepted the penalty. A very large majority of those 345 both-commit rounds produced the cooperative result. That is not surprising given the strong direct payoff cue, the subtler forward induction cue early, and the accumulation of experience later. Among the 690 individual opportunities for betrayal in the 20-point game, there were only 21 actual betrayals, of which 11 came from just 2 of the 32 players.

But in the 10-point game, though the number of accept-the-penalty interactions is almost the same (345 in the 20-point game, 354 in the 10-point game), the payoff nudge to break free of a zero-sum default is weak. Although there remained the forward induction concern to cue a shift to the payoff-maximizing frame (1b), betrayals were now almost as common as mutual cooperation. Players mostly did make the cooperative choice (563/ 708) when they had that choice to make. But since it takes two cooperative choices to avoid a betrayal, that left 145 betrayals among 354 pair-wise opportunities (versus 21/345 with the 20-point penalty). Total earnings fell to half what they were in the 20-point version. So the first inference clearly holds. Betrayals indeed are conspicuously more common in the 10-point game.

And within that 10-point game as the second conjecture anticipates, players accept the penalty more often as they gain experience, and betray less. In the strongest comparison, in the first round 15 (of 32) players accepted the penalty, which produced four accept-the-penalty matches, three of which yielded betrayals. Among the 8 opportunities to betray, there were 4 betrayals (one a dual betrayal involving both players in a match). In the final round, 25 of the 32 players accepted the penalty, yielding 18 opportunities for betrayal, of which 3/18 occurred, in contrast to 4/8 in round 1. All this is as would be expected on the cascade conjecture that betrayals are likely to be seen in the 10-point game, but due to adverse defaulting rather than intrinsic zero-sum preferences.

This evidence for adverse defaulting to the zero-sum frame is only suggestive. Whatever might prompt betrayals – perhaps an intrinsic taste for spiteful behavior not adverse defaulting – would prompt more of it when betrayal is cheaper. The contrast between betrayals in round 1 and in round 50 favors the adverse defaulting explanation, but is also not clear-cut. That might have been mostly because players who naively declined the penalty would have cooperated in round 1 if they had accepted the penalty. But by round 50, many more are following Strategy X, getting to play, hence show up among the 25 acceptors in round 50 instead of being hidden among the 17 not-acceptors in round 1. The detailed data do not really support that. But it is enough for the NSNX + cognition view to claim only that the test is consistent with the conjecture. The accumulation of other evidence to come strongly reinforces the cascade interpretation.

Some of that is in the balance of this chapter. More will come later, in particular in Chapter 9, where we will see data that incidentally, but emphatically, tests for a propensity to actual zero-sum preferences. If players betray because they are often actually spiteful then we should see plenty of spiteful behavior when it costs nothing at all to be spiteful and when in addition the players face provocation that would give reason to exercise spite. But in the data in Chapter 9, we will see very marked reluctance to impose costs on another player even when provoked by nasty behavior from the other player, and even though no cost to self would be involved. The puzzle in Chapter 9 will be to account for a deficiency of nasty responses in a context where nasty responses would seem normatively appropriate.

### The inverted Public Goods game

How to interpret what looks like spiteful choice is even more prominent in the inverted Prisoner's Dilemma game, where that is the only straightforward explanation and has been the standard explanation. On a "spite" reading, the Japanese and Canadian players in these games are not motivated exclusively by spite. They do not single-mindedly value doing better than fellow students over cooperation that increases payoffs for everyone. Rather, spite is tempered by greed, so on average they contribute about half their tokens, and withhold the other half. But the data (Figure 7.2) show very nearly as much cooperation when spite must compete with greed as when spite would be reinforced by greed. The open-circles data in Figure 7.2 (for the inverted trials) show no hint of either the holdup of contributions in round 10 or the high contributions in round 1 that would make sense if motivation was spite qualified by greed. Several players actually contributed more when contributing reduced their payoff (the 7/10 return) than when it increased their payoff (the 10/7 return).

All that suggests that spite and greed are not really insightful categories for understanding what generates these results. Rather, the data show a pattern of choices consistent with NSNX motivation *distorted* by an adverse default in the cascade. But in this case (in contrast to that of the convertible Prisoner's Dilemma), it is an adverse default on the cooperative rather than competitive branch. Players respond as if they recognize the context as cooperative, which indeed fits the logic of the game they are in. But on the logic of the game they should escape the *risky* cooperation default (2a). There is zero free-rider risk. The more you contribute, the more you profit. Responses, however, fit the default anyway. They reveal "neither selfish nor exploited" concern about being exploited if cooperating more than others, and they do so starting in round 1, before there is any reason to suppose that would happen.

But if adverse defaulting accounts for what is happening, we want to be able to say why the cooperative character of the game is transparent to the players in this inverted Public Goods context while the also cooperative character of the convertible Prisoner's Dilemma game is missed by the players. And we want to say why, having seen the context as cooperative, players then fail to see that cooperation is easy (they can just think about coordination), since there is no free-rider risk in this game. But with the notions we now have in hand, neither is hard to do.

In the convertible Prisoner's Dilemma, a player has to tease out the implications of the payoff matrix, adjusted for the implications of the opportunity to accept or reject the penalty provision, and then for the opportunity to accept or reject actual play of this round. None of this seems at all difficult, but in the aggregate it is also not trivial on the scale of the difficulties that yield terrible performance in the puzzles of Chapter 6. In contrast, the Public Goods game does not have that logically modest but perhaps cognitively substantial additional layering of difficulty. Relative to the difference (again) between a base rate presented as 34 out of 100 versus the same base rate presented as 0.34, the incremental difference in complexity between the inverted Public Goods game and Neugebauer's presentation of the convertible Prisoner's Dilemma is not inconsequential.

Players come to the game with normal human experience of cooperation. The game looks like a situation every player has encountered often, where contributions to a group effort plainly benefit everyone. But some members of the group might be tempted to shirk. And what players miss in the inverted game is the unusual feature which makes the immediate return from a player's own contribution so large that shirking would be stupid. A person does best, even in terms of narrow self-interest, to contribute everything he can. So although social experience would prompt a person to expect a free-rider issue to be present in this interaction with anonymous others, here it isn't. Intuitions need to be adjusted to catch that. But over and over in Chapter 6, we saw that choosers are frequently caught by a neglect default that leaves them cognitively blind to such details.

The patterns of contribution in Figure 7.2 for the inverted game look almost indistinguishable from the patterns for a game which in fact does entail a free-rider risk. Somehow players act as if they did not notice that for the inverted payoff rounds, returning 10/7 token per token contributed instead of 7/10. The quantitative information, which logically shifts the game into the coordination frame (2b), where there is no free-rider concern, is not cognitively effective enough to overcome the default tendency to respond in a common pool situation as if there were a free-rider risk. But we have more than once had occasion to notice parallel insensitivity to large quantitative shifts in other contexts.

What appears to happen here is that players generally escape the default first branching of the cascade, but then are caught on the weak cooperation frame on the cooperative branch. They respond to the familiar context of a group endeavor by favoring the cooperative over the default competitive branch. But they then sufficiently neglect an atypical quantitative detail to be caught by the risky cooperation default on that cooperative branch. There "neither selfish nor exploited" intuitions prompt players to be wary of cooperating more than others, lest they be exploited, though there is actually no way they can be exploited. Players act as if there were a free-rider risk, even though there is no free-rider risk. Illogical though that may be, it is apparent in Figure 7.2 that that is how players are behaving. The cascade conjecture tells us how it could be that choosers do that.

It is a conjecture that what we are seeing again are NSNX choices revealing the force of adverse defaults. But it is not a conjecture that players act *as if* that were so. Whatever the cause, the data, not the cascade conjecture, show the restrained cooperation characteristic of NSNX responses to free-rider incentives in a context where that makes no sense. But that is consistent with the adverse defaulting which seems to govern responses to Neugebauer's convertible Prisoner's Dilemma, though here the adverse default is on the cooperative branch, not a defaulting failure to even reach the cooperative branch.

But if there remains, perhaps, some plausibility to the contrary conjecture that somehow the choices we see in this game, and also in the convertible Prisoner's Dilemma game, can be explained with the help of a *spite* motive, that pretty dim prospect becomes vanishingly remote in the light of the example coming next. Spite in the two games considered so far would be quite stupidly pursued, and hardly typical of how students usually respond to anonymous interactions with other students, but if you are desperate enough for an explanation, that might seem tempting. But we can turn now to an example where "spite" is not available even as a perverse and barely plausible possibility.

### The degenerate Minimum game

Strategy uncertainty has been the standard explanation of how rational choice in the Minimum game (Table 7.2) can lead players to their worst possible level of coordination. Within a very few rounds coordination is focused on the lowest payoffs, which are about half of what is available. But each player is tempted to choose low by what indeed turns out to be correct anticipation that someone else will choose low. I will return to the game in Chapter 10, to show that this standard explanation might in fact reflect intuitions among analysts of the game captured by the same illusory mechanism that captures players within the game. But here we deal with an entirely uncontroversial case of illusion.

In the degenerate game we have the "money back guarantee" described earlier in this chapter. A player can only gain, never lose (even relative to other players), by offering to contribute the maximum. There is no spite incentive even for a player who would be spiteful if she could, and also no chance of being exploited. Every player in every round gets exactly the same payoff. But in the inverted Public Goods game we have just seen how neglect of qualifying information could miss that. A can't-lose context is somehow seen as looking like a free-rider context. And the same possibility here would have the same consequence in a slightly different form.

The data starkly show players in the degenerate Minimum game treating an opportunity for profitable, risk-free cooperation as subject to a free-rider concern that does not exist. Since this is overwhelmingly evident in round 1, it cannot be somehow explained as a reaction to what other players have done. Nor can it be revealing some perverse propensity of players to spitefully value doing better than others even when the alternative is doing just as well as others. That cannot happen no matter what the chooser does or what anyone else in the game does. Everyone gets the same payoff, which can be larger or smaller contingent on player choices, but is always exactly the same for every player. In terms of the cascade, players act as if they are caught in the risky cooperation frame (2a) when in a completely unambiguous way they are in a pure coordination context (2b).

A modest degree of translucency turns out to be enough to yield the logic-defying choices in this game. After ten rounds of the standard Minimum game, Van Huyck offered his subjects a no-risk game in an additional five rounds. That was essentially the same game as the Valencia no-risk game, but more starkly transparent. Van Huyck's players had just played ten rounds of a real Minimum game. Now they play five rounds of the degenerate game. The explicit payoff Table 7.1 now is changed into a schedule that no longer imposes a penalty for choosing more than the round minimum. And with this degree of experience and transparency, even though there are many more players in a group than in Valencia, only 14 of 91 Van Huyck's players started with the blunder made by 19 of 24 FNJ players. But although one game makes the situation harder to miss than the other, this is a distinction between speaking clearly and shouting. Why do players have to be shouted at to notice something clearly in their interest to notice?

What should we make of what looks like severe aggravation of vulnerability to adverse defaulting, which we have been seeing repeatedly, due to a modest change in the transparency of the situation? Think of a tennis player instructed to keep her eye on the ball, and having no doubt about what makes sense on this point. Nevertheless, as every tennis player knows, she will sometimes take her eye off the ball. Why is it so hard to avoid that? Presumably because outside a few specialized contexts (like playing tennis) we do best keeping our eye on what is ahead of us. We watch the road, not our hands on the wheel. So it is understandable that keeping your eye on the ball, not on where your opponent might be moving, might go against some well-entrenched default. Then, if concentration flags momentarily, the usually advantageous default can slip into place, even though we know that while playing tennis that is not helpful at all.

And here, on the cascade conjecture, the default in a potentially cooperative situation is to guard against exploitation by free-riders. Players in the no-risk game have received instruction and testing about how the game works, but they have not had anything like the repeated experience that a tennis player gets but still is insufficient to avoid lapses even among professionals. A bit of translucency turns out to be sufficient to make players vulnerable to a default that prompts responses that make no more sense in this context than the usual illusory responses to the puzzles in Chapter 6.

If the situation is stark enough, we get a jolt sufficient to displace the default propensity to neglect a piece of secondary information. But if the clue is only translucent, not completely transparent, the jolt is cushioned, and the default might stay in place. Here we can observe that for most players, it does stay in place. But, reprising a point already made, if effects like these can prompt players to damage their own interests in an only mildly translucent experiment, then in far less transparent natural situations the same effects which here prompt players to visibly nonsensical choices might also generate enough unfortunate choices to make effective social cooperation difficult. It could hardly take more than a moment's discussion to correct the misbehavior in the degenerate Minimum game. But in a difficult natural setting, where nothing will be so starkly apparent, correcting a misperception of what makes sense may not be easy at all. Situations marked by perversely inappropriate responses should be uncommon. But especially under novel conditions, they ought to be sometimes encountered, so that something consequential might be learned by careful attention to anomalous results in the vastly simple, artificial, but far more amenable to analysis, realm of social choice experiments.

# 8 NSNX effects in the Public Goods game

Without stark demonstrations, no one would suppose that *visual* misperceptions like the Müller-Lyer illusion in Figure 8.1 could occur. Similarly, gross *logical* illusions parallel to the surprising but indisputable visual illusions would not seem plausible without examples strong enough to catch the person who needs to be convinced. But we now have examples at hand where sophisticated subjects (such as people who might read a book like this) are prompted to clear intuitions that make no sense, as all of us see an unmistakable apparent difference in length that does not exist in the Müller-Lyer drawing. And without the evidence of experiments like those reviewed in Chapter 7, defaulting to inappropriate *social* contexts would seem implausible, though here it is harder to convince a reader that she too can be caught. But I will make an attempt in Chapter 10. We have enough in hand (from Chapter 7) to leave no reasonable doubt that students in experiments can be strikingly caught, which in fact makes it rather naive to doubt that professors can be caught too.

Sometimes illusory effects must be only an artifact of odd conditions peculiar to an experiment. But there is no reason to suppose that the effects only occur in a laboratory, since it is certainly not only in a laboratory that people sometimes face contexts that are unfamiliar and lacking the dense and usually redundant cues of natural situations. So as I have urged more than once, the possibility that adverse defaulting might play a perverse role in real situations warrants attention. To get to that we need to have in hand some experience in applying NSNX reasoning to data. But in Chapter 7, I specifically avoided experiments which could provide an occasion for that, since what we wanted were results which were not contingent on NSNX or any other

*Figure 8.1* The Müller-Lyer illusion. Both lines are identical in length.

form of other-regarding motivation. So examples were selected for the special property that purely self-interested and purely group-interested motivation would yield the same results from a player responding sensibly to the incentives she faces.

And it was easy to find experiments in which players did not respond sensibly at all. Exploring what might account for that in Chapter 7 allows us now to turn to data that might profit from a NSNX analysis, and which indeed require some allowance for other-regarding motivation to make any reasonable sense. But we do that armed with an account (from Chapters 6 and 7) of how players might be vulnerable to distortions of their own preferences. As I write, efforts to account for positive contributions in cooperation games in terms of error-prone but essentially strictly self-interested motivation still continue. I don't think I distort the situation to treat this as a fading enterprise. An account solely in terms of NSNX, however, also is unlikely to be sufficient, given the strong cognitive effects we have been seeing. Therefore we need an analysis in terms of NSNX + cognition, since an account in terms of NSNX alone (or in terms of any other model of motivation alone) that is missing a cognitive component may cripple the attempt to gain insight from data.

An exchange between two Nobel laureates (Paul Samuelson and Milton Friedman) is relevant here. Friedman had made his argument for boldly unrealistic assumptions, using the example of ignoring resistance of the medium in analyzing free fall. This indeed is how Galileo proceeded, with memorable results. But, Samuelson (1963) objected, what if the object you are analyzing is a parachute? Plainly, it is nice to keep things simple. But two simple things at work can yield what seems hopelessly complex unless you allow for both components.

I start from some fresh analysis of two particularly well-known sets of Public Goods data, and then consider a recent (and still unpublished as I write, hence citations to working papers) but particularly suitable set of variants on the standard game.[1]

Start with a few general remarks, some in the nature of review of points made earlier but specifically needed here. In the basic Public Goods game, all players share equally in a pool of contributions. The return to each player per token in the pool is less than 1, but the sum shared among all players is greater than 1. So it goes against the self-interest of a player to contribute (since the return is <1, there is a free-rider incentive), but it is profitable to contribute as part of a mutual commitment of all to contribute (the shared return per token is >1). But mutual commitment is not available. The experiment guarantees anonymity, and strictly forbids communication or any other means by which commitments might be made, intentions shared, punishments or rewards implemented. These features were intended to maximize the prospect that (at least by the end of a series of rounds), cooperation would be nil. This would provide a baseline from which to investigate design of institutions which could yield successful cooperation. But it turned out that while contributions typically decline over the series of rounds, the baseline could rarely be reached.

Characteristic results of this basic game have proved to be highly consistent across experiments. Nationality, gender, and various subtler distinctions have made little difference. (Still the most widely cited review is Ledyard 1995.) But as mentioned in Chapter 7, across the entire range of subject pools, players in every culture come to the game with experience with common pool problems. They are a pervasive aspect of social life, encountered in some form every day at home and work and even in chance encounters with strangers. We can expect players to recognize that the context of a common pool game is on the cooperative branch of the cascade introduced in Chapter 7. And then we can also expect subjects to ordinarily respond to the risky cooperation frame (2a) that correctly matches the context the game puts them in. But we saw puzzling choices in Chapter 7 that turned on the difficulty of escaping this default when the game is altered to make that inappropriate – and in either direction. We saw degenerate games in which a cooperative frame (even the weakly cooperative 2a) is a mistake, and we also saw degenerate games in which failing to move from the weak cooperation to the strong cooperation frame (2b) is a mistake. In both directions players seemed vulnerable to being inappropriately caught by the default. We see choices that the chooser herself would find puzzling.

In a standard (not degenerate) Public Goods game, the "ordinarily" qualifier in the previous paragraph is needed to allow that some subjects of a particularly cooperative bent might escape the risky competition default (frame 2a in the cascade) for the coordination frame (2b). They might (initially, for they are almost certain to find things otherwise) take it for granted that fellow players will also see the game that way. At the other end, a player well drilled in the standard economic model of rational self-interest, and since this is after all a game and games are usually played competitively, might be on the competitive branch of the cascade though with cues adequate to escape from the zero-sum frame (1a) to the payoff-maximizing frame (1b). Neither of these responses involves adverse defaulting in the invidious sense developed in Chapters 6 and 7. A bright player could find herself seeing the game in either of these ways and defend her view of the game as reasonable. But since typical results are much the same across experiments and across subject pools, propensities to both departures are apparently not very different across subject pools. We ought to find NSNX effects that generalize across subject pools.

## The *updown* effect

As in all standard Public Goods games, parameters in the experiments of the first half of this chapter were chosen such that the group does best if everyone contributes their entire endowment, but each individual does best for herself if others contribute while she keeps her endowment. Let *give* = a player's choice in the current round, *pool* = sum of all *gives* in this round, $y$ = endowment per round, $n$ = number of players in each group, and $a$ = return to each player for each token in the common pool. A player's total payoff for the round will be $y - give + a*pool$. The cost of contributing a token is $1 - a$ (a fraction of each token given comes back to the donor). The gain to the group from any player contributing a token is $n*a - 1$, since each member of the group (including the donor) gets the return from any member's contribution of a token.

The value ratio (G'/S') on the right in the NSNX equilibrium condition would then be subject to various complications noticed in Chapter 1, but that ratio would be anchored on $(n*a - 1)/(1 - a)$. So other things equal, the value ratio increases with increases of $n$ or $a$. But W on the left of the equilibrium condition (W = G'/S') responds to how a player's contributions look relative to what others are contributing. To catch that aspect of a Public Goods game, define *gavg* as the *give* of a player in a round relative to the average *give* of other players. So $gavg = give / ((pool - give)/(n - 1))$.

Further interpretation is tied to the Darwinian argument that underpins NSNX in Chapter 1. Darwinian variation is blind and selection near-sighted, which creates a challenge for any account that postulates choice motivated by group- as well as self-interest. The problem is not insurmountable. In SA&R (Chapter 3), I suggested that an evolution of gene linkages across traits that could favor selection "as if" a longer view were effective. But the main point of the Darwinian argument, sketched in Chapter 1 here, is that we can see that human beings exhibit a degree of other-regarding as well as self-interested motivation, and thinking in Darwinian terms about how that might be sustained leads us to the pair of NSNX rules, which in turn imply the NSNX equilibrium condition.

But concern for Darwinian plausibility warns us not to treat the G'/S' ratios of the NSNX model as more than ordinal. A creature might get by with only a sense of greater-than or lesser-than to manage choice between alternatives. Nicely refined quantitative assessments would be better (if there were no costs to managing that and a feasible evolution pathway were available), but it does not look like we have been provided with that until cultural rather than genetic evolution yielded such things as literacy and recording devices. Our deeply entrenched propensities long antedate that.

So the Darwinian view allows for and indeed at least weakly predicts the predominance of qualitative over quantitative effects we have seen repeatedly, yielding the sometimes startling insensitivity we have seen of intuitive judgments to even quite gross shifts in parameters. Several examples in Chapter 7 exhibited the stickiness of neglect defaults in the face of starkly contrary quantitative cues. And as mentioned there, parallel insensitivity to quantitative parameters have been noticed in many other studies entirely unconnected with data from cooperation experiments. The effect of quantitative cues is likely to be weaker than logic would warrant. And the value ratio is several steps removed from the cues. A general consequence is that we should not expect more than comparative statics inferences from the NSNX argument as presented. But as will be seen here, that is sufficient to yield strong results.

Under strictly self-interested choice, players would contribute nothing to a Public Goods game, on a variant of the backward induction argument in the 100 PD game noticed at the end of Chapter 1. But NSNX players should ordinarily be willing to contribute something to a common pool (even when there is no way to punish a free-rider), with the "ordinarily" qualification allowing for the various atypical cases mentioned earlier. The positive contributions expected under NSNX, however, should show the effects of "neither selfish nor exploited" mixed motivation, which would be adversely affected by the difficulty in coordinating contributions which the standard conditions (anonymity, etc.) are in fact designed to impose.

An easy comparative statics inference from Rule 1 (NSNX efficiency), however, is that even without explicit coordination, contributions should tend to increase with increasing return per token from the pool and also with increasing membership in the group that will benefit. On the standard account players should not contribute at all. But increasing cooperation with increasing return is easy to accommodate even in terms of the standard account. Given that (for whatever reason) players contribute at all, it would be surprising if they did not tend to contribute more if the per token cost of contributing $(1 - a)$ falls. And this is a well-marked feature of Public Goods data. On the other hand, a tendency for contributions to also increase with increasing $n$ is puzzling on the standard account (Ledyard 1995), since a player concerned only with self-interest tautologically does not value a better return to the group, only lower cost to self. On that logic, increasing $a$ motivates contributing but increasing $n$ does not, even allowing that somehow players do contribute. But contributions do generally increase with increasing $n$ as well as with increasing $a$, as NSNX would expect. Since the NSNX argument was published in 1982, generally increasing cooperation with increasing $n$ as well as for increasing $a$ is confirmation of an implication antedating the observations.

On the prevailing view, some fraction of players can be labeled "conditional cooperators," and attempts to sort that out typically find the fraction to be large. And since an immediate consequence of the NSNX equity rule (p. 8) is that *in general* players must be conditional cooperators, that observation, in terms of NSNX, must hold. But NSNX implies that efforts to "type" players as conditional cooperators or not conditional cooperators should lead to only superficial results. "Types" (other than conditional cooperators) should usually be unstable, so that it does not take much to reveal that they are conditional cooperators after all. I will have occasion to provide several examples as we proceed. Even the player who sees the game competitively will ordinarily be a NSNX player who is seeing free-riding as akin to bluffing in poker – just part of the game, not a strictly self-interested player who recognizes the game as cooperative but is indifferent to norms of reciprocity.

Unlike a strictly self-interested player, a NSNX non-cooperator's frame might shift as cues to what kind of game he is in accumulate during play. On the other hand, a cautious player who in fact would be willing to contribute all his tokens if he knew others would, might start by contributing zero, waiting to see what others do. At another extreme, a bold player, but one seeing self-interested choice as a hard-nosed but not unfair way to play, might still contribute some chips in early rounds to encourage others to give enough in later rounds to make that profitable. And another player might give his entire endowment, or give nothing, but for no better reason than that he misunderstood the instructions or let his attention wander.

So as every experimenter learns, no inference can be drawn from the behavior of one subject, and especially one subject's choice in one round. But strong effects can show through these atypical responses. If NSNX is right, players are ordinarily trying for a "neither selfish nor exploited" balance, and overall results should reflect that even through the noise in the data introduced by complications of the sort I've just sketched.

The most obvious such inference is that on the "neither selfish nor exploited" argument, a player who has given more than the average in her group ought to be more inclined to give less in the next round than a person who has given less than the average. Other things equal, when a NSNX player sees she has given more than others, then directly from Rule 2, W increases. But, other things equal, G′ and S′ are the same. The see-saw on p. 10 would, consequently, tilt toward more weight to self-interest. The player's sense of how she stands with respect to a "neither selfish nor exploited" equilibrium shifts toward the exploited side. And we should see a converse tendency if she has given less than others in her group. Hence if *gavg* is high (player's *give* is big compared to what others in the group have given), the propensity to give in the next round should fall. And more generally, if motivation is NSNX the prospects of cooperation in future rounds must vary with whether some players are contributing a lot and making minimal gains while others are contributing nothing and gaining a lot, as against the case where everyone is contributing and gaining about as much.

Players are not ordinarily given information about the distribution of contributions, and in the data used here they were not. The average given by others is implicit in a player's own payoff for the round, but it is not transparent, which would reduce its impact in the unfamiliar context of an experiment, as repeatedly seen in the odd cases of Chapter 7. And even when detailed information on giving by others is available, the weakness of quantitative inputs relative to qualitative impressions will diminish its impact. Consequently, in addition to what a player might surmise about how her contribution compares to what others have contributed, the propensity to contribute less (or contribute more) in the next round would also be influenced by a comparative *give/get* effect, which more directly confronts the chooser and requires only a qualitative perception.

A player who gave more in the previous round but got less can hardly fail to notice that disagreeable news, and must be moved towards feeling exploited, hence be more likely to give less in the current round than to give more. A player who gave less but got more should tend to give more in the next round. If he changes his contribution, it should be more likely to change up than to change down.

But the "gave-more/got-less" influence should be stronger than the "gave-less/got-more" influence, since for "gave-more/got-less" there is a double effect favoring giving less in the next round but for "gave-less/got-more" two opposing effects. *Ex ante*, a player has to rely on some intuition about G'. He knows S' (it is coming out of his pocket), but until he gets feedback after the round, he does not know the value of choosing as he has. If he were to turn out to be the only cooperator, G' cannot be anything but negative. There is no social value in rewarding a bunch of free-riders, and all the more so when the sole contributor ends up with a loss, while free-riders profit. On the NSNX norms logic of Chapter 1, that is not likely to be seen as a social gain at all. In a natural situation, details might be such that something different is seen. The sole contributor might be reciprocating prior behavior or expecting reciprocity tomorrow, or be far better off than others, or in various other ways be quite willing to be the only contributor. But in the artificial context of a Public Goods game marked by anonymity and no communication, there is not much opportunity for that.

Ordinarily the player who gave more but got less should feel exploited, and in addition in simple stimulus/response terms he was punished for that choice (got less). Call this the *exploited & punished* case. Among *exploited & punished* players who change their contribution in the next round, what I will call *fractiondown* should be high. For the converse "gave-less/got-more" *selfish & rewarded* case, *fractiondown* ought to be lower (a smaller fraction of changes should be to give less). But that must be a weaker effect since here the NSNX effect and the stimulus/response effect go in opposite directions.

Table 8.1 tabulates these effects for the "high gave, gave more, got less" case, using data from the two widely cited series of experiments mentioned earlier, which happened to be among the earliest sent to me. The results are very similar for other datasets. The main effects prove to be both large and robust, not only in the 13 experiments reported in Table 8.1, but in many others I have had an opportunity to test. An interested reader can use the "template" described in the Appendix to run this and other tests on data of her own choice. The difference (*exploited & punished* versus *selfish & rewarded*) is exhibited for all nine experimental conditions reported in Isaac, Williams, and Walker (1994) and for all four conditions reported in Fehr and Gachter (2000).

Could these strong results reflect merely regression to the mean? Table 8.2 reports summary results that control for level of contribution. The stratified data cover the great majority of non-zero choices (all non-zero *gives* divisible by 5), arranged into High, Mid, and Low with respect to "*gavg*".[2] The fourth

*Table 8.1* The results for 13 experimental conditions: all 9 of the Isaac, Williams, and Walker (1994) experiments, plus all 4 conditions of the Fehr and Gachter (2000) series.

| Summary | | Fraction down | |
| --- | --- | --- | --- |
| XP | | | |
| IWW 1994 | Choices | Exploited | Selfish |
| 10.3 | 1600 | *0.77* | 0.32 |
| 10.75 | 1000 | 0.77 | 0.16 |
| 4.3 | 680 | 0.89 | 0.21 |
| 4.75 | 400 | 0.70 | 0.22 |
| 40.3 | 4800 | 0.80 | 0.31 |
| 40$×3 | 800 | 0.86 | 0.41 |
| 40$.3 | 800 | 0.78 | 0.23 |
| 100.3 | 3000 | 0.78 | 0.31 |
| 100.75 | 1000 | 0.72 | 0.24 |
| FG 2000 | | | |
| S–S+ | 480 | 0.89 | 0.09 |
| S+S– | 240 | 0.89 | 0.22 |
| P+P– | 160 | 1.00 | 0.29 |
| P–P+ | 240 | 0.92 | 0.14 |

The Isaac, Williams, and Walker (IWW) conditions cover groups of 4, 10, 40, or 100, some playing for course credits, some for cash, some with a return per player per token contributed of 0.3, others of 0.75. The Fehr and Gachter (FG) data are for both "stranger" and "partner" experiments, each either following or preceding a set of rounds with punishment. For the IWW series, "40.3," for example, refers to IWW trials with 40 players in a group and a return per token of 0.3. There were in all 4,800 choices within IWW 40.3: twelve 40-player groups and 10 rounds per group. For the FG series, "S–S+" is a strangers' series (groups reshuffled at each round), with a no-punishment preceding an (unannounced) punishment series. "P+P–" is a partners' series (groups are fixed) with the punishment series preceding the no-punishment series.

Data points in the analysis are about half as large as total choices, since there is no prediction until round 3 (of 10), and then predictions only for choices that change from the previous round.

The data are for the "gave more and got less" versus "gave less and got more" cases, averaging between an upper bound result which includes "*gives*" of 0 and *y* (entire endowment) and a lower bound result which excludes these cases. The upper bound is biased in favor of the prediction since a player cannot give less if she has given 0, or give more if she has given *y*. But the lower bound is biased against the test, since it excludes just the cases where, on the theory, the effect should be strongest. The summary results here therefore give the mean of the upper and lower bound results. As expected, the differences are typically even larger (in the predicted direction) for the "gave more and got less" versus "gave less and got *less*" cases.

column for each contribution level sums the results for that level. If the results in Table 8.1 reflected merely random regression-to-the-mean, we would see no effect looking across the High, Mid, Low columns within contribution levels. Instead, we should see a big effect looking at the summed results across levels. To the extent that the results are pure NSNX effects we should see the opposite. And what you can see scanning across contribution levels in Table 8.2 is that there is no sign of regression to the mean, but ample evidence of the NSNX tendency of *fractiondown* to respond to *gavg* in the predicted way. The only clear anomalies are in cells where data points are so sparse that occasional anomalies would be expected.

## "NSD" effects

If others are contributing in a cooperative game, the salient choice for a NSNX chooser will be to contribute about as much as others, as in the everyday situation of restaurant tipping, people mostly want to do about what others are doing. But how could the player be confident that others are seeing it the same way and playing the same way? On everyday intuition as well on the NSNX-constrained norms sketched in Chapter 1, it would in fact be socially perverse to allow exploitation unless that was sufficiently (meaning, more than just barely) offset by the gains to cooperators. Consequently the social value of a contribution (G′) will be influenced not only by the return to the group it will bring in the current round but also by what giving in prior rounds suggests about the prospect of sustaining fair cooperation in future rounds.

Define *nsd1* as the normalized standard deviation of contributions in round 1 (the standard deviation among *gives* relative to the mean *give*). High mean *give* favors low *nsd1* (the denominator is large), but so does more or less equal sharing of effort even if the mean is low (the numerator is small). On the argument, prospects for sustaining cooperation should be affected by how coordinated the group happens to be in round 1. Low *nsd1* should enhance and a high *nsd1* diminish G′ adjusted for this effect of the prospect of fair cooperation in future rounds. So from the NSNX perspective, a group that fortuitously starts off well coordinated should have a better chance to stay in step than a group that starts off badly coordinated. In a "before seeing data" note soliciting datasets for this project, I suggested that if NSNX is right, giving to the pool averaged over all later rounds should correlate with what I am here calling *nsd1*. Call this a *firstgrand* effect.

In contrast to the *updown* effect, this *firstgrand* effect should be seen only in "partners" experiments, where group membership stays fixed across rounds, and not in a "strangers" experiment where players are shuffled after each round, allowing no chance for a coherent tendency across rounds.[3] The effect would be clearest at the extremes, reflecting the dichotomizing ("twoness") tendency seen elsewhere. A log regression would fit such data better than a linear regression. The charts in Figure 8.2 consequently plot log regressions for giving over all remaining rounds (*grandmean>1*) against the fortuitous coordination in round 1 measured by *nsd1*.[4]

Figures 8.2a, 8.2b, and 8.2c plot log regressions for data from the most

*Table 8.2* Table 8.1 data stratified by level of contribution

| | 5 | | | | 10 | | | | 15 | | | | 20 | | | | 25 | | | |
|---|---|---|---|---|---|---|---|---|---|---|---|---|---|---|---|---|---|---|---|---|
| | hi | med | lo | All | hi | med | lo | All | hi | med | lo | All | hi | med | lo | All | hi | med | lo | All |
| less | 21 | 6 | 88 | **115** | 83 | 27 | 107 | **217** | 39 | 19 | 20 | **78** | 109 | 31 | 6 | **146** | 225 | 53 | 2 | **280** |
| same | 4 | 0 | 25 | **29** | 16 | 4 | 35 | **55** | 8 | 6 | 3 | **17** | 10 | 19 | 9 | **38** | 82 | 19 | 1 | **102** |
| more | 4 | 2 | 90 | **96** | 25 | 8 | 160 | **183** | 21 | 13 | 31 | **65** | 25 | 40 | 2 | **67** | 104 | 61 | 4 | **169** |
| All | 29 | 8 | 203 | **240** | 124 | 39 | 292 | **455** | 68 | 38 | 54 | **160** | 144 | 90 | 17 | **251** | 411 | 133 | 7 | **551** |
| | *0.72* | *0.75* | *0.43* | **0.48** | *0.67* | *0.09* | *0.37* | **0.48** | *0.57* | *0.50* | *0.37* | **0.49** | *0.76* | *0.34* | *0.35* | **0.58** | *0.55* | *0.40* | *0.29* | **0.51** |

| | 30 | | | | 35 | | | | 40 | | | | 45 | | | | 50 | | | |
|---|---|---|---|---|---|---|---|---|---|---|---|---|---|---|---|---|---|---|---|---|
| | hi | med | lo | All | hi | med | lo | All | hi | med | lo | All | hi | med | lo | All | hi | med | lo | All |
| less | 226 | 7 | 0 | **233** | 230 | 1 | 0 | **231** | 389 | 4 | 0 | **393** | 179 | 1 | 0 | **180** | 491 | 3 | 0 | **494** |
| same | 41 | 9 | 0 | **50** | 43 | 3 | 0 | **46** | 92 | 2 | 0 | **94** | 79 | 1 | 0 | **80** | 514 | 32 | 0 | **546** |
| more | 118 | 7 | 0 | **125** | 162 | 0 | 0 | **162** | 163 | 1 | 0 | **164** | 90 | 0 | 0 | **90** | 0 | 0 | 0 | **0** |
| All | 385 | 23 | 0 | **408** | 435 | 4 | 0 | **439** | 644 | 7 | 0 | **651** | 348 | 2 | 0 | **350** | 1005 | 35 | 0 | **1040** |
| | *0.59* | *0.30* | .... | **0.57** | *0.53* | *0.25* | .... | **0.53** | *0.60* | *0.57* | .... | **0.60** | *0.51* | *0.50* | .... | **0.51** | *0.49* | *0.09* | .... | **0.48** |

(Continued)

*Table 8.2* (Continued)

The bottom row in each box shows "fractiondown" for the stratified choicer of "*give*" shown in the upper left of each box. The data have been aggregated across the 13 Public Good conditions reported in Table 8.1. To the extent that the strong and robust effects reported there are contaminated by mere regression to the mean, we should see a marked trend upward in the fraction in bold in the lower right corner of each box, but no effect in the italic components showing how (within a contribution level) "fractiondown" varies with how the chooser's "*give*" compared to the average of others in the group.

The FG data (with $y = 20$) are aggregated to as nearly as possible match the fractions for the IWW data ($y = 50$). So FG "*give*" = 5 is an aggregate with IWW 10, FG 10 with IWW 25, FG 15 with IWW 40, FG 20 with IWW 50. Detail for individual experiments is included in the Working Paper (note 2). The "less," "same," "more" labels on the columns refer to choices where gang (own *give*/others' average) was more than 1.3, within the interval 0.9–1.1, or less than 0.7. The integers are the number of data points in each category.

The relative small numbers for low "*givers*" reflects the reduced tendency to choose a number divisible by 5 when the "*give*" is close to zero. And the largest category of "*give*" is 0, which is not in the table since "fractiondown" from 0 can only be 0. But the second most common "*give*" was the entire endowment.

It is apparent that there is no hint of regression to the mean, but rather marked support for the NSNX prediction of a downward trend across the "*give*" categories.

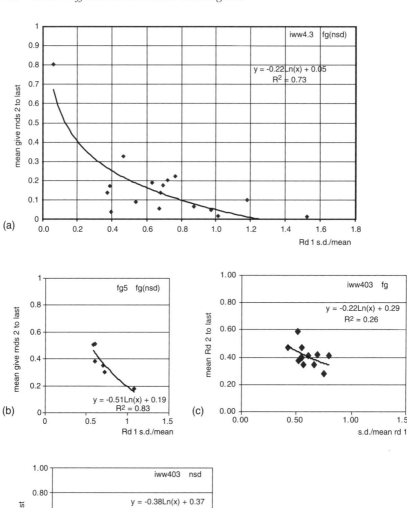

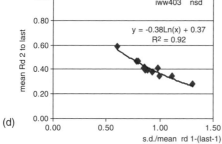

*Figure 8.2(a)–(d)* Log regressions for data from the series used for *updown* tests.

relevant experiments from the series used for the *updown* tests (IWW1994 *n* = 4 and *n* = 40 trials with *a* = 0.3, plus the FG2000 partners trial, FG5, which was not conditioned by an immediately preceding series of rounds with punishment).[5] The predicted effect is evident, but with a cognitive nuance.

The data divides into contrasting modest payoff cases (here IWW4.3 and FG5) and high payoff cases (here IWW40.3). For the modest payoff cases, a player who gave well above the mean of what others in the group gave would be left a payoff below her original endowment.[6] A player in this situation can hardly fail to notice she is being exploited. But for the high payoff case (with $n = 40$, $a = 0.3$) each token in the pool yields 12 tokens to be shared, so that even if there were many complete free-riders – it is an interesting point to be taken up in a moment that in fact there were very few complete free-riders – a generous contributor still comes away with a profit. A player can do very well even if grossly exploited relative to free-riders in her group.

Hence we might expect that the relative importance of standard deviation and mean in round 1 would be different for the two cases. And as the figures show, there is indeed a strong *firstgrand* effect, but separately plotting *grand-mean>1* against *standard deviation(rd 1)* and against *mean(rd 1)* suggests the effect is dominated by one or the other component. We see either a response mainly to *standard deviation(rd 1)* or a response to *mean(rd 1)*, rather than a simple response to the ratio. Again, a reader can examine this using the "template" described in the Appendix, which includes the data for these and many other experiments and which can easily take in new datasets of a reader's choice. The dichotomous effect is governed in the way just suggested. In modest-payoff experiments (where exploitation is easily severe) the response is mainly to *standard deviation(rd 1)*, and the converse in the high-payoff experiments. A related and perhaps more striking feature will be seen in the *lastround* effect coming later.

Contrary to what a first glance might suggest, the effect for the IWW 40.3 (Figure 8.2c) case is not very different from that for the $n = 4$ cases. The range of variation is much narrower in IWW 40.3 than in IWW 4.3. Within the narrower interval, the effects are very similar despite the difference in the dominant aspect just discussed.

Although these experiments have been studied for several decades, the relations apparent in these figures have not been noticed, most likely because almost all experiments are in the modest-payoff category. But the effect of the mean is weak there; it is the effect of the standard deviation in round 1 that is strikingly large. It is a significant point in favor of NSNX, I think, that what had not been noticed over several decades of discussion of Public Goods experiments was found almost immediately here, since the theory quite directly demands what turns out to be a fruitful conjecture.

Is the marked effect in Figure 8.2a only an artifact due to an outlier? The very similar effect in Figure 8.2b suggests it is not, as does the theory. But as with the *updown* effects, an interested reader can use the template to check such effects in data of their own choosing.

Finally, Figure 8.2d shows a stronger-looking but harder to interpret result. This example uses the IWW 40.3 experiment, plotting the *grand-mean>1* for each of the 12 groups as a function of the average normalized standard deviation across all of the first 9 rounds of these 10-round experiments (in contrast to Figure 8.2c, where the independent variable is *nsd* for round 1 only).

In Figure 8.2d, the round 10 *nsd* is excluded from the across-rounds average since there are no future rounds it could influence, and *mean(rd 1)* is excluded from the grand mean since there is no prior round *nsd* to influence it. The correlation is very tight indeed, but since in 8 of the 10 rounds (rounds 2–9) a term of the denominator of the independent variable also contributes to the dependent variable, some inverse slope could hardly be avoided. Trials with random data, consequently, also show tight fits on this measure. But for actual data the variance across groups, the slope of the regression, and the r-squared values are all about twice as large as for random data. And *strangers* data, where partners are reshuffled from round to round, show no overall *nsd* effect. But since random data show a spurious correlation, why should there be no such effect with real data from a strangers experiment? Perhaps that is somehow due to player responses to the absence of expected responses by their "partners," even though they have been told there are no partners. So this result is puzzling. Nevertheless, the contrast between real data and pseudo-data is sufficiently strong that *something* of interest is apparently going on here.

## A lastround effect

The groups in all the IWW trials were drawn by random assignment of players from a common pool of students in introductory economics courses. With an interesting exception to be noted, payoffs were in extra course credits not money, but calibration with trials with real money at stake showed no systematic difference. The striking contrast was that the IWW results for groups of 40 with a return per player of 0.3 look very different from the results for groups of four with the same return. But that should be expected if motivation is NSNX. Direct social value of giving (G′ with no adjustment for prospective cooperation) is ten times as large when $n = 40$. As already mentioned, for IWW 40.3, each token given to the pool produces $40 \times 3 = 12$ tokens for distribution across the group, while IWW 4.3 yields only $4 \times 0.3 = 1.2$ tokens per token given. With $n = 4$, it takes 100 percent cooperation to make a social gain unless gain to the free-rider is treated as a social gain rather than as socially perverse. And in terms of contributors' self-interest, it is emphatically perverse: they are left worse off than if they had not played at all. If there were a free-rider and three contributors in a round, each giving some common amount, then with $n = 4$, the three contributors would all be worse off than if everyone gave nothing.

But with $n = 40$ contributors of some common amount would gain even if 90 percent of the remaining players (36 of 40) were free-riders. These contributors might very reasonably see themselves as exploited by the free-riders, but they would not be outright losers. So we might expect, and certainly NSNX would expect, a difference in behavior between the $n = 4$ and $n = 40$

cases. And there is indeed a large difference. The point requires serious care in drawing any generalizations about cooperation outside the lab from the far more common small *n* experiments. For although the IWW large group trials are atypical relative to other experiments (where $n = 4$ is the most common), it is large group results (not small group results) that are more typical of empirical situations in which free-rider difficulties become critical. Outside the lab, Public Goods contexts where cooperation is problematical involve numbers that are large not small, and the value of the Public Good provided by all contributions is often vastly larger for each individual than the cost to the individual of his own contribution. In an actual situation in which *n* is small (as in nearly all experiments), the anonymity and no-communication conditions imposed on the experiment would be highly unusual.

Consider, for example, the incremental value of a pristine rather than rubbish-littered beach against the slight inconvenience to any individual in carrying her own rubbish to a basket. Relative to this, the social gain from cooperation in small group experiments is quite trivial. With $n = 4$, $a = 0.3$, perfect cooperation yields only a 20 percent improvement in payoffs relative to no cooperation at all.

So it is not a surprise (in terms of NSNX: for the standard theory, as mentioned earlier, it did come as a surprise) that propensity to cooperation increased in moving from IWW 4.3 to IWW 40.3 (from $n = 4$ to $n = 40$, with $a = 0.3$ in both cases). And in contrast to the robust tendency for contributions to decline over the 10 rounds, cooperation with $n = 40$ here did *not* regularly decline. For about half of the 12 IWW $n = 40$ groups, contributions did not significantly decline at all across rounds, and the decline even in the least successful groups was never close to complete free-riding. Baseline trials IWW ran for real money had already shown that behavior in $n = 4$ games did not noticeably depend on this. But it is interesting to note that the second most cooperative $n = 40$ group was a group playing for real money. And the most cooperative group of all was a group also playing for real money but with experience (having already played the game once). This is consistent with NSNX and seems sharply at odds with the many attempts to account for contributions as errors.

Another test also yields a striking result. The *lastround* choice is a player's last chance to move toward NSNX "neither selfish nor exploited" equilibrium. Figure 8.3 displays *lastround* choices for the $n = 40$ groups conditional on players' relative prior contributions over prior rounds.

> Set DIFF = *(last round contribution)* – *(average contribution for the prior* $n - 1$ *rounds)*
>
> *Gavg\* = mean own contribution up to the last round, relative to others' contributions*

So if a player gives more in the final round than her prior average gives, DIFF is positive; and if she gives less, DIFF is negative. *Gavg\** is the grand average for *gavg* over the first *n* − 1 rounds. If *Gavg** > 1, a player has given more on average than others, and if *Gavg** < 1 she has given less. Figure 8.3 then plots DIFF on the vertical axis against *Gavg** on the horizontal.

You can see a dichotomous response, in which about half the players who gave more than others gave nothing (the streak slanting down from the left), while the other half mostly *increase* their contribution over their prior round average. The figure shows a blurred "zero" line slanting down since player average *gives* across the 12 groups are not identical, so while the DIFF of a 0 final *give* must grow as *gavg** grows, it is only roughly not exactly in proportion across players.

The simplest interpretation of the dichotomous result is that it is akin to the response we all have to gestalt drawings, like the duck/rabbit, young girl/ old hag, faces/vases. In each case, there are two ways to see the drawing. But at any moment we see just one. For players in the IWW small-*n* trials, this is not very significant. A person who has contributed conspicuously more than others will not have done much better from participating in the game than if she had been allowed to just opt out of the game. In fact, she may easily have done worse, ending up with a net payoff less than her endowments. So we should expect a definite tendency to give less in the final round than whatever her average was prior to the final round, and a great majority of players do so.

But in the large-*n*, *a* = 0.3 tests, even players who contribute the most do very well. Consequently, in contrast to the *n* = 4 case, here two gestalts are available. The "exploited" gestalt which alone is easily prompted in the *n* = 4 case is available here, but also a "success" gestalt enhanced by reciprocity towards other contributors. Both make sense, as the gestalt drawing can reasonably be seen as either duck or rabbit. Heavy contributors have indeed

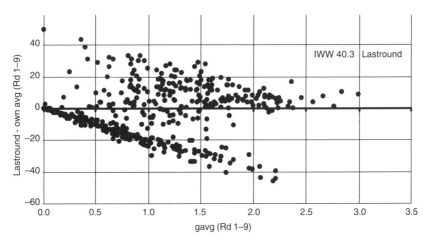

*Figure 8.3* The chart reveals a dichotomous last round response as explained in the text. Most choices are either zero (in the blurry line at the bottom) or more than the chooser has given in earlier rounds.

been exploited by low contributors. But they have done very well anyway. And they cannot punish their exploiters without also punishing their fellow contributors. So it is not surprising (in hindsight: I do not claim to have foreseen this) that we would see the dichotomous response the scatter-plots reveal.

Putting this duck/rabbit interpretation in terms of the NSNX equilibrium ($W = G'/S'$): if weight to self-interest (W) is salient, from Rule 2 it must look large relative to a player's starting expectation. The player has given clearly more than others, and giving nothing in the final round will be the salient choice. But if it is your gain that is salient, then you see a big social gain (you and others who have been generous now have many more tokens than you were originally given). So $G'/S'$ is large, and giving generously in the final round remains salient. And since some see the W "duck" while others see the $G'/S'$ "rabbit," we can get the dichotomous response which is so apparent in Figure 8.3.

But it is a cognitive point, not a rational choice point of any sort, that we are prone to such either/or, duck/rabbit dichotomies: here with choice dominated by one side or the other of the equilibrium, not a balance between the two when (in this case) the shifts push in competing directions.

The next point, which is certainly important, can't be seen in Figure 8.3 and has been essentially ignored in the very extensive literature on Public Goods games. Contrary to what might be expected on the standard theory, *complete* free-riding is far less common in the large group, $a = 0.3$ setting than in the small groups with the same return. Of 68 players in IWW 4.3, seven were complete free-riders, never contributing at all. But of 480 players (from the same subject pool) in IWW 40.3, there were only six complete free-riders.

This is the first of several occasions when we will encounter quite sharp reason to doubt that "types" (conditional cooperators versus self-interested versus full cooperators) often reported in analyses of experimental data are permanent types rather than transient and tactical. We have an almost ten-fold difference in propensity to be a complete free-rider which here cannot possibly be anything but an effect of the change in conditions.

But a puzzle can be seen in the large group response to an improvement in the per-token payoff. Players in the $n = 4$ trials were sensitive to the return they got per token in the pool. Raising return from 0.3 to 0.75, which lowers the net cost of contributing a token from 0.7 to 0.25, made a big difference. This remained true for $n = 40$ but only with respect to a difference in cooperation between $a = 0.03$ and $a = 0.3$. This ten-fold increase in return – reducing the net cost of giving a token from 0.97 to 0.7 – produced a more than ten-fold increase in cooperation. This is not hard to understand, since with the very low return of 0.03 as few as seven (out of 40) free-riders would leave most contributors as exploited losers. But a further increase from 0.3 to 0.75 in the $n = 40$ case (and also in several $n = 100$ trials) produced no increase at all in contributions. Players contributed no more when it cost only 0.25 tokens to give a token ($a = 0.75$) than when it cost 0.7 ($a = 0.3$).

The results grossly violate the one generalization in economic theory most routinely designated a "law": that lower price yields higher demand. The Law of Demand is suspended here, and absent any special conditions which make sense of such an observation in a few other contexts. But this insensitivity to quantitative effects relative to qualitative (for the large number case, even exploited players are doing very well whether $n = 40$ or $n = 100$) is consistent with the insensitivity to quantitative effects relative to qualitative already seen repeatedly. It is more evidence of insensitivity of choice to other than gross quantitative cues in unfamiliar contexts, which looks like an aspect of the strength of neglect defaulting central to the account of the cognitive illusions of Chapter 6. And it is yet more indication that any rational choice account of social choice, including NSNX, is likely to get into trouble unless serious allowance is made for cognitive effects.

### Standard versus Best Shot versus Weakest Link games

Now consider to a more intricate dataset from Croson, Fatas, and Neugebauer (2006) (CFN). The CFN starting point was a standard 10-round Public Goods game, run with a surprise (to the players) restart after round 10. In all, the CFN series provides data on the basic game and two variants of the basic game, each played under three payoff conditions, and with new groups of players in each of the nine variants. Figure 8.4 shows the round-by-round results for the nine games, each played out for 20 rounds with a surprise restart at round 11.

The baseline VCM game (first panel of Figure 8.4) uses the "voluntary contribution" mechanism of a standard Public Goods game. The two variants use a Best Shot Mechanism (BSM) where payoffs depend solely on the *highest* contribution in a group, or a Weakest Link Mechanism (WLM) where payoffs depend solely on the *lowest* contribution (Harrison and Hirshleifer 1989). There are always four members in a group, an endowment of 50 tokens per round, and a return arranged to be the same across all variants when everyone makes the same choice. In VCM a player gets two tokens per token in the pool for the *average* contribution,[7] in BSM for the *highest* (Best Shot) contribution, and in WLM for the *lowest* (Weakest Link) contribution. A player's payoff for the round is then the sum of what he gets from the pool plus any tokens kept (not contributed to the pool). If all players give the same, they all get the same payoff under any of these schemes, since then the average, highest, and lowest *give* are all the same.

The three payoff conditions were: (1) the games just described, with no adjustment of payoffs; (2) an exclusion game (VCM-EX, BSM-EX, WLM-EX) in which the player (and ties unless all *gives* were identical) who gave the least forfeits any payoff from the pool; and (3) an exclusion with redistribution game (VCM-EX-R, BSM-EX-R, WLM-EX-R) in which any forfeited payoff is divided among the remaining players. In Figure 8.4 the VCM, VCM-EX, and VCM-EX-R results are in the panel at the top, BSM,

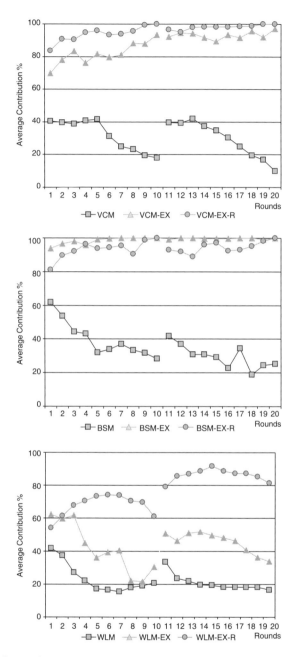

*Figure 8.4* Nine variants of the Public Goods game from Croson, Fatas, and Neuge-bauer (2006).

BSM-EX, and BSM-EX-R in the middle; and WLM, WLM-EX, and WLM-EX-R at the bottom.

I had occasion to mention at the start of this chapter that the bounce-back at the restart in the VCM game is a robust feature of Public Goods experiments. It always happens. This is a mystery for accounts in terms of self-interest, where confusion must play a large role in accounting for contributions. For it is certainly puzzling that a verbal instruction to start over and play another ten rounds would return players to whatever state of confusion they were in before play started at all. The replays always look very similar to the original sequence, as they do here. One experiment (Cookson 2000) even followed a surprise restart with another surprise restart and then yet another surprise restart. Each restart produced a pattern similar to what is seen for the basic game here, with the repeated restart sequences looking much like the original sequence.

So we want to give an account of that, and more generally we want to use this interesting array of variants to consider how we might gain insight into what is happening in a poorly understood situation from what we can learn from how choices went in a related, but better understood, situation. Here I want to move from the most familiar game (VCM) to increasingly harder-to-analyze games, taking advantage of what we have learned from the results of prior games. The VCM game is by now familiar. The Best Shot game is unfamiliar, but relative to the Weakest Link game is easy to analyze. We save the hardest for last.

Start from some general points about how the elements in the NSNX equilibrium (W, G', S') would respond to the changing incentives across the CFN variations.

From NSNX Rule 2, which conditions W (weight to self-interest) on a player's contribution relative to others in the group, W will be smaller to the extent that others' past and perhaps anticipated future cooperation become larger.

G' will reflect both a direct effect of a choice on payoffs to the group within the current round, and also (until the last round) possibly some adjustment for effect of a choice on the prospects for enhanced payoffs in future rounds.

S' will have a direct cost offset by any expected return from the pool, and perhaps also by a share in any prospective value for G'. When the CFN exclusion conditions are in play, the effective cost of contributing (*net* S') needs to be also adjusted for the prospect of exclusion. The higher the *give*, the less chance of exclusion. Giving 50 guarantees against exclusion, since 50 cannot be less than others have contributed. Giving 0 guarantees exclusion. No one could give less.[8]

Against that background, consider what NSNX implies with respect to the results you see in Figure 8.4.

### VCM versus VCM-EX versus VCM-EX-R

The VCM results are in the lowest line of the first panel. They are entirely "normal" for a Public Goods game with a return/token as high as 0.5. The conspicuous restart effect is also entirely normal, as already stressed, and has a ready NSNX interpretation. Players are left frustrated by the modest level of cooperation by the tenth round and readily take up a suggestion to try again. And on that explanation of the restart effect, of course there is no reason for a restart effect when cooperation is succeeding not failing, and the Best Shot and Weakest Link data also show a resistor effect when cooperation is failing and not so where cooperation is succeeding.

Between VCM and VCM-EX, on any reasonable account (and with no need to allow for other-regarding motivation) contributions should move quickly toward 100 percent. If they didn't (but you can see in Figure 8.4 that they do) an account explaining some severe cognitive distortion would be needed. In VCM a player who gives 0 gets a better payoff than a player who gives any positive amount. The more you give, the less you get, providing the tension between self-interested and social motivation that is the heart of the game. Unless others are also giving, a player motivated by "neither selfish nor exploited" concerns ordinarily does not want to give. A player motivated only by self-interest does not want to give at all. But in VCM-EX, a player who gives 0 guarantees he will be excluded from what promises to be a very profitable pool (no one could give less). A player who gives a positive amount but not his full endowment (50) risks ending the round with a loss (relative to his endowment). He has moved tokens from his private account to the pool, but might be excluded and get nothing back from the pool.

But a player who gives 50 loses only if the other three players together do not at least match that, which in fact rarely happens in round 1 of any Public Goods game, and becomes especially unlikely to happen under the exclusion rule. And even in that never-occurring worst case, the player has risked only 25 tokens (since half his 50-token contribution will come back) to enhance the prospect of gaining $10 \times 50$ tokens over the run of the game. It is not surprising that at least one player in every group in these trials gives 50. But then a player who gave < 50, but wants to do better than just keep his endowment, must enter a kind of reverse auction against other players who want to share in the pool, where the only safe choice is to give 50. Self-interest alone is then enough to drive contributions up towards 100 percent. So it is scarcely surprising that contributions are high from the start, indeed push towards 100 percent compliance, and with no restart effect, since in this game cooperation does not fail.

And under VCM-EX-R (exclusion + redistribution), the prospect for complete cooperation becomes overwhelming. Only in some very improbable condition could it fail to be profitable, while giving zero means getting nothing from the pool and giving a positive amount less than 50 risks exclusion. Even if no one else contributed, giving the entire endowment is profitable, since if others give zero the sole contributor collects all earnings from the pool, which doubles her contribution. But given the strength of the VCM-EX > VCM inference there could hardly be room for much more improvement. Overall we should expect VCM-EX-R > VCM-EX >> VCM. Further, the bizarre choices seen in Chapter 7 for the inverted Public Goods game, defying the logic of the game, can hardly occur here, though there is no reason to suppose these players would do any better in the Chapter 7 games. For the threat of exclusion (or experience of exclusion, since at least one player will be excluded until all are fully contributing) pushes choices in one direction – up – a push lacking in the Chapter 7 situations.

Finally, by way of an exercise in the mechanics of the NSNX formalism, notice that *net* S' for *give* = 50 becomes negative (the cost is actually a gain) under VCM-EX as expected contributions rise (giving 50 becomes essentially certain to increase own payoff). G'/S' becomes negative, hence necessarily W > G'/S', since W is positive by definition. So the see-saw (Figure 1.2 in Chapter 1) must tilt towards self-interested choice, though all three elements of the NSNX equilibrium have changed to favor group-interest in VCM-EX relative to VCM. But if S' is negative (it pays to give rather than costs to give) and G' positive, then there is no conflict between group- and self-interested choice. *Give* = 50 is best for the group, but it is also best for self-interest, so the effect through the NSNX equilibrium is odd but not perverse. This technical point has already been noticed in the discussion of Chapter 1.

### BSM versus BSM-EX versus BSM-EX-R

If payoff from the pool scales with either the average (VCM) or smallest (WLM) contribution, then the socially best outcome is for everyone to contribute their entire endowment, yielding each player double their endowment. But under the *Best Shot* rule only one player need contribute a full endowment to give everyone the maximum payoff from the pool (double the endowment). Any contribution beyond one person contributing the maximum is pointless. If players could communicate, they would arrange for one full contribution and three zero contributions, ending up with payoffs almost triple their endowment.[9] But no communication is allowed, so players must gamble.

Once exclusion is added to the Best Shot game the analysis is far simpler. With exclusion, giving zero guarantees getting nothing from a pool that (if 50 were given) guarantees a return of 100. Choosing any number in the interval between 0 and 50 risks exclusion. That forces the inverse auction noticed in VCM-EX, to avoid being the low contributor, but in even starker form since no matter what others do, giving 50 guarantees getting 100 from the pool, and giving anything less than 50 risks getting nothing from the pool. It is not surprising on any account (NSNX, pure self-interest, or whatever) that we see almost 100 percent contributions from the start and literally 100 percent contributions in almost all remaining rounds. The clear comparative statics inference is that BSM-EX >> BSM, as indeed is seen in Figure 8.4.

But BSM-EX-R (Best Shot with exclusion + redistribution) yields a surprising result. In terms of self-interest, the incentive to contribute 50 is even stronger than in BSM-EX (exclusion *without* redistribution). For there is a chance someone will give < 50, be excluded, and leave his share to be divided among those not excluded. The incentive to contribute 50 is a bit stronger. But the result is the reverse. The top line in the Best Shot panel is for BSM-EX. In defiance of players' self-interest, the BSM-EX-R result never exceeds the BSM-EX result, but instead falls below it in almost every round.[10]

This makes no sense for self-interested players, who would see only one effect of redistribution. Expected payoff (if she gives 50) is slightly higher. Consequently, in terms of self-interest the results seen in Figure 8.4 should not happen. If, however, NSNX motivation is in play, then the result is correct. For with NSNX motivation there are two effects, not one from giving 50. There is the self-interested effect already noticed, strengthening the incentive to give 50. But there is also a group-interest effect, since exclusion no longer lowers overall group payoff. In BSM-EX, a low contributor's payoff from the pool disappears. In BSM-EX-R that payoff is not lost but only redistributed.

Consequently, adding redistribution yields a pure NSNX result. Under BSM-EX, *give* = 50 is the only sensible choice for self-interest, and group-interest reinforces that. So BSM-EX must yield more cooperation than BSM alone (no exclusion) even without NSNX, but NSNX reinforces that. But in BSM-EX-R the group-interested reinforcement of self-interest favoring *give* = 50 no longer holds. With redistribution, exclusion can never entail any loss whatever to group payoff. Rather total group payoff is improved. In the Best Shot game, any contribution beyond one 50-token *give* can yield no increase in payoff from the pool. But in BSM-EX-R, if a player is excluded by his low *give*, his payoff is not lost but only redistributed. Total group payoff *increases* by avoiding a redundant contribution.

A perfectly group-interested player would be willing to make that sacrifice. But it is hardly conceivable that a NSNX player (who attends to self-interest as well as group-interest) would. But even a strictly self-interested player confused or uncertain about how the game works, or revealing a lack of concentration, or caught by the here inappropriate free-rider default in the cascade, might give less than 50 and be excluded. That chance would not increase in BSM-EX-R relative to BSM-EX. But with NSNX motivation, losing the group-interest component of the incentive does make *give* < 50 more likely. That is the clear NSNX inference, though without the results we can see in Figure 8.4, we could hardly have expected an effect this subtle to be strong enough to be noticed. In Figure 8.4 that effect, though small, is nevertheless large enough to be very easily seen. That is probably because another player – not a player making a mere blunder – could recognize (or in an earlier round notice) that someone might give 0, that at least one other will give 50 (essentially certain here), so creating a case such that a minimal *give* > 0 contribution might both share in the group payoff and save some endowment (save 49 of 50 tokens if *give* = 1). And this would improve *both* own payoff and aggregate group payoff.

Further, even if this looks like (and indeed is) a rather reckless gamble, it is significant for NSNX that it is a risk only for the chooser himself. If he feels like taking a fling it is only his own payoff he is putting at risk. No payoff is lost to the group. From the group perspective, it is a nice thing to do.

So NSNX suggests more deviation from *give* = 50 in BSM-EX-R compared to BSM-EX, while self-interested motivation alone does not. The incentive to be alert is softened. And even if fully alert, a player who feels like fooling around in some rounds would see no social harm in it. Rather, it is socially efficient. Hence in contrast to VCM and (as will be seen next) WLM, adding redistribution to exclusion does not imply higher propensity to contribute, but marginally the opposite. This is a surprising turn in the logic. But in the data in Figure 8.4 the effect turns out to be strong enough to be readily apparent.

### WLM versus WLM-EX versus WLM-EX-R

WLM is the same game, differently presented, as the Minimum game discussed in Chapter 7.[11] Cooperation is modestly more successful here. Groups do not quickly sink to their lowest payoffs. Contributing 0 in the Weakest Link game here, as the note explains, is the same as coordination on "1" in the Minimum game. The difference in results (poor in WLM rather than downright terrible in the Minimum game) is most easily accounted for by the small size of the CFN groups (four players) relative to Minimum game experiments (usually at least seven players). As I mentioned in Chapter 7, I will eventually try to show that there is a significant *cognitive* puzzle in why players do so badly in these games. But I continue to set that aside. We will be only concerned here with comparative statics across the WLM versus WLM-EX versus WLM-EX-R games. Given the results of the WLM game, what should we expect in WLM-EX and WLM-EX-R? And if a puzzle arises, can NSNX resolve it?

For any player, define *MIN* as the lowest another player chooses. Under WLM, a choice < *MIN* lowers own payoff and everyone else's as well, a choice > *MIN* wastes tokens, yielding nothing to either the chooser or anyone else. So it is not a puzzle that over the sequence of rounds contributions tend towards settling on some common level, with the minimum rule biasing that toward the low end of the range of initial responses.

With exclusion, incentives change but whether cooperation should increase is unclear. WLM-EX incentives are dichotomous. At equilibrium no one gives anything is possible (and everyone just keeps their endowment). Everyone gives the maximum is also possible (no one is excluded and everyone gets the maximum payoff). But there is no viable option in the middle. A player who moves up puts pressure on lower players to either move up (otherwise they will be excluded) or move down to zero (which keeps a chooser's endowment intact, but gives up on any prospect of making a profit from the game). A player who moves down (and he should move down to zero, since being *at* the minimum otherwise makes no sense at all) pressures everyone else to follow, to everyone's disadvantage, including the initiator.

With exclusion, then, the minimum within a group must be expected to move *either* up towards full cooperation, or collapse to no cooperation. The intermediate levels shown in Figure 8.4 for WLM-EX (and EX-R) are averages across all players. Within any group, though, the result is that either contributions move up towards full cooperation or down towards no cooperation. In terms of self-interest alone, risk aversion would seem to make moving down salient. It takes only one choice = 0 to make a positive *give* costly to anyone else, and everyone knows that. The experimenters expected that. But exclusion of the low giver would also provide a player who started from a middling level a clear incentive to give more in future rounds. And if motivation is NSNX, punishing the least cooperative player is socially benign in a context where cooperation could double payoffs for everyone, as indeed even a player risking punishment is likely to allow. So although it is unclear how these effects would net out, in terms of NSNX it is certainly not surprising that cooperation can in fact be observed to increase into WLM-EX relative to WLM. That can be seen in the first series (rounds 1–10), and it becomes clearer as players with experience from rounds 1–10 are given a chance to try again in rounds 11–20.

In turn this yields a stronger inference for WLM-EX-R. NSNX yields no clear prediction about WLM-EX relative to WLM, in contrast to standard models, which yield a definite prediction, but it is wrong. But NSNX does imply WLM-EX-R > WLM-EX. Given that adding exclusion improves cooperation, adding exclusion + redistribution must improve it more. For suppose that in WLM-EX-R a *give* leads to exclusion. That is no worse for self-interest than in WLM-EX. But if it does not, a player probably does better and never does worse than in WLM-EX. And group-interest is clearly better served in WLM-EX-R relative to WLM-EX, since everyone other than the excluded gets a bonus and a person excluded is no worse off than under WLM-EX. A strong point, however, is that NSNX motivation softens the severity of the choice. A middling choice might result in exclusion, but for a player with "neither selfish nor exploited" motivation, it is not so selfish as giving zero, and not so vulnerable to feeling exploited as giving 50. And the exclusion is socially fair and socially useful (recalling the discussion of contributors to G′ in Chapter 1). All this must make a player tempted to bail out (choose zero) more willing to take a chance on a middling level, and a player at a middling level in the prior round more likely to head up rather than head down.

So the NSNX inference is that players should do better under WLM-EX-R than under WLM-EX. And the data in Figure 8.4 show that players indeed do better, and very strikingly they do better when given an opportunity to replay the game (rounds 11–20) with experience.

So reviewing the entire CFN set, the basic Public Goods games show one familiar but never actually explained effect (the bounce-back at restart) which makes easy sense in terms of NSNX motivation. Adding *exclusion* and *exclusion + redistribution* to Voluntary Contribution yielded almost perfect cooperation, but in a way that is easily explained even in terms of self-interest alone. NSNX motivation only reinforces what self-interest alone can explain. But adding *exclusion* and then *exclusion + redistribution* to the Best Shot and Weakest Link games provides results (subtle for the Best Shot games, impossible to miss for the Weakest Link games) which no available model other than NSNX seems to make sense of.

But other than the dichotomous result of the *lastround* test (Figure 8.3) cognitive effects have not played much of a role in this chapter. The surprising results in the Best Shot and Weakest Link games get an explanation which is essentially pure NSNX. That will change in the next two chapters, where interactions of cognitive effects with NSNX are prominent throughout.

# 9  Reciprocity puzzles

Normal situations sometimes yield abnormal behavior. We know there are serial killers, pathological liars, paranoid psychotics. But they are uncommon enough that unless your line of work is psychiatry or criminal investigations, they would not be prominent in your understanding of people's behavior. But in data from experiments it is not so unusual to see a major fraction of choices violate what both common experience and essentially universal social norms would lead us to expect. The problem is not that players may behave differently in the lab. Something of that has to be expected, since no lab experiment can capture exactly the conditions of choice outside the laboratory. But the sort of problem I want to explore here arises when choices in an experiment look so completely different from what we might expect that there is a challenge in conjecturing what kind of context might prompt such abnormal responses from apparently normal people.

We know that can happen, since we have already been through a set of examples (in Chapter 7). But there the odd results had a comical flavor. What we have every reason to expect were reasonably intelligent, and certainly sometimes highly intelligent, subjects were making choices that are hard to describe as anything but very stupid. The material in this chapter has a different character, because essentially it is about *character*. We will be looking at a set of games in which subjects seem to reveal weakness of character that is as hard to believe as the weakness of intellect that seems to be revealed by the examples in Chapter 7. We will see players (students in Barcelona and Berkeley) who seem immune to normal human responses to generous treatment, and also normal human responses to bad treatment. Since the same players reveal both, we are not speaking of *bad* character but of *weak* character. I will be giving an account, as you will now expect, in terms of adverse defaulting interacting with NSNX motivation, to yield choices which are sometimes selfish, sometimes unselfish, but in both directions often severely inappropriate.

The Trust game is often cited as an experimental demonstration of reciprocity. A and B each are given ten tokens. A sends as much as he wishes to B, which is then tripled. B sends whatever he wishes back to A. Trustees (B) by a large majority return tokens back to the trustor (A).[1] But define *full* reciprocity as when the trustee returns the tokens the trustor put under his control, and then fully shares profit from trustor putting his endowment at risk. If A sends ten tokens, full reciprocity occurs if B returns the ten tokens and also shares the 20 token profit equally. That rarely happens. But when it does, if each starts with ten, each ends with 20, which if communication was allowed is what a competent trustor would demand and what a reasonable trustee would agree to. Trustor is doing what he knows is efficient. Trustee is reciprocating by doing what he knows is fair.[2]

Against this standard, reciprocity can then run from 0 (no return to the trustee) to 1 (full profit-sharing). Allowing that reciprocity is a matter of degree, not dichotomous, there is still evidence of reciprocity in Trust game data, but it is usually evidence that reciprocity is feeble. In a large fraction of Trust game interactions, trustors do not even get back as much as they send. The trustee pockets the profit and keeps some of the trustee's tokens as well. On average, trustors are doing well in these games if they end up with some modest gain from putting endowment at risk. If this was the usual result of trusting in real life, we would see very little of the cautious, qualified, sometimes disappointed, but still substantial not feeble trust that plays an essential role in successful economies. But much more extreme failures of reciprocity can be found in experimental data, and the focus of this chapter is on a salient example of that.

The anomalies which were the focus of Chapter 7 showed that experimental results could violate any coherent account of what to expect from subjects with normal intelligence. It should not then be surprising that subjects who fail to follow their own clear interests even when simple self-interest is all that is needed might also fail to follow norms to the extent that people usually do follow norms outside the lab. Conforming to norms is certainly imperfect, as stressed in Chapter 3, but a very long way from inconsequential. List, writing with Harrison (2004) and with Levitt (2005), has built a strong argument that subjects in the laboratory often behave better than people unobtrusively observed in natural settings. That is certainly true. But a broader look reveals that the opposite is also true. Players sometimes are less social in the lab. And sometimes, we have seen in Chapter 7, players are just stupider in the lab. In this chapter we will see the same holds for the moral dimensions.

In everyday life we take it for granted that if A is nice to B, then B will feel some obligation to be nice to A, and even if A is someone he will never see again. B might not in fact do the nice thing, but if not we look for an explanation. If B can do the nice thing at very little cost to himself, but still doesn't, that is stranger. If B treats people who actually have been nice to him worse than he treats people who have done nothing for him, that is strange. Or if A is *nasty* to B and B in return is nice to A, that is strange. If C sees A is being wantonly nasty to B that would normally affect C's inclination to be nice to A. If she doesn't, that is strange. And so on.

It is easy to find examples in experiments of all the choices I have been labeling strange, other than the last. I will return to that significant exception.

But given what we have seen already of self-damaging choices apparently prompted by adverse defaulting, we might consider how strange behavior with respect to reciprocity also might be governed by adverse defaulting.

Rabin (1993) proposed a model of other-regarding choice that turned critically on reciprocity. Charness and Rabin (2002) (CR) then reported on a set of 32 simple games which appear to have been designed to explore reciprocity effects. But reciprocity turned out to be almost invisible. CR note that, but neither they nor anyone else commenting on this very widely cited paper has offered any explanation, or indeed explicitly viewed the results as puzzling, though most experiments indeed show at least the qualified reciprocity of typical Trust games. But if you think about what the data seem to show, you will agree that indeed these results demand some explanation.

Table 9.1 shows the 32 CR games, the number of players in each, and the results. The notation A(**x,y** *or* B(**w,z** *or* **m,n**)) means Player A can exit the game by choosing *left*, which takes **x** for himself with **y** to Player B. Or A can chooses *right*, which passes the choice to B, who must choose between **w** for A, **z** for B *or* **m** for A, **n** for B. By changing the structure and parameters (the values of **x,y,w,z,m,** and **n**) many different situations can be set up. Sometimes (a change in structure) in games of this sort A makes a choice between a pair of possibilities (he has no "exit" option, and then B makes a choice in response, as in the Trust game I described a few paragraphs back. CR did not use this structure, but they did use variants in which there is no A choice, just a B choice (B is "dictator"), or in which a third party (C) chooses. Throughout, players are in sessions of four games, where in most a player makes both an A and a B choice (or in several an A and a C choice[3]), anonymously matched at each choice with a different player among the several dozen in the experiment.

Start with CR23, where the choice was B(800,200 or 0,0). B is dictator. If he chooses left, an anonymous A would get the 800, and he would get 200. Or B could choose right, yielding 0 for both. Here Bs unanimously (36 of 36) chose 800,200. No one is spiteful. The CR players, and players in choice experiments very generally, prefer equal payoffs if there is no reason or temptation to depart from that. Players in all these games show some preference for equality. But on any plausible model for other-regarding motivation, the preference for equality should not extend to no payoffs (which of course are perfectly equal) when there is no reasonable question of fairness. But here the player getting the larger payoff (A) did not in any way choose that. So this is an easy case to understand.

But in a slightly more complicated game we begin to see odder results. Falk, Fehr and Fischbacher *et al.* (2000) tested A(8,2 or 8,2); B(8,2 or 0,0). So they offered their As the degenerate choice 8,2 or 8,2 immediately before Bs made the proportionally identical choice just considered in the CR game. Translating tokens into dollar payoffs, the CR and Falk *et al.* games involved much the same stakes. But now 20 percent of Bs chose 0,0, apparently to punish As for the one-sided allocation, though As had no more actual input

*Table 9.1* Charness and Rabin (2002) "simple tests" (in sequence . . . 4 games each session)

| Game | # | Choices | A: Left/ Right | B or C:Left/Right |
|------|-----|---------|------------|-------------|
| CR1 | (44) | A(550,550 or B(400,400 or 750,375)) | .96/.04 | .93/.07 |
| CR2 | (48) | B(400,400 or 750,375) | | .52/.48 |
| CR3 | (42) | A(725,0 or B(400,400 or 750,375)) | .74/.26 | .62/.38 |
| CR4 | (42) | A(800,0 or B(400,400 or 750,375)) | .83/.17 | .62/.38 |
| CR5 | (36) | A(550,550 or B(400,400 or 750,400)) | .39/.61 | .33/.67 |
| CR6 | (36) | A(750,100 or B(300,600 or 700,500)) | .92/.08 | .75/.25 |
| CR7 | (36) | A(750,0 or B(400,400 or 750,400)) | .47/.53 | .06/.94 |
| CR8 | (36) | B(300,600 or 700,500) | | .67/.33 |
| CR9 | (36) | A(450,0 or B(350,450 or 450,350)) | .69/.31 | .94/.06 |
| CR10 | (24) | C(400,400,x or 750,375,x) | | .46/.54 |
| CR11 | (35) | A(375,1000 or B(400,400 or 350,350)) | .54/.46 | .89/.11 |
| CR12 | (22) | C(400,400,x or 1200,0,x) | | .82/.18 |
| CR13 | (22) | A(550,550 or B(400,400 or 750,375)) | .86/.14 | .82/.18 |
| CR14 | (22) | A(800,0 or B(0,800 or 400,400)) | .68/.32 | .45/.55 |
| CR15 | (22) | B(200,700 or 600,600) | | .27/.73 |
| CR16 | (15) | A(800,800,800 or C(100,1200,400 or 1200,200,400)) | .93/.07 | .80/.20 |
| CR17 | (32) | B(400,400 or 750,375) | | .50/.50 |
| CR18 | (32) | A(0,800 or B(0,800 or 400,400)) | .00/1.00 | .44/.56 |
| CR19 | (32) | A(700,200 or B(200,700 or 600,600)) | .56/.44 | .22/.78 |
| CR20 | (21) | A(800,800,800 or C(200,1200,400 or 1200,100,400) | .95/.05 | .86/.14 |
| CR21 | (36) | A(750,0) or B(400,400 or 750,375)) | .47/.53 | .61/.39 |
| CR22 | (36) | A(375,1000 or B(400,400 or 250,350)) | .39/.61 | .97/.03 |
| CR23 | (36) | B(800,200 or 0,0) | | 1.00/.00 |
| CR24 | (24) | C(575,575,575 or 900,300,600) | | .54/.46 |
| CR25 | (32) | A(450,0 or B(350,450 or 450,350)) | .62/.38 | .81/.19 |
| CR26 | (32) | B(0,800 or 400,400) | | .78/.22 |
| CR27 | (32) | A(500,500 or B(800,200 or 0,0)) | .41/.59 | .91/.09 |
| CR28 | (32) | A(100,1000 or B(75,125 or 125,125)) | .50/.50 | .34/.66 |
| CR29 | (26) | B(400,400 or 750,400) | | .31/.69 |
| CR30 | (26) | A(400,1200 or B(400,200 or 0,0)) | .77/.23 | .88/.12 |
| CR31 | (26) | A(750,750 or B(800,200 or 0,0)) | .73/.27 | .88/.12 |
| CR32 | (26) | A(450,900 or B(200,400 or 400,400)) | .85/.15 | .35/.65 |

CR 1–12 were played in Barcelona, CR 13–32 in Berkeley. Two games run in both locations (1 and 13, 2 and 17) yielded closely similar results. A (if he has a choice) can let payoffs be determined by B (or sometimes by a referee, C), or he can take the choice on the left. Choices (left or right) by B or C concern what player does, assuming A chooses right. So in CR1, if A and B both choose *right*, A's payoff is 750, B's is 375. If A chooses *left*, A and B each get 500. All choices are blind, and each player makes both choices, matched to different anonymous partners, with no information about what others have chosen.

than in the CR game. It is as if B noticed only the situation A's choice had put him in, but not the alternative if he had not done that. B acts as if he did not notice that A in fact had no choice. A reader who recalls what happens in the puzzles of Chapter 6 and the degenerate games of Chapter 7 might recognize this behavior. Somehow, players know what situation they are in but seem to be neglecting information highly relevant to responding to the situation. This possibility will play a large role here, since you will see that choices in the CR data over and over seem to be tied to this, on the face of it, exceedingly unlikely possibility.

But this case is only mildly puzzling compared to many others. In CR28, A can exit the game by accepting 100 while B gets 1000. Or he can force B to choose between 75 or 125 for A, with B getting 125 (instead of 1000) whichever he chooses. Since each point was (contingently) worth a penny, an A player who forced B to choose has deprived B of $8.75, apparently in the hope that B will respond by rewarding him with an extra 25¢ rather than punish him by 25¢. And half of the A players do throw away $8.75 of B's $10 payoff on a gamble that this will make themselves better off by 25¢. In the B role, players then respond to the possibility that A has done this. The apparent judgment of players who make the risky and greedy choice in the A role then proves sound. Two-thirds of the B choices do reward the A choice which throws away most of their payoff. We appear to have A players who are quite viciously selfish and apparently expect B players will mostly turn out to be masochists who will respond favorably to this treatment. And they are apparently correct to suppose that.

But in the CR games, within each game (and across the four games in a session), each player makes an A choice, and (anonymously matched against a different player) also makes a B choice. A players and B players are the same people. Taken together, the choices reveal that players are quite viciously selfish but also extraordinarily indifferent to losing most of their earnings. And looking across the subject pool, these players are also extremely altruistic as well as intensely selfish. In CR15, facing B(200,700 *or* 600,600), 73% surrendered 100 points of own payoff to provide a gain of 400 points for their partner. And in the A role in CR14, rather than keep all the tokens for themselves when facing A(800,0 *or* B(0,800 *or* 400,400)), a third were willing to share equally even though this not only involved a large sacrifice to benefit an anonymous other player, but also the risk that a B player might take advantage of their generosity and just keep all 800 for himself.

Which leads to a startling next result. Almost half (45%) of the beneficiaries of A's generosity in CR14 did keep all 800 for themselves. In this A(800,0 *or* B(0,800 *or* 400,400)) game, even a pathologically selfish person might see that reciprocity is called for. Being pathologically selfish, he will not reciprocate anyway. But it seems hard to understand how anyone could fail to notice what is called for. A could just keep 800 (worth $8). But he doesn't. He allows B to split the 800 equally, even though this allows the chance that B will just pocket all for himself. And almost half then do pocket the entire payoff for themselves! So in addition to being viciously selfish and masochistic and altruistic, CR players are also about as likely as not to be utterly immune to the normal propensity to reciprocate kind treatment, even in a really clear case that calls for it.

And there is more. In CR14, the fraction who shared when the A choice risked 800 in hand to allow an equal split turned out to be almost exactly identical to the fraction who shared in CR18, where choosing *right* involves no risk at all. Here the choice is A(0,800 *or* B(0,800 *or* 400,400)). A can choose to get 0 or allow B the opportunity to share. Unsurprisingly, all subjects were willing to give B an option to share. The fraction of Bs who then did share when reciprocity was irrelevant (56%) turned out to be higher (insignificantly, but higher not lower) than when reciprocity was plainly in order (55%). That in one case A had run a major risk by allowing B to choose to keep all or to share, and in the other took no risk whatever, seems of no interest to these players. Any propensity to reciprocity is again utterly invisible.

And we can conclude with an even more extreme example. In CR2 and its replicate (CR17), B's choice is 400,400 *or* 750,375. B can improve the outcome for A by 350 if he is willing to give up 25. So contrast that with CR3 or CR4 or CR21, in all of which the B choice is the same as in CR2 or CR17, but now after A has risked 400, and in one case (CR4) also sacrificed at least 50, to gain at least 375 for B. We have a baseline for judging the effect of reciprocity by noticing that in the first case (no reciprocity at issue) half of Bs were sufficiently generous to A to accept a loss of 25 (from 400) to gain 350 for B. But after As have run the risk that they could be abused by a really selfish B's response, the result is different. Now less than 40% (not fully 50%) are generous. A clear majority (above 60%) of Bs return A's favor with abuse rather than pay a very small price to reciprocate this generosity.

A Nobel laureate (Amatya Sen (1977)) wrote a well-known article under the title "rational fools," where the rational fool was the economic man of the standard model. But at least Sen's targets were rational. Sen, however, relied on everyday intuitions about everyday situations. As he intended, readers easily saw his postulated behavior not so much as exemplifying pure self-interest as exemplifying social idiocy. As his title anticipates, a reader sees Sen's examples of pure economic men as fools. However, what all the games reviewed here have in common is an absence of any familiar connection with the choices to be made. As is usual, in none of the games here are players allowed to talk to others in the game, or know who their partner might be. The only thing players can easily recognize is that they are players in a game, and we all know that in a game you should try to win. Most often that means doing better than the other player. But everyone also has experience with games where you win by cooperating with a partner, as in bridge or charades.

Players in these games ordinarily sit at computer consoles, matched anonymously with some unknown individual at another console, whose identity changes from round to round. Making a choice consists of looking at a diagram like one of the game trees in Figure 9.1 and clicking a button on a screen. Although it is a strong tradition within the experimental economics

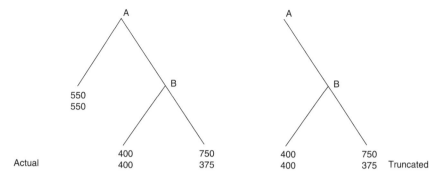

*Figure 9.1* A game tree from Charness and Rabin (2003) (left) and the truncated tree (right) that would guide intuition if neglect defaulting was left in place.

community never to lie to subjects, players in fact have no way to be sure there is actually any other player to be affected by their choice. But since actually telling subjects (in the degenerate game described at the start of Chapter 7) that there are no real partners does not have a huge effect, that source of uncertainty is not likely to be a problem. But the severe shortage of cues that link to the world of visceral experience, could nevertheless yield odd effects. Even the simple tree diagrams in Figure 9.1, though transparent to anyone who has worked with this sort of notation, might be considerably short of transparent for many subjects, parallel to the difficulty subjects might have with the Prisoner's Dilemma matrix in Chapter 7.

Our brains are set to be alert for orienting cues. Absent strong cues even weak cues can have strong effects. And absent even sufficient weak cues, we fall back on defaults that guide intuition when it is unclear what to do. From the defaulting argument and examples of Chapters 6 and 7, in the impoverished environment of the CR games, we might even expect defaulting to play a significant role, and we find it.

Individually, but especially in the aggregate, the CR games reveal multiple challenges to essentially universal moral intuitions, or to common sense, or both. The CR games are not unique in this. But it is especially easy to see in this data where we have responses from the same player in both the A and B roles (against different anonymous partners) usually making in all eight choices in a session of four games. These players turn out to be neither reliably self-interested, nor reliably other-regarding. Sometimes they behave the way their mothers taught them, but often they don't. Almost no one is a consistent conditional cooperator, though in other experiments that is often reported as the most common "type."[4] Players seem to jump from type to type across choices, like someone who sees the well-known gestalt drawing as a duck one moment but as a rabbit the next, and while seeing things in one gestalt comprehending things the other way is completely out of sight. I will be showing that gestalt shifts of very much this sort seem to resolve a series of puzzles in the CR data, where the gestalts are frames within the *cascade* developed in Chapter 7.

The *neglect* default developed in Chapter 6 comes into the argument because the data show us B choices that seem to make no sense unless players are in fact *neglecting* the payoffs they would receive if A does not choose to pass the decision on payoffs to B. Players in a CR game see a decision-tree like that on the left in Figure 9.1 (which is the game tree for CR1). But if the neglect default were left in place, a player might respond as if the game he was playing was the truncated game on the right. Logically this makes no more sense than the illusory responses that subjects overwhelmingly give to the puzzles reviewed in Chapter 6. In particular, it makes no more sense than the very common response of sophisticated subjects to the puzzle that concludes Chapter 6, where they appear to neglect conspicuous and obviously relevant details of the simple diagram in Figure 6.1, as here players respond as if they saw only their bare choice that might be coming from A, and neglecting the alternative A might have chosen. I will call that a response to the *truncated* situation on the right in Figure 9.1, in contrast to a response to the situation in the *actual* game they face, on the left in Figure 9.1 Sometimes B should be very pleased with the choice he has been offered, sometimes B should be appalled. But the B responses mostly seem to have gotten things backwards. It is instructive to consider in detail what would happen if indeed adverse defaulting (defaulting that on reflection the chooser herself would regard as inappropriate) was shaping responses.

Figure 9.2 reprints the cascade introduced in Chapter 7, the competitive branch is the default relative to the cooperative (if in doubt, better treat the situation as competitive); and within the competitive branch, the zero-sum frame is the default. But a rational agent would be alert for a cue pointing away from the zero-sum (1a) to the payoff-maximizing (1b) frame. It would be dangerous not to guard against the possibility that an unclear situation will turn out to be zero-sum. But it would be self-damaging to unnecessarily fail to maximize payoff. And a NSNX agent would also be alert for a cue that would prompt a shift across the cascade to the cooperative branch, where cooperation subject to free-rider concerns (2a) would become the default (what to do if you're not sure what to do).

Cooperation is weak in frame 2a in the sense that a person sees cooperation

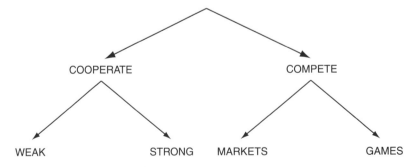

*Figure 9.2* The NSNX cascade.

as a possibility, but might not cooperate anyway. Choice is under the "neither selfish nor exploited" tension fundamental to NSNX motivation. But in a context where free-riding does not seem an issue, the strong cooperation frame (2b) comes into play. An agent who sees the context as one where he is not tempted to free-ride or worried that others will be tempted sees the choices as a pure coordination problem (like driving on the right in a country where everyone else is driving on the right). But this gestalt can also govern cases less simple. You tell guests at a party to toss their coats on your bed, without worrying that you had better follow them into the bedroom to make sure they don't steal anything.

Even in the strong cooperation frame, and of course also in the weak cooperation frame, an agent does not always make generous choices. If the choice is with respect to someone who has behaved badly, punishment not reward is what is likely to seem socially appropriate. But in the coordination frame, ordinarily choice would yield benefits for others, and in the weak cooperation frame choice sometimes benefits others even at a cost to self.

Here is the situation described in terms of the NSNX formalism introduced in Chapter 1. On the competitive branch an agent seeks to maximize S(elf-interest), but in frame (1a) the argument of the self-interested utility function is the difference between own payoff and other's payoff, while in frame (1b) it is own payoff. In frame (2b) on the cooperative branch, an agent seeks to maximize G(roup-interest), governed by his own sense of what would be socially good, as discussed in some detail in Chapter 1. In frame (2a) however, agent does not directly seek to maximize anything, but rather tries to move as close as is feasible to a "neither selfish nor exploited" equilibrium, where $W = G'/S'$, again as developed in some detail in Chapter 1.

And applying this to the CR games:

(1) Without a potentially threatening agent in sight (meaning an agent with an opportunity to respond adversely), and where a player's choice would not affect own payoff (so there is no risk of being exploited), the default context for a NSNX agent would be coordination (2b). Only social concerns are immediately salient. This is the situation for the several CR games (CR 10, 12, 16, 20, 24) in which a referee (C) chooses the response, but also in four of the games in which B responds (CR5, 7, 28, and 32). A NSNX agent would favor a generous choice unless something recognized in the situation makes punishment seem more appropriate.

In the converse case where B's choice does change own payoff (with no active agent in sight), the NSNX default would be the "neither selfish nor exploited" (2a). B then might or might not in fact sacrifice something from own payoff to benefit his partner, contingent, as in the pure coordination case, on whether the partner seems to deserve that generosity, but also on how much a generous choice will cost relative to the benefit it could provide. This situation holds for eight games in which B's choice is 400,400 *or* 750,375, for three games where B's choice is 0,800 *or* 400,400, and for a variety of choices in ten other games (CR6, 9, 11, 19, 22, 25, 27, 28, 30, and 31).

(2) But suppose there *is* a potentially threatening agent in sight. The cautious zero-sum frame (1a) is then the default. This holds for all A choices in the CR games. But that the zero-sum frame is the default for this kind of situation does not imply that a player is likely to be caught by that default. Risk that own payoff will be harmed in response to a zero-sum move would push a player towards the payoff-maximizing frame (1b). A shift from the zero-sum to payoff-maximizing would be particularly easy within the CR games, since in these games zero-sum play in fact makes no sense (there is no payoff for doing better than the other player), so that once pushed to look closer, a player would be unlikely to remain caught by that default.

Finally, for NSNX agents in the A role, a cue suggesting a cooperative context could shift the frame all the way over to the cooperative branch of the cascade. In the CR games, B has no opportunity to provide an explicit cue. But there is a cue built into the structure of the games. Except for CR18, each of the CR response games essentially asks A either "Are you willing to run a risk to improve your competitive outcome?", as in CR1 and ten others, or "Are you willing to run a risk to improve the cooperative outcome?", as in CR3 and eight others. So the framing might suggest the perspective appropriate for assessing the risky choice: competitive in the first case, cooperative in the second. The nudge towards the competitive branch in the first case would reinforce starting from the default competitive branch. But the nudge towards the cooperative branch in the second case might be enough to move a NSNX agent over to the cooperative branch of the cascade. The question, I think, is not whether there is such a nudge in the framing of the games. Of course there is, and it could hardly be entirely avoided. But is it consequential? Theory cannot say, but as will be seen, the data give us a clear answer.

(3) But the sampling of CR results earlier in this chapter suggests we also need to consider the possibility that in these games players somehow are caught by the *neglect* default developed in Chapter 6. In a real situation anywhere near as transparent as these games, that should essentially never happen. But we have already seen many examples (in Chapters 6 and 7) where in the impoverished environment of an unfamiliar game things of that sort do seem to happen. And here, when we come to the data, what certainly looks like a blindness of B choosers (in the CR response games) to what is right in front of them will be apparent. Instead of responding to the situation, B seems to respond to what I have already called the *truncated situation*.

Chooser notices that A has put a choice to B, but neglects the payoff B would get if A had not provided that choice. In some of the CR response games, the A choice (no matter which way B responds) would make things much better for B. In the rest, the A choice usually makes things much worse for B, and again whichever way she chooses. Responding to the situation should prompt positive reciprocity in the first case and negative reciprocity in the second. But neglecting the alternative can reverse the response, and the particular games in the CR set happen to be such that indeed usually the affective response would be reversed.

In an influential paper, Zajonc (1980) reported a series of experiments showing an immediate, ordinarily covert, *affective* response to whatever is the focus of attention, which then colors the response to the situation. For a B player who neglected the alternative A could have chosen, it is the bare choice he faces (the truncated situation) that prompts Zajonc's visceral response. And the bare choices B sees do vary in their affective character. The choice 400,400 *or* 750,400 does not *feel* the same as the choice 400,400 *or* 750,375, even though the difference in B's payoff is barely more than 6%. It is not hard to see why that might be so. Making someone else better off at no cost (even if this makes them now better off than you) is more comfortable than making someone better off than you by making yourself worse off. And we have repeatedly encountered the cognitive force of qualitative as against quantitative cues.

In terms of the cascade effects just introduced, 400,400 *or* 750,400 for the B choice would prompt the coordination frame in the cascade, but 400,400 *or* 750,375 would prompt the weak cooperation frame, where choice is under "neither selfish nor exploited" tension. A NSNX agent would be seeing the situation from frame (2a) where he might make the generous choice, but unless he has a cue which makes one choice clearly appropriate, he would tend to feel uncomfortable about being confronted with the choice. With a little bit of luck, he would not have been home.

Similarly, 300,600 *or* 700,500 for the B choice looks stressful relative to the quite similar 200,700 *or* 600,600. Even 0,800 *or* 400,400 does not look stressful relative to 400,400 *or* 750,375, though the cost in payoff of a generous choice is much larger. If so, that would presumably be because a person often faces such choices and comfortably handles them. If you look in your pocket and find two dollar bills you didn't realize you had, you would hardly offer one to the person next to you even if she is your best friend. But if you find two cookies in your box lunch and the person next to you finds none in his box, it would be quite odd if you did not offer to share, even if he is a complete stranger. Unless seen as imposed by the other player, a choice between an inferior payoff and no payoff for either does not seem to be stressful. As mentioned earlier, 36 of 36 players chose the positive payoffs from 800,200 *or* 0,0, which hardly seems likely if players found this choice difficult.

A point to note in this discussion is that framing within the cascade relates to the Zajonc effect but does not mechanically govern it. A choice from the weak cooperation frame (2a) is more likely to be aversive than a choice from the strong cooperation (coordination) frame (2b), since there is a "neither selfish nor exploited" tension to be dealt with in the first but not in the second. But sometimes a risky choice is easy (there is a risk but you are confident about how you want to deal with it) and sometimes a pure coordination choice is difficult (you suspect someone who could benefit really deserves punishment, but you are not sure).

But, restating the reason for this Zajonc discussion, if B indeed is somehow neglecting A's alternative and responding only to the truncated situation, the Zajonc prompt covertly coloring the B choice could only come from the bare choice A has put to B, which might be the opposite of the Zajonc response to the full situation.

Finally, neglect defaulting would also play a role in A as well as B choices, and of an even odder sort. When a CR game provides an A choice, it is always between an *exit* option (choose *left*), which takes a known payoff, versus taking the risk of passing the choice of payoffs to B (choose *right*), which yields payoffs which might be better or might be worse than just choosing to exit, conditional on what B then does. A has no way to assess this risky choice if she neglects what B's options would then be. So in the A role, players should escape the *neglect* default. As A, a player has a very strong cue to pay attention. The same holds for the two games in which a third party (C) with no personal stake responds to a choice by A. C acts as referee, deciding whether A gets a very big payoff and B a very small payoff, or the reverse. His only clue to which might be more deserving is the choice A made to set up C's need to respond. So it is again hard to see how this player could be vulnerable to the neglect default. Like A with respect to B's possible response, though for a different reason, C has a strong cue to focus attention on his partner's choice. But players in the B role have no such sharp prod to look at the other player's choice, but just at their own.[5]

But when A looks at how B would react to the choice if offered, he must be prompted by the same visceral affect as B. If B's immediate feeling about the choice is prompted only by the truncated situation, so will A's, and with the same impression as B. This would be a strong assumption if A and B choices were made by different subjects. But here no assumption is needed. This is a case in which A does not need any actual empathy to be prompted to the same visceral response to the B choice as B would feel. Recalling how the CR data was gathered, in these experiments the person making an A choice is the same person who also makes a B choice. Each subject makes both choices. If the visceral response to that choice is positive (prompting A to feel a tacit sense that an advantageous response from B is likely), that would embolden competitive play when the question is whether to risk gambling for more payoff at B's expense. And it would also embolden cooperative play when the question is whether to risk own payoff to try for a better social outcome. All CR response games ask one question or the other.

So now look at the data, keeping in mind that B responses concern what choice B wants to govern her payoff in the event A presented the choice. So in CR1 presenting the choice is rare (only 4%), but all B responses are to that A choice if it were made.

A reader will notice that many of the results, even looked at in isolation, will obviously be statistically impressive and some others not. But neglecting results that piecemeal do not reach conventional statistical significance is not actually defensible. What most of all needs to be considered is the chance that all the effects reported here will so consistently go the way the analysis expects them to go, which plainly is zero to as many decimal places as anyone would want to know.

(1) Is the evidence clear that Bs (responders) are mostly neglecting to notice whether A has made a generous or nasty choice? Very much so. In noting that reciprocity seems to be missing in this data, I am only repeating what Charness and Rabin themselves reported. All I have added is that failures of reciprocity as extreme as seen in this data would ordinarily only be seen if either the situation is plausibly an actual zero-sum situation (if your opponent in tennis hits a weak return, you do not feel you ought to be nice and hit an easy return back) or if responders were somehow unaware of what another person had done to create the situation. But here the situation is completely described by the game tree the player is shown, not reasonably seen as zero-sum, but somehow normal reciprocity fails anyway. Over and over, A takes a big risk solely to help B, and Bs mostly respond with utter selfishness. Or A makes an aggressively selfish move, hurting B, and Bs mostly respond by being nice to A.

Of nine games in which B responds to a generous A choice (CR3, 4, 6, 7, 9, 14, 19, 21, 25), only two show a majority of generous responses (CR14 and 19), and as will be seen, in both there is strong reason to doubt that the "nice" responses here are in fact mainly responses to A's generosity. And of eight games in which B responds to a nasty A choice (CR1, 5, 11, 13, 22, 28, 30, 32), the only CR1 that shows clear evidence of reciprocity for a majority of B choices. But CR1 is a game that makes the unreasonable character of the A choice especially hard to miss. The fraction of nasty responses to a generous move by A reaches 94% in CR9. And if you look at the games in Figure 9.1, you will see there is nothing subtle about the A moves. The generous moves are *very* generous. The nasty moves are *very* nasty.

Nor could it resolve the puzzle to suppose that nasty responses to generous moves just show the importance of self-interest. That would not explain generous responses to nasty moves. Nor where the generous moves ungenerously responded to come from. Nor how such contrasts in motivation could make sense when all these moves are made by the very same people.

As Table 9.1 shows, there are many generous as well as many nasty choices by both A and B. What is puzzling is that B's choices, whether generous or nasty, so often seem inappropriate to the circumstance, and what is puzzling about the A choices is that so often the same player seems cooperative making one choice and narrowly self-interested making another. But the first puzzle could be resolved if indeed Bs are frequently caught by the neglect default. And the second puzzle could be resolved if the cue to how a player should be seeing the context implicit in the question he faces is indeed nudging players towards the cooperative branch of the cascade in some games and towards the competitive branch in others. We want to see if the data provide some clear evidence of these effects.

(2) On the earlier discussion, B responses guided by a Zajonc-like visceral reaction to the *truncated situation* are responses to the choice B faces that

neglect how that choice would look relative to the situation for B if A did *not* offer that choice. But if the covert visceral response to the truncated situation is aversive, that would color the choice in a way that suggests A does not deserve a reward for presenting that choice to B. Or if B's covert visceral response to the truncated situation is positive, that would color the choice in a way that suggests A does not deserves punishment for presenting that choice. In either case, the visceral response to the truncated situation could be – and given the particulars of the CR games in fact usually are – the opposite of what a normal reciprocity response to the actual situation would be. The data provide striking tests of whether these effects are present and important.

I start with the most difficult case for this account. In CR1, B responds to a nasty A choice. In CR2, the B choice is the same but A is only a bystander. This provides the one example in this data of a substantial overlap between a normal and a truncated response from B. The effect is really big. Only 7% of responses are generous in CR1 but 50% are generous with the same 400,400 *or* 750,375 B choice in CR2. This is consistent with truncated responses, but also consistent with normal reciprocity. If a player escapes the neglect default, of course he will not surrender even more of the payoff A has destroyed to reward A's aggressively nasty move. But A's refusal to accept the conspicuously fair and efficient 550,550 looks so conspicuously unreasonable that A's rejection of it might get B's attention even if in these games it is hard to catch B's attention. So we might be seeing one game out of 19 CR games with a B response to A which actually yields a normal reciprocity response. On the other hand, a bit later you will see why some large part of what looks like a normal reciprocity effect might be in fact a *truncated situation* effect which in this case happens to coincide with normal reciprocity.

But in every other game there is very little ambiguity or no ambiguity at all. Under a later heading I will consider CR 14 and CR19, where we see appropriately generous responses that are clearly more plausibly attributed to the truncated situation effect, since a comparison is available that crowds out any significant normal reciprocity effect. In CR28 and 32, B faces a viscerally nice choice of whether to improve A's payoff at zero cost to himself. By two to one, B does what is generous, though in each case it is in response to an A choice that is very nasty. In CR22 a truncated view of B's situation looks *really* nice. B can choose to help A and at the same time help himself. B rewards A's exceedingly nasty choice by 97%–3%, rather than forgo a small fraction (1/8) of his payoff to punish a really nasty A move, although in numerous replications of the Ultimatum game players are ready to accept much more severe costs to punish much less severe insults. In CR9, B responds selfishly to a really generous A move by a margin of 94%–6%. And so on.

(3) The clearest evidence for the relative strength of truncated as against normal reciprocity responses from B comes when (a) the truncated and normal responses would go in opposite directions, and (b) the data allow a comparison between B choices with A as bystander and the same B choice responding to A. This yields an unambiguous prediction that generous choices will

increase if one element (truncated or normal) dominates and decrease if the other dominates. The CR data provide two opportunities to look at this test. Both show the truncated effect dominating any plausible normal reciprocity effect, though certainly at least some subjects in each game are seeing what is actually there and giving normal reciprocity responses, which here would reduce the apparent strength of the truncated situation effect. In both, quite amazingly in terms of what we could usually expect, Bs are *more* likely to respond nastily to A when A has been very nice to B than when A has done nothing for B.

For CR6 (responding to an exceedingly generous move from A), normal reciprocity would yield more generosity from Bs than in CR8, where B faces the same choice but with A as bystander. The A choice in CR6 definitely sacrifices 50 tokens, and puts an additional 400 tokens at risk, to help B get a 400 token increase in his payoff. But the bare B choice (300,600 *or* 700,500) is not comfortable, as discussed earlier. It is efficient (total payoff of 1200 rather than 900) but perhaps not fair, unless of course B attends to how generous A has been to make this choice available to B. But if caught by the neglect default, B misses that. A truncated response then would yield less cooperation here (where the Zajonc prompt affect would be negative) than in CR8, where A is only a bystander, not the agent who put this aversive choice to B. And indeed, B is less generous (25%) to A when positive reciprocity would be in order than when A has done nothing for B (33%). One in three B choices sacrifice to improve the aggregate payoff when A has done nothing to earn that. But only one in four B choices do that in CR6 where only a moral idiot could fail to see what is in order. Since these games were within the same session in Barcelona, the reversal of normal behavior here involves exactly the same players across the two games.

An instructive auxiliary comparison is provided by CR19. This cannot provide an unambiguous result since normal reciprocity and a truncated response go the same way. But the B choice is similar to the choice in CR8, but now comfortable rather than aversive. The B choice is 200,700 *or* 600,600, rather than the CR6 B choice of 300,600 or 500,700. In CR6, the generous choice is efficient but out of context somewhat unfair (and specifically unfair to B). But for 200,700 *or* 600,600, the generous choice is both efficient and conspicuously fair. This yields what looks like a normal reciprocity response. Generous choices are higher in CR19 (with A presenting the choice) than in CR15 (with A as bystander). But the comparison between CR15 (where 73% of Bs are already generous even though A is only a bystander) and CR19 (78% generous) leaves very little room for normal reciprocity once any effect of truncated responses is allowed. Given the striking truncated response effect where the conflict with a normal reciprocity response makes that starkly visible (in CR6), what could be interpreted as a mild normal reciprocity response that coincides with a truncated situation response looks essentially dismissible as just an artifact of that coincidence.

The second opportunity to examine conflicting normal and truncated responses yields the same morally perverse result as in CR6. In CR2 (and its replicate, CR17) half of B choices are generous to A, sacrificing 25 tokens to gain 350 for A, though A is a bystander who has done nothing to earn that. But in CR4 and again in CR5, after A has risked 400 or more tokens to give B a large instead of 0 payoff, the fraction of generous B responses drops to under 40%. As in the CR6/CR8 comparison, normal reciprocity would increase cooperation in response to a really generous A move. But a truncated response to the out-of-context aversive 400,400 or 750,375 choice would go the other way. And again, the data go the other way.

(4) A different test is available when we have a pair of games which are identical except that in one the B choice could be expected to yield a positive visceral (Zajonc) prompt response and in the other a negative Zajonc response. If the truncated situation argument is on target, we should get a clear result, which indeed we do. As background, note that comparing CR5 in Barcelona versus CR29 in Berkeley, both of which offer the same B choice (400,400 *or* 750,400), the results are essentially indistinguishable though in CR5 the choice is in response to a nasty A choice while in CR29 A was only a bystander. No truncated situation effect is visible, but also no normal reciprocity effect. But the null effect could be because some fraction of normal reciprocity responses (here negative) are canceling the truncated responses which for this choice would be positive.

And we can see that indeed that is very likely by comparing CR5 with CR1. The only difference between the two games is that in CR1, B faces the aversive 400,400 *or* 750,375 choice instead of the agreeable 400,400 *or* 750,400 choice in CR5. B's payoffs from a generous B choice differ by only 1/16. But on the account here, this quantitatively unimpressive difference shifts the frame in the cascade from (2b) to (2a). And the effect turns out to be huge. In CR1 only 7% of B choices reward A for a really nasty move. In CR5 this soars to 67% in response to the identical nasty A move.

(5) In introducing oddities in the CR data earlier in the chapter, I already mentioned the anomalies that can be seen among the trio of games where B's choice is 0,800 *or* 400,400. B shares 55% of the time in CR14 and 56% in CR18, but only 22% in CR26. But the logic of the games says that sharing should be less common in CR14 (where it entails a risk of betrayal) than in CR26 (where it doesn't). And a normal reciprocity response would make B more likely to share with A in CR14 (where A could have just kept the 800 tokens) than in CR18 (where A had no such choice). But none of this happens. Mere common sense fails badly. But if B is caught by the neglect default he would see no difference between CR14 and CR18 (and from the results, it is apparent he doesn't); and if the truncated situation is what guides B's intuition, B would be more generous to A when A's choice puts him in that situation even when (in CR18) A has actually done nothing in any way generous to put him there. Again, the data fit an analysis in terms of cascade effects and neglect defaulting.

(6) But, recalling the Falk *et al.* set of experiments mentioned in

introducing the CR data, Falk reports a very different result from a test which on the face of it is essentially identical to CR27. In both, the A choice is whether to accept an equal division of the total payoff (in CR27: 500,500, in Falk: 5,5), or make the risky aggressive move of presenting B with the ultimatum choice between giving 4/5 of the payoff to A or refusing and getting zero payoff. In CR27, 91% of Bs then accept the severely unequal split, far higher than in numerous equivalent "ultimatum" games, where this move could be expected to generate almost as many refusals as accepts. In Falk's game, 44%, rather than the 9% in CR27, refuse what they see as an unfair offer.

But in Falk *et al.* there was a fork in the left as well as right branch of the A choice. A's generous choice was not just to end the game as 5,5 but to let B choose 5,5 *or* 0,0. So the nasty choice was identical to that of CR27, but the generous choice required explicit attention from B, who to get the even split had to explicitly choose it over 0,0. Further, both choices were made as part of a set of eight choices over four games (with two choices in each game) where the A alternative to 8,2 *or* 0,0 was systematically varied. The complete set of A alternatives to offering 8,2 *or* 0,0 included the degenerate choice mentioned earlier plus 10,0 *or* 0,0 and the self-sacrificing 2,8 *or* 0,0. So indeed, there was a large difference between the CR game and the Falk game in the fraction choosing 0,0 from 8,2 *or* 0,0 where A could have offered 5,5. But there was also a more than adequate difference in conditions to account for why truncated responses would be very much more likely in the CR game than in the Falk game.

(7) So far we have considered *truncated situation* effects on B. But for the reasons I've pointed to in setting up this series of tests, there should also be *truncated situation* effects on A, even though A cannot be blind to B's alternatives in the way that on the defaulting argument B can be blind to A's alternative. If as B a player usually attends only the truncated situation, then as A that same player (and recall that in the CR games it is the same player) would also usually see just B's truncated sense of the situation in considering B's possible response to his move. How could it be otherwise, since if looking at B's situation when considering the A move is *not* truncated, how could that fail to inform how the same situation looks to this same player when making the B choice? If A notices a conflict, a closer look will prompt a normal reciprocity response from B, since on reflection no one would be in doubt that a response to the actual situation not the truncated situation is what she wants.

That "look closer" shift in perspective certainly must sometimes happen. There is severely deficient evidence of normal reciprocity in the CR games, but far from a complete absence of it. There are always some, and often many appropriate responses. But if A mostly sees only the truncated situation B faces, a positive Zajonc affect that for B makes it more likely he will make the nice choice would make A more optimistic about taking a risk. This encourages a cooperative choice when the risk on offer puts his own payoff at risk to do better as a group, but it would also encourage a competitive choice when taking the risk might make A better off at B's expense. So we would see more nasty A choices, as well as more generous choices. And all this would point in the opposite direction when the B choice is aversive for B.

Is there evidence of this in the data? An appropriate test here is to consider A's tendency to risk putting the choice in B's hands conditional on whether B's truncated situation is 400,400 *or* 750,375 vs. 400,400 *or* 750,400. As already noticed, the B payoff is almost the same in either choice, differing by only 1 part in 16. But from a small quantitative difference we have a big affective difference. The most striking illustration comes from a pair of games already discussed but with respect to the B choices. We want to compare A's propensity to risk a nasty but potentially profitable move in CR1 to the same nasty choice in CR5, which differs only by that 1 part in 16 in what B will get from a nice response to this nasty move.

Both games are with the same subject pool (both in Barcelona). They differ only in that in CR1, B has the aversive 400,400 *or* 750,375 choice and in CR5, B has the nice 400,400 *or* 750,400 choice. We have already noticed that in CR1, only 7% of B responses to a nasty A move are generous, while in CR5 that skyrockets to 67%. And if, as the argument here expects, A's Zajonc affect when he looks at the B choice is like B's, that ordinarily covert but prompt affect will be negative in CR1 and make A cautious about taking the risk but make A bolder and positive in CR5. Very emphatically, that is what we see. In CR1, just 4% of the A choosers made the nasty but risky choice. But in CR5, 61% of A choosers made the same nasty but risky choice.

The effect is also very apparent in the converse situation, where the risk on offer is to risk own payoff to gain a better cooperative rather than a better competitive outcome. We see a sharp demonstration across three Barcelona games where choosing *right* is generous (not nasty, as in CR1 and 5). As already noticed, the B response to an exceedingly generous A choice in CR3 and 4 by B's facing 750,375 is 62% nasty. But in CR7, facing the nice 750,400 rather than the aversive 750,375, nasty B responses plummet to 6%. So look at A choices in these same games. A generous choice is a little easier in CR3 than in CR4, but the pair yields an average of 22% generous A choices when B will then face 750,375. In CR7, B faces 750,400 with its benign affect, rather than 750,375 with its aversive affect. Generous A choices now more than double, to 53%.

And note that these are indeed truncated situation effects, enormous for B but also big for A. Looking at the actual situation there is no reason for any significant difference in CR3 and 4 as against CR7 for either A or B choices. In CR3 and 4, the B choice would be from frame (2a) in the cascade, not from frame (2b) as in CR7. So B in CR3 or 4 would have to resolve the "neither selfish nor exploited" tension characteristic of that weak cooperation frame. But the situation is one in which it is obvious (responding to an A choice which risked a great deal to help B) that the generous choice is what is called for. B responses to the actual situation would be overwhelmingly generous not overwhelmingly punishing. And an A who shared that sense of the full situation B would face would not be inhibited by a sense that it would be dangerous to trust B because the generous B payoff would be 25 tokens less than in CR7. So without the truncated distortion affecting A as well as B, the difference of more than a factor of 2 between willingness to make the risky cooperative choice in CR3 and 4 as against CR7 would be mysterious.

The inferences here should also apply to CR21, which also does show the effects, but just barely. But CR21 is a decided outlier on any view. See note[6].

(8) Can we distinguish whether the effects in (7) are really due to Zajonc's "emotions come first," where conscious processing of a choice is colored (usually covertly) by a very fast visceral response, as against A successfully intuiting how B will choose, and responding accordingly. This is a side issue for the account here. The former seems the more pure Zajonc effect (positive affect encourages A to take a chance). But the latter would also be contingent, though less directly, on a Zajonc effect (A senses that B will be inclined to be nice, which comes from B's Zajonc response to the truncated situation). The adverse defaulting conjecture is not at risk. But the point is still consequential, since seeing which way this possibility goes is likely to prove helpful in interpreting what is happening in other experimental settings.

On the "payoff" view, A is not directly put in a positive mood by the covert visceral prompt, but correctly judges how likely B is to be generous, hence making his risky alternative look more risky or not so risky contingent on his intuition about B's sense of the situation. On the "emotions come first" view, A is influenced by sharing in B's covert visceral response, not by correctly intuiting how B is likely to choose. As with the competition between normal reciprocity and truncated responses, we want to look for situations in the CR data where the payoff interpretation would yield different behavior from the directly visceral interpretation. The data give us two opportunities to test this, both of which strongly go against the payoff possibility and support the direct version.

On the logic of the games a player making the A choice in CR14 should be *less* likely to be willing to share (since B then has the option to betray A and just keep the tokens) than to make the risk-free choice to share as the B choice in CR26. The choice 0,800 *or* 400,400 looks nice for B, as discussed earlier, but in CR26 it implies no particular propensity to be generous. Rather, it looks nice because it offers B a guilt-free option to do whatever he feels like doing. By a wide margin (78% to 22%) B does *not* share in this game, as by a much wider margin even very generous people do not ordinarily share half of what they have with random strangers. So if A is responding to his reliable intuition of what B will do, that would further strengthen the already strong inference that the risky offer to share in CR14 must be rarer than the risk-free choice to share in CR26. On the other hand, if it is Zajonc's visceral response that is directly influencing A, the positive affect of this choice would encourage A to take the risk. So we have starkly contrasting inferences. On the payoff mechanism, we get an emphatic inference that the fraction inclined to share must surely decrease between CR26 and CR14. On the direct Zajonc mechanism, it should increase. And in fact the fraction willing to share does increase from 22% in CR26 to 32% in CR14.[7]

We have another opportunity to test for a direct Zajonc effect in the results from CR9 in Barcelona and CR25, its replicate in Berkeley. The B choice in this game is 450,350 *or* 350,450, which is certainly agreeable. And it is not surprising that overwhelmingly, given a guilt-free choice between more for you and more for me I cheerfully prefer more for me. In CR9, 94% make that choice. But this would be a guilt-free choice only for someone who neglected to notice that his payoff would be zero if A had not very generously put part of his own payoff at risk by making it available. In the actual context, it is a nasty choice after A has taken a risk solely to help B. If A is intuiting that perverse B choice (the payoff motive), he would hardly offer the choice. On the other hand, on the direct Zajonc argument, A is influenced by the visceral response to the choice, which is positive, not to the likely pick from this choice, which from A's perspective is outrageous. So on the payoff response, A should never offer this choice, but on the visceral response view, A should be tempted to take the socially nice risk. And almost a third do, so that instead of just pocketing 450 tokens, they trust B to respond reasonably, which *these same players*, in their B choices, then do not do.

This is the starkest example in the CR data of a gestalt shift that yields what appear to be utterly incompatible responses between a player's choice as A and the same player's choice as B. Since many more A choices are generous than B choices respond to that generosity, it is necessarily the case that a large majority of players who as A trust their partner not to betray their generosity then as B do betray A's generosity. In the trial in Berkeley (CR25), 12 of 32 players risked making the generous offer as A. Nine of the 12 betrayed as B. In Barcelona (CR9), 11 of 36 players took the cooperative risk as A, and as B every one of them betrayed a person who made that generous choice. The fraction of generous As who betray as B is even larger than the raw data in Figure 9.3 suggest, since most players did not take that risk, not all of whom betrayed another player who did.

(9) But, as noticed in (8), except for the atypical CR9 and 25, a B choice that prompts a positive visceral sense will always favor a generous to A response. Consequently, the visceral response to the B choice that prompts A to make the risky A choice (and again whether it is a risk to gain payoff at B's expense, or a risk of losing payoff to help B) will prompt B towards indeed making the generous choice. Hence, if we set aside the two plays of the atypical game (CR9 and 25), the fraction taking a risk as A in all but these contrary cases should correlate with the fraction of B responses that reward that risky choice. Figure 9.3 plots all relevant tests, distinguishing the contrary cases just described. The figure speaks for itself.

(10) In CR10, a third party with no own payoff stake (C not B) makes the final choice facing 400,400 *or* 750,375. C's choices favor the larger but unequal payoff, but by only 54%–46%. So it looks like equal payoffs indeed are very

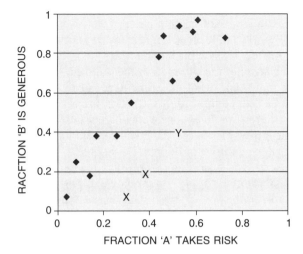

*Figure 9.3* Risky A choices vs. generous B choices.

The puzzling outlier (Y) discussed in note 11 is easy to spot, as are the pair of points (X) expected to be outliers relative to all the other risk-by-A, reward-by-B pairs. The data include all games with a B response to A's choice, *except* CR18 (no risk at issue) and CR30 and 32, where a payoff-maximizing A would not be tempted.

nearly as attractive as larger aggregate payoffs when a cost – even a small cost – is imposed on the trailing player, and even when the choice is made by a referee with nothing of his own at stake. Choices favoring the larger but unequal payoffs are barely more common when the referee chooses than when B makes this choice about his own payoff in CR2 in Barcelona and its replicate in Berkeley, CR17. In both trials, B makes the choice equally both ways. But why? If these players could talk they would easily agree that the sensible preference is for more payoff, and very obviously so in these games where everyone gets both an A and a B payoff.

But apparently in the impoverished environment of these abstract games, even a third-party chooser (C), with no own payoff stake in the choice, cannot easily escape a sense that they may be making a choice about some continuing game where it would be unfair to give one player an advantage. We see yet another indication that in the impoverished environment of an experiment, players tacitly impute some richer but more familiar context than is actually there, in which they know what to do from ample experience. Sometimes this will be just what is appropriate or just what the experimenters had in mind in designing the experiment. But sometimes it won't, as seems to be the case for half the players here. But when B's payoff becomes slightly larger, so that giving A a larger payoff does not cost him anything (CR29), B is nice to A by far more (69%) even though this still results in a large disparity in payoff favoring A.

We like to think of experimenters providing a context and incentives to subjects, whose choices then reveal their motivation and the consequences of that motivation in the experimental context. But here, as in examples throughout this study, we can see that it is the players not the experimenters who provide the context, influenced but not always controlled by the cues that experimenters provide. Even explicit statements are only cues. What governs choice is the tacit sense of the situation inside a subject's head, which is open to influence by more than what experimenters intend their instructions to convey. And a further complication is that if subjects respond to NSNX incentives, their motivation may appear incoherent in terms of standard theory, as it conspicuously does in this data, since no standard theory allows for the gestalt shifts in perspective of the NSNX cascade.

(11) On a related point, since zero-sum play makes no sense in the CR games (there is no payoff for doing better relative to other players), we cannot expect many zero-sum responses. Even when players are prompted to make the A choice from the competitive branch of the cascade, they should be quite easily nudged by a prospect of payoff loss over to the payoff-maximizing frame (1b) of the cascade. But if indeed players making the A choice can be caught by a zero-sum default, we could expect to see some non-trivial fraction of players who are slow to notice that the situation is not one where a zero-sum choice makes any sense.

In two games with obvious B choices for any alert player, players never miss. In CR18, all 32 players see that choosing *right* (passing the choice over to B) cannot lose and might gain, and in CR23, all 36 players see no reason to punish A at a cost to themselves for a one-sided allocation of payoffs in which A is only a bystander. But if mere blunders are rare, we can at least roughly estimate the fraction of zero-sum choices typical of the CR games by looking at games where a *right* choice by A can make sense only as a zero-sum move. There are two such games. In CR30, A cannot gain, only harm B by choosing *right*. In CR32 the zero-sum motive is even more extreme, since A hurts his own payoff in order to hurt B worse. We see 23% of these perverse A choices in CR30, and 15% even if the more extreme CR32. So we do find a remnant of zero-sum choices, as would be expected as a cascade effect.

But as another indication of the dominance of truncated B responses in this data, note the fraction of B choices which respond with generosity to these aggressively perverse A moves. In CR30, 88% of B choices reward A for his nasty choice rather than give up the small remaining balance of their payoff (200 left after A has refused to let B have 1200). Even in CR32, where it costs B nothing to punish an especially nasty A choice, 65% reward him.

(12) Comparison across games within the same session (hence comparing choices by the same players across games) provides evidence bearing on the reality of the stable "types" commonly reported by experimenters, as in Houser and Kurzban (2005). As I mentioned in Chapter 1, in terms of NSNX, highly atypical cases aside, these contrasting types should not exist. Of course there will be a wide range of individual difference, so that some people could be cued quite easily into the cooperative or competitive frame of the cascade and others would be hard to budge. Further, every player comes to the game

with experience of their own which may make them inclined one way or the other given the immediate circumstances. So it is not surprising that careful experimenters would find what seems to be clear evidence for "types," especially since the type that is usually by a wide margin the most common is the type that in terms of NSNX everyone should be. A NSNX agent is by definition a conditional cooperator, seeking to be "neither selfish nor exploited."

But if there are stable types (selfish, conditioned, cooperators, pure cooperators), we should be able to see them in the CR data. The simplest test comes from comparing choices across individuals within a session. I will give just one example of many that can be teased out of the CR data.

If we can take the players in CR9 as an unbiased sample of the population (and it is not apparent why not), there would be almost no consistent cooperators and also almost no conditional cooperators, since 93% of B responses violate any plausible interpretation of how such players should respond to a selfless move by A solely on their behalf. And extending the argument to other games would only reinforce that. Over and over players choose as if they were one type in the A role and another in the B role. But since on the argument here B choices are very often distorted by truncation, we might imagine there really are stable types, obscured by adverse defaulting.

But defaulting effects would not weaken an inference about types from A choices, since as discussed, A choices would not be vulnerable to truncation. An intrinsically competitive type would never take a risk to benefit the other player. A cooperative type would not make an aggressively selfish move merely because the Zajonc affect encouraged him to feel he could get away with it. So consider the replicate of CR9 in Berkeley. We are here comparing choices across games within the same session, hence involving the same players. The session covers CR25 (the replicate), 26, 27, and 28. Only 12 players (of 32) make the risky choice to allow B to choose the payoffs. There may be other cooperative types among the 32, but too cautious to run the risk of being betrayed. But clearly the 12 bold enough to accept that risk cannot be competitive *types*. Their choice cannot benefit themselves at all. Its only consequence is to risk losing 100 tokens in order to help the other player.

So we can identify 12 players who on the usual taxonomy of types must be either conditional cooperators or committed cooperators. But if that is so, we could predict that in CR27 within the same session, they would not refuse an even split of the gross payoff in order to put an unfair ultimatum to B. And in CR28, they would not destroy 875 tokens that would otherwise go to B on the chance that B will actually reward them for this by 25 tokens. But of the 12 players who make the risky cooperative move in CR25, 11 make an aggressively selfish choice in either CR27 or 28, or both, which is hard indeed to explain in terms of stable types.

And continuing on that line, I next want to show some consequences of the NSNX view of types as artifacts in other experimental data, and also show what looks to me like a potentially important, intrinsically social, cognitive illusion which can be teased out of the widely discussed Minimum game.

# 10 Social illusions

Return to the Minimum game introduced in Chapter 7 and the payoff matrix in Table 7.2 (p. 115). This is not the commons dilemma of a Public Goods game. In a commons dilemma, everyone would be better off if all cooperate, but each individual can do even better by shirking while others cooperate. In the Minimum game, however, there is nothing to be gained by free-riding. But cooperation can't be managed anyway.

Over a sequence of rounds, each player reports a number from 1 to 7. The best payoff in a round declines by 10¢ at each step that the minimum choice drops. If everyone reports "7", everyone gets $1.30. But if there are players who choose < "7", the lowest choice determines the payoff schedule for that round, which declines by a dime at each step. A player who matches that lowest number then gets the best payoff available in that round. For each step a player's choice is above the round minimum, the player's payoff is cut an additional 10¢. So if the minimum is "4", a player who reported "4" gets $1, which is down three dimes from what everyone would get if everyone picked "7". A player who reported "7" when the minimum turns out to be "4", gets 70¢, down another three dimes from the best available when the minimum choice is "4". At the extreme, if the round minimum is "1", a player who reported "1" gets 70¢ (down six dimes), but a player who reported "7" in a round where the minimum is "1" gets 10¢ (down another six dimes).

So everyone does best when everyone can coordinate on choosing "7". But the higher the number a chooser reports in any round, the more risk of an incremental loss in that round. All this might seem complicated as written out, but the players are provided with the payoff table, which makes it easy to see how the game works. It is rare that a player finds it difficult to understand the game.

A player who wanted to fully analyze the situation, somehow estimating how others will choose, would face a complicated case of strategic uncertainty. But Schelling long ago showed that players who know it is in their mutual advantage to coordinate on a common response often are able to recognize a salient choice. If we look for that here, it is not hard to find. For "7" is the most prominent number as the table is displayed. And everyone can see that this most prominent number also would be best if everyone could coordinate on it. And since the game runs 10 rounds, there is not very much at risk in staying with "7" in round 1. Risking a few dimes here could yield improved payoffs from the overall game of several dollars. So before seeing any results, we might suppose that players would mostly stay with "7" in round 1 to see how things stand with other players.

The result, however, is drastically different. A large fraction of players, usually upward of 2/3, chooses < "7" from the start. For groups of non-trivial size, the round 1 minimum will usually be some number intermediate between the payoff-maximizing "7" and the payoff-minimizing "1". It is not often "1" but also almost never "7". And a more puzzling surprise then follows. The long-run cost of a middling minimum in round 1 would be modest if in successive rounds players could edge back up toward "7". In round 1 a player has no way of knowing how low a number someone in the group might choose. But after round 1, everyone in the group has demon-strated how low he was moved to go to guard against a low choice from someone else. It is now hard to see any sensible reason for even a very cau-tious player to go further *down*. Indeed, since it seems to make no sense for anyone to go further down, choosing one notch higher than the previous minimum seems to risk just a dime for the prospect of a much larger gain over the balance of the game.

So even if there is no immediate coordination on "7", by the end of a series of rounds we might expect to get coordination back to 7, or at least approach-ing "7". And if NSNX (or any other allowance for other-regarding motiv-ation) is in play, that would reinforce the expectation. A lower minimum is bad for self, but also bad for everyone else.

But the results are entirely different. The minimum quickly falls to "1" and stays there. Some players try to edge up, but beyond $N = 2$ the minimum never goes up. Weber (2006) summarizes the results of many Minimum game experiments with Table 10.1.

Prior experience with the game does not help. Indeed, it seems to aggravate the problem. After doing badly players do not seem surprised, nor are experimenters commenting on the game. Apparently even the fall in the min-imum beyond round 1 does not violate the intuitions of sophisticated obser-vers, though if directly asked about it no one suggests why players would do that. Overall, on the prevailing interpretation, players are doing what makes sense in a difficult situation. The usual appraisal (see, for example, Camerer 2003) is that players *correctly* suspect someone will choose low and respond correctly to that. With respect not only to the coordination games discussed here but more generally, Camerer's book is an essential complement to this one, providing an exceedingly thoughtful and thorough "mainstream" behavioral survey of the experimental work. Anyone interested in this work will learn a lot from reading him. But on many points the NSNX + cognition view here runs against such views. On the Minimum game, it is tautological that if players feel sure someone will go low and act on that, then indeed they

*Table 10.1* Percent of groups at a minimum after five rounds in the Van Huyck game and various replications, by size of groups.

| 1 | 2 | 3 | 4 | 5 | 6 | 7 | Group size | N | Source |
|---|---|---|---|---|---|---|---|---|---|
| 5 | 0 | 0 | 3 | 3 | 3 | 86 | 2 | 37 | VHBB 1990, Camerer & Knez 2000 |
| 37 | 15 | 15 | 11 | 0 | 4 | 18 | 3 | 27 | Knez & Camerer 1994, Camerer & Knez 2000 |
| 80 | 10 | 10 | 0 | 0 | 0 | 0 | 6 | 10 | Knez & Camerer 1994 |
| 100 | 0 | 0 | 0 | 0 | 0 | 0 | 8 | 5 | Chaudhuri *et al.* 2001 |
| 100 | 0 | 0 | 0 | 0 | 0 | 0 | 9 | 2 | Cachon & Camerer 1996 |
| 100 | 0 | 0 | 0 | 0 | 0 | 0 | 14–16 | 7 | VHBB 1990 |

Even groups of two sometimes fail to coordinate efficiently. Groups of three mostly are doing badly. In larger groups efficient coordination appears to be hopeless. From Weber (2006).

will be correct in anticipating that the minimum will fall. The puzzle, though, is why would players expect that?

I want to argue that we are seeing something akin to what is happening in cognitive illusions like Monty Hall or three-cards in Chapter 6, but even harder to correct. People looking at the results of the Minimum game (such as you and me) are vulnerable to the same illusion that catches players in the game, as nearly everyone first encountering Monty Hall or three-cards is vulnerable to the probability illusions those problems prompt. But there is now a *social* complication.

When first seeing the Monty Hall puzzle, and sometimes long after first seeing it, very few people are immune to the intuition that there is no advantage in switching. But since the puzzle can be turned into a physical experiment no one can reasonably remain indefinitely caught by the illusion. But the Minimum game cannot be converted into a physical experiment with results that can't be denied. So if it is more difficult to escape the adverse intuition, and since that is shared across people (so that it seems "everyone knows" that it is only reasonable to choose < "7") there is no puzzle to be noticed.

If a player feels uncertain about what to do, a middling choice (like 4 or 5) will appeal as a compromise between the biggest risk (choosing "7" and it turns out someone chose "1") and the poorest payoff (choosing "1" when coordination on "7", if achievable, would pay almost twice as much). But what could possibly account for the further decline to "1" if that worst case has been escaped in round 1? And if the round 1 responses are taken to be responses to strategic uncertainty, it is to *myopic* strategic uncertainty, just within round 1. With respect to the whole game, why wouldn't the sensible response to strategic uncertainty be the one mentioned earlier, which is to stay at "7" for that first of ten rounds, to see how things stand with other players? The behavior we see can be *described* as a response to strategic uncertainty. But from the NSNX perspective it is at least questionable that it can be *explained* as a response to strategic uncertainty. Why do players so totally miss what is in their common interest when self-interest alone might be enough to make it sensible to wait at least one round before going lower?

I will argue that indeed something odd is happening that turns on what can be usefully identified as a form of *social* illusion. Cooperation falls to its lowest possible level, and under conditions where logically nothing that players do not already know is needed to sustain full cooperation. Players need only respond with minimal sophistication to what is visibly in each player's own best interest. But they don't.

That this can happen in experimental games we already know from the degenerate games of Chapter 7. But there was no essentially *social* character to more faulty responses. A player who escaped the illusion could unilaterally improve her expected payoff by some change that involved no risk of a loss of payoff. In the Minimum game, however, a player who escapes the illusion (as no doubt many do) faces a dilemma. If others are caught by the illusion, unilaterally going against that is going to lose payoff. There is no commons dilemma here (where everyone would be better off if all cooperate, but each individual can do even better by shirking while others cooperate). In the games in this chapter there is nothing to be gained by free-riding. But cooperation can't be managed anyway, even if many players in fact do escape the dilemma. Weber (2006) used student players from universities with more competitive admissions than in Van Huyck's game. In the control runs, half the players stayed with "7" in round 1, compared to less than a third in Van Huyck. But every group soon collapsed to its worst payoffs anyway.

And of course if some sort of cognitive illusion especially hard to escape because of its social character is governing the outcomes, it would be important to take notice, and consider whether that sort of difficulty could arise in natural settings. A first intuition might be that since players can be prompted to illusory choices in contexts where they could unilaterally escape (Chapter 7), it is not surprising and so perhaps not especially interesting that they could be misled in a context of what I am calling social illusion. But an opposite insight is likely to be more important. If individuals can unilaterally escape an illusion, then in a natural setting over time we could expect illusory behavior to fade. More and more people, perhaps reaching a tipping point, can see what is sensible. But in a context of social illusion insight cannot easily spread, since even those not caught by the illusion have an incentive to act as if they were.

Here is a stripped-down version of the Minimum game that may sharpen the argument. Allowed choices are narrowed to just "7" or "1", and the choice in round 1 will be binding over all 10 rounds.

The payoff table that would go with this simplified, all-10-rounds-at-once game would be:

|  |  | Minimum from another player. . . . | |
|---|---|---|---|
|  |  | 7 | 1 |
| You choose | 7 | $13.00 | $1.00 |
|  | 1 | $7.00 | $7.00 |

And indeed it looks risky to suppose that out of six or more players none would make the cautious choice. Should anyone fail to stay with "7", you would earn 10¢ per round rather than 70¢ per round that could be guaranteed by choosing "1".

But suppose you were not required to make an all-at-once choice. Rather, you can make a trial choice of "1" or "7" for only 10% of the stake, and after you see the result of the 10% trial you can choose "1" or "7" for the balance (9-rounds-at-once). A strategy you might consider is to report "7" in the trial round, but continue with "7" only if indeed that is the trial minimum. For if everyone stays with "7" in the trial, all almost double their payoffs by just continuing to do what everyone has already demonstrated they are inclined to do. The risk may not seem severe, and the stakes are certainly within what you can afford. If you judge that indeed, if everyone chooses "7" in the trial that is very likely to hold in the balance, then the effective trial round payoff table for this 1 + 9 game would then be:

|  |  | Minimum from another player. . . . | |
|---|---|---|---|
|  |  | 7 | 1 |
| You choose | 7 | $13.00 | $6.40 |
|  | 1 | $7.00 | $7.00 |

where you stand to gain $6 at a risk of only 60¢. If the riskier choice fails, you get only 10¢ in round 1, but you then get nine times 70¢ for the balance.

And if on reflection your intuition about how sensible it would be to stay with "7" in round 1 changes (for this version with a single trial round followed by an all-at-once choice for the remaining nine rounds), how could it revert for an even safer 10-rounds condition? Then you *never* have to risk a bad result for more than 10% of the aggregate stake? But now we are back to the Minimum game.

Extending the discussion to consider a moderate choice (say 4 or 5, rather than 1) would complicate but not undermine the argument. But it is apparent not only in the behavior of players within the game but also in the comments on the game from experimenters, that this way of looking at the round 1 choice rarely governs how the game is seen. Indeed, it generates responses like responses to the simple explanations of three-cards and Monty Hall in Chapter 6. It is hard to put your finger on what is wrong with the argument (because in fact there is nothing wrong with the argument), but the illusory intuition does not readily go away anyway.

We want to consider why. But the many examples of puzzling choice from earlier chapters suggest an explanation. We want to account for the propensity to make a middling choice in round 1 (not allowing even one round to see how high the payoffs might be kept though the prospective payoff from risking several dimes here is several dollars over the 10 rounds). And the explanation for that round 1 effect should be such that it extends to explain the even more puzzling further collapse of the minimum beyond round 1. But in terms of adverse defaulting within the NSNX cascade introduced in Chapter 7, the required explanation will be familiar.

The Minimum game is intended to capture the incentives of team production, in contrast to the Public Goods game, which is intended to capture the incentives of a common pool problem. But getting a good result in the Minimum game is strictly a matter of coordination. There is no free-rider temptation, since the only way to maximize own payoff is to fully cooperate. But this is not the team production problem as encountered in natural settings, where team production is always subject to free-rider problems, and in two forms. I might risk delaying the team project by slack effort. I plan to be on time (my own interest is harmed if I am late) but if something goes awry, I have not allowed enough leeway to be on time. Everyone has an incentive to do just barely enough, since more than that is wasted. But if everyone aims to do just barely enough then someone is likely to have an unexpected problem and the entire team suffers.

So there is a free-rider problem (the player who puts the team at risk by not leaving enough margin for the inevitable occasional slips). My expectation may be improved by shirking (I don't want to be late, but I am only late once in a while I gain whatever advantage tempts me to shirk every time). But team expectation is diminished, since when I am late it imposes a cost on everyone, not just me. *Some* risk of being late must be efficient, since the aggregate cost of never being late at some point must exceed the value of never being late. Shirking here is what is in excess of that.

And a more familiar sort of free-rider temptation might make my work shoddy as well as slack, diminishing the value of the team effort (or putting a burden on others to straighten out my shoddiness). But neither sort of free-riding is at issue in the Minimum game. If I report "7", that is it. There is no such thing as a tardy "7" or a shoddy "7".

Consequently the Minimum game is not actually like any team production context players would know from experience in the world. From what we have seen earlier of player difficulties in escaping defaults, we could expect players in this game to recognize the context as cooperative (so with the qualifications discussed in Chapter 8, they escape the competitive branch on the right in the NSNX cascade in Figure 7.3, p. 119) but it would be difficult to reach the coordination frame (2b) on the cooperative branch, since there is no strong jolt away from the default "neither selfish nor exploited" weak cooperation frame (2a). In a context where efficient coordination should not be difficult it then turns out to be essentially impossible, since the salient "neither selfish nor exploited" choice for a player in an unfamiliar setting is some middling level of response. Many players are caught by the default, and respond with intuitions guided by a frame within the cascade (2a) that does not match the actual context they are in (2b). In the language I have been using, they are *neglecting* features of the situation that mark it as a coordination game, not the default risky cooperation game.

The data show players choosing at least *as if* that were so. Players choose *as if* the neglect defaults defined in Chapter 6 leaves them caught in a default frame that does not match the context of the game they are actually in. Or players are in the appropriate frame but with an inappropriate sense of some essential feature of the situation, as seen repeatedly in the Charness and Rabin games considered in Chapter 9. Here, many players certainly respond *as if* they were in a Public Goods context though the incentives define a coordination context. In that frame, it will be hard to escape the intuition that even if I stay with "7" others probably won't, and I will be exploited by free-riders. We would (in round 1) then see many middling responses, as if we were in round 1 of a Public Goods game. And this would also account for the even more puzzling further decline of the minimum in later rounds. For in later rounds, groups would be at risk to the sort of choices (recall the *updown* effect explored in Chapter 8) characteristic of players in an actual Public Goods game who chose high in round 1, and were with good reason left feeling exploited by free-riders. Again, players are responding as if they were in a Public Goods game, though if explicitly asked they could correctly describe the Minimum game they are in. But this is not at all the only time we have encountered such a disconnect between what players at a conscious level know and what at a tacit level guides their intuitions.

A player who might in an actual Public Goods game give 0 would be tempted to choose "1" in the Minimum game, for any of the various reasons sketched in introducing the Public Goods games in Chapter 8. But when that player looks at the payoff table he gets a jolt that would push almost anyone to think more carefully, since it yields a payoff of only 70¢, which is low relative to most possibilities in the payoff table, and in particular low compared to the possibilities that left-to-right reading habits make most prominent. So parallel to what was seen in the 20-point penalty condition in the convertible Prisoner's Dilemma (Chapter 7), a player is pushed to think again, back off and pick some higher number. But a player inclined to give a middling or higher amount gets no jolt and is likely to be left feeling comfortable with that inclination.

Is there evidence for this account? In fact there is a great deal, either in the way of really strong manipulations which jolt players away from the risky cooperation default (hence yield strong cooperation), but also several variants in which what might be supposed to be adequately strong manipulations fail to overcome the difficulty.

A follow-up experiment by Van Huyck *et al.* (1993) reversed the bleak result by *auctioning* the opportunity to play. Only half the subjects were actually admitted to the game, after all had been prompted to look closely to assess how high it made sense to bid. Hence those who would actually choose would be just those self-selected through a public procedure (the auction) as being most confident that a high level of coordination could be achieved. Players did not always start fully coordinated but if not, groups went up not down

Another strong manipulation that works is providing really emphatic advice on what to do. Chaudhuri *et al.* (2002) ran groups of Minimum game subjects as a sequence of "generations". Each new generation is given advice from all members of the predecessor generation. At NYU and then again in a replication at Wellesley, if groups were given really emphatic, unanimous, and publicly shared advice that it would be stupid not to choose "7", then in round 1 all players would indeed choose "7". And then this payoff-maximizing coordination on "7" would almost always be sustained throughout. Players coordinated on their best result, instead of deteriorating to coordination on their worst result.

What might appear to be another sufficiently strong manipulation (Weber 2006) obtained only qualified success. Weber's games started from just two active players. With only two players efficient coordination can almost always be quickly reached. After five or six rounds, active members were gradually added, one by one, until twelve were active. Throughout, all twelve sat in the same room, with those waiting to join watching as coordination on "7" was gradually extended. So those not yet in the active group could see successful coordination starting from the group of two and usually being sustained for at least some additional rounds as, one by one, active players were added. This produced far more efficient outcomes than the standard game. Nevertheless, only 1 of 9 groups sustained fully efficient coordination throughout. Two other groups were nearly successful. But six of nine groups in this benign situation failed to come close to full cooperation. Similarly, in the Chaudhuri manipulation, merely giving players really emphatic advice in writing but not *reading it aloud* clearly improved chances that players would stay with "7", but not enough to avoid the usual collapse.

So we can see that the tendency for cooperation to collapse is hard to block. Even strong manipulations can fail. To work, it seems that a really forceful jolt away from the default is needed. How forceful is surprising, yet not *more* surprising than the many strange details we have by now seen in experimental data, but which can be comprehended if indeed adverse defaulting occurs in the strong form I have been proposing. The Weber experiment is particularly instructive. When Weber adds another player to the game while full cooperation is still being sustained, that new player is joining a group all of whom are fully cooperating, and who had been continuing to cooperate as new members joined. When coordination on "7" breaks down, there usually remain multiple future rounds, and fully cooperating maximizes payoff for everyone. Why would there be sufficient strategic uncertainty about what profitably coordinating players are likely to do in the next round to lead to a breakdown of that maximally profitable level of coordination? But if players are vulnerable to the adverse defaulting I've described, then even if overcome for some rounds it can return, as even after being convinced that it pays to switch in Monty Hall the illusory intuition can return. And the more active players, the more likely at least one will suffer the illusion.

On the other hand, if this certainly strange account of what is happening is right, we ought to be able to find more specific evidence for it. There turns out to be quite a lot.

1. We have already seen (in Chapter 7) that in a variant of the Minimum game in Valencia that totally eliminated strategic uncertainty a large majority of players give middling responses anyway, not only in round 1 but continuing through many successive rounds. Strategic uncertainty is literally zero. But players continue to act as if they are concerned that they need to guard against a concern that does not exist.

2. A restart in the Minimum game, in contrast to the Public Goods game restart seen in Chapter 8, failed utterly to yield the renewed effort at cooperation which is a robust feature of Public Goods games. By the end of Van Huyck's ten rounds, essentially all choices were at or very near "1". Apparently prompted by this dismal result in the first group, each of six more groups (91 players out of the total of 107) were asked to continue with five rounds of the "can't lose" variant described in Chapter 7. As described there, attention is more emphatically directed to the elimination of strategic uncertainty than in the Valencia game, and here by round 15, all players were choosing "7". A restart with these 91 thoroughly experienced players, with coordination on "7" in place, then yielded an even more dismal result than the first ten rounds. The fraction of players who immediately dropped to the bottom at the restart hugely increased relative to round 1 (from 2/107 to 24/91). And that can be understood since relative to an actual Public Goods game, where a restart returns players very nearly to their round 1 choices, in this game the loss from choosing high when someone else chooses low is much more severe and these players have experienced that.

Yet even though the overall restart choices are far below the round 1 choices, the fraction who stayed with the maximum choice hardly changed at all. A NSNX conjecture then is that players who stayed with "7" in round 1, who would have the strongest reason to feel exploited, would be reluctant to do that again at the restart. But those who went against that strong move down would likely include many players who reported less than "7" from the start in the original series, who would be more likely to feel selfish rather than exploited now. Since the fraction staying with "7" was essentially unchanged in the replay, the NSNX perspective would prompt us to ask: did "types" persist, or did types reverse as on a NSNX account they well might?

And among the six groups given the opportunity for a restart, the players who chose "7" were indeed overwhelmingly different in the round 16 restart compared to round 1. Among the 91 players given the restart opportunity, only 8 of 23 choosing "7" at the restart had been among the 25 choosing "7" in round 1. Those who chose "7" in the replay were by a large margin those who contributed to the collapse by starting off at <"7" in the original play.

A similar effect can be seen in Weber's data. Among 5 groups of 12 run as controls (so they started with all 12 players active), choices of "7" in round 1 were much more common than in Van Huyck's game (33/60 versus 31/107 in Van Huyck). All groups, nevertheless, quickly collapsed to the minimum. Only one player immediately chose "1" in round 1 (here parallel to Van Huyck, where only 2/107 did that). On the NSNX conjecture of the previous paragraph, those first to drop to "1" would be especially likely to be players who stayed with "7" in round 1, who would feel most exploited. In the four groups where this can be tested there were, counting ties, six players first to choose "1". And of 26/48 who stayed with "7" in round 1, 6/6 were first in their group to later plummet all the way to "1". Again players are responding *as if* motivated by "neither selfish nor exploited" concerns that are logically not present in this game.

3. Chaudhuri, having replicated the NYU result at Wellesley, considered what would happen if the coordination game was replaced by a standard Public Goods game. Chaudhuri wondered if players might still "talk themselves to efficiency". It turns out that advice from a prior generation that firmly counseled staying on the team, not be selfish, yielded close to 100 percent coordination on the optimal group behavior of contributing the full endowment to the common pool. Changing the game from one where the free-rider concern would be illusory to one where it was actually in play made remarkably little difference.

Without strong advice and listening to that advice as a group, many choices in the Minimum game (given the rules, one such choice in a round is enough) responded as if chooser was seeing the game as a free-rider problem, as (unsurprisingly) did players in the game with an actual free-rider problem. With strong advice and listening to that advice as a group, players uniformly framed the Public Goods game as a coordination game. This turned out to prompt a reframing but not an illusory reframing, since in fact the manipulation here was sufficient to orient the players to pretty nearly act as a team. If you are motivated, as NSNX supposes, to be "neither selfish nor exploited", and you expect others to cooperate, then even from the free-rider context (2a) it is likely to seem reasonable to risk cooperating at least through round 1, and to continue that way when that anticipation of cooperation was confirmed.

Chaudhuri's results here were complementary to the striking effect which started this discussion of the Minimum game. Lacking *cognitively* effective cues away from default responses, Valencia students in the logically trivial game described in Chapter 7 acted as if they faced "neither selfish nor exploited" choices when no such risk existed. American students at Wellesley chose as if there were, or as if there were not, good reason for free-rider concerns whether in a Public Goods game (where that is an issue) or in the Minimum game (where it isn't), in either case contingent on whether or not they were prompted to expect a high level of cooperation, not on whether there actually was a free-rider risk.

4. A telling detail of the Minimum game results is that although coordination problems of course become increasingly severe as group size grows, choices do not reflect that. Table 10.2 reprints Camerer's (2003: 383–4) tabulation of results across experiments, showing that "distribution of first-round choices is surprisingly invariant to the number of subjects in the group", prompting his comment that "subjects in larger groups should realize that the minimum in a large group is likely to be low, and should choose much lower numbers than in small groups". But if strategic uncertainty is (correctly, of course) directed to the money payoffs at the end of the game, not myopically to the paper tally at the end of round 1, and if NSNX motivation governs, then responses from NSNX players might reveal just such invariance.

Recall the remarks near the beginning of Chapter 8 on the contrast between standard models and NSNX on the effect of increasing group size. For a NSNX player *not* caught by adverse defaulting, staying with "7" in round 1 remains a reasonable response to strategic uncertainty, since the increasing risk of low choices with increasing group size would be offset by the increasing aggregate value of keeping coordination high. Perhaps that increasing group value of staying with "7" (more players will be hurt by going low) would not fully offset the increasing risk of a low choice by someone else. The theory does not imply which way that would go. But the offsetting effect might be strong enough that players *not* caught by adverse defaulting would respond very similarly in large and small groups.

On the other hand, a player who *is* caught by adverse defaulting would be giving responses anchored on intuitions more appropriate for a Public Goods game than for the Minimum game they are playing. Under NSNX motivation, as discussed in Chapter 8 and as can be seen confirmed in the actual Public Goods game data in Chapter 8, players in the "neither selfish nor exploited" frame also will not be one-sidedly prompted to lower choices by increasing group size. They are not likely to choose "7", but the middling

*Table 10.2* First-round choices contingent on group size (from Camerer 2003: 383).

| Group size | Number choice | | | | | | | Total sample size |
| | 1 | 2 | 3 | 4 | 5 | 6 | 7 | |
| --- | --- | --- | --- | --- | --- | --- | --- | --- |
| *Distribution of first-period choices (percent)* | | | | | | | | |
| 2 | 28 | 3 | 3 | 7 | 21 | 0 | 36 | 28 |
| 3 | 8 | 5 | 8 | 17 | 7 | 2 | 41 | 60 |
| 6 | 18 | 7 | 13 | 16 | 7 | 7 | 39 | 114 |
| 9 | 0 | 11 | 28 | 39 | 5 | 0 | 17 | 18 |
| 12 | 25 | 4 | 13 | 8 | 16 | 4 | 29 | 24 |
| 14–16 | 2 | 5 | 5 | 17 | 32 | 9 | 31 | 104 |

levels favored by this frame would not be much affected by group size. So whether players are caught by adverse defaulting or not, on the account here we have reason to doubt that increasing group size will push choices lower. Standard views, as Camerer makes clear, emphatically say the opposite. A large body of data, across many replications of the Minimum game, show that the standard view is wrong.

5. But what seems to me the most striking support for the NSNX + cognition account comes from Van Huyck's subsequent results in a game where payoffs were determined not by the *minimum* choice in a round, but by the *median* choice (Van Huyck *et al.* 1991). There were nine players in each group, using the payoff matrix in Table 10.3. As before, the game would run for ten rounds. But now the governing choice in each round would not be the *minimum* choice in the round, but the *fifth lowest* among the nine choices (the median).

In the Minimum game a player would lose by staying with "7" if even one of the eight other players fails to do the same. But in the Median game, staying with "7" is the most profitable move unless at least five of the eight other players choose < "7". What is required is 5/8 choosing < "7", not 5/9, since if the chooser herself is needed to provide the fifth, she won't. So it is far less risky to choose "7" in this Median game than in the Minimum game. And in addition the payoff matrix now makes it costly to choose lower than whatever turns out to be the governing number, rather than (as in the Minimum game) only costly if the choice is above the governing number. So in this way also any temptation to choose low must be less. Finally, since the median is determined by what most players choose, even in round 1 most payoffs will be either in the upper left or lower right quadrant. But payoffs in the upper left are conspicuously bigger than in the lower right.

Even a player who responded only to that grossest feature of the game has a strong prompt away from the competitive right branch of the cascade in Figure 7.3 (p.119). The better payoffs are only available if players jointly

*Table 10.3* Van Huyck's Median game payoffs. As discussed in the text, logically there are multiple reasons to expect higher first round choices here than in the Minimum game.

| | | *Median value of X chosen* | | | | | | |
|---|---|---|---|---|---|---|---|---|
| | | 7 | 6 | 5 | 4 | 3 | 2 | 1 |
| Your | 7 | 1.30 | 1.15 | 0.90 | 0.55 | 0.10 | −0.45 | −1.10 |
| choice | 6 | 1.25 | 1.20 | 1.05 | 0.80 | 0.45 | 0.00 | −0.55 |
| of | 5 | 1.10 | 1.15 | 1.10 | 0.95 | 0.70 | 0.35 | −0.10 |
| *X* | 4 | 0.85 | 1.00 | 1.05 | 1.00 | 0.85 | 0.60 | 0.25 |
| | 3 | 0.50 | 0.75 | 0.90 | 0.95 | 0.90 | 0.75 | 0.50 |
| | 2 | 0.05 | 0.40 | 0.65 | 0.80 | 0.85 | 0.80 | 0.65 |
| | 1 | −0.50 | −0.05 | 0.30 | 0.55 | 0.70 | 0.75 | 0.70 |

produce a median that makes the high payoffs available. But a player who neglected further details (that is, a player caught by the *neglect* defaulting introduced in Chapter 6) would then be caught by default in the "neither selfish nor exploited" weak cooperation frame (2a). A player caught by that would respond about the same in this Median game as in the Minimum game. For a player neglecting the difference between the Median game and a Public Goods game is scarcely likely to be alert to the difference between the Minimum game and the Median game. In both games (Minimum and Median) players caught by neglect defaulting would tend to exhibit myopic responses to strategic uncertainty, and would tend to middling choices that look much like choices in round 1 of a Public Goods game (but with the lowest choices deterred in the way mentioned earlier in this chapter).

On the other hand, a player who did *not* neglect all but the grossest features of the game would not be caught in the "neither selfish nor exploited" frame, since there is no free-rider risk here. A player not caught by neglect defaulting would be nudged away from that default over to the coordination frame (2b). Schelling long ago (1960) reported that when he asked people how they would respond if they would win a prize if they make the same choice as another person between "heads" and "tails", that 36 of 42 chose "heads". Here players have the certainly easier coordination problem of choosing between more money and less money. If not caught by adverse defaulting, when players make their choice in round 1 of this 10 round game it would hardly be difficult to see that everyone should want to help get a median in the upper left quadrant.

But set aside what is best for the group and also set aside what is best looking ahead. Unless a player thinks the median will be 3 (or less), anyone who actually responds to the payoffs in Table 10.4 can see that choosing "5" dominates choosing "3" even considering only expected own-payoff within the current round. That five of the eight other players would then choose 3 (or less) looks negligible bordering on impossible. Consequently, for a player alert to what is at issue in this game, the relevant portion of the payoff matrix collapses to Table 10.4.

And now, unless you felt almost sure the median would be "4" (but how could you?), you would certainly choose at least "5", since "5" could lose only

*Table 10.4* Median game payoff table for payoffs that could plausibly occur.

|  |  | Median value of X | | | |
|---|---|---|---|---|---|
|  |  | 7 | 6 | 5 | 4 |
| Your | 7 | 1.30 | 1.15 | 0.90 | 0.55 |
| choice | 6 | 1.25 | 1.20 | 1.05 | 0.80 |
| of | 5 | 1.10 | 1.15 | 1.10 | 0.95 |
| X | 4 | 0.85 | 1.00 | 1.05 | 1.00 |

5¢ if the median is indeed "4" and otherwise is better, aside from improving prospects for a better median in the nine future rounds. An iterated dominance argument here would yield "7" as the unambiguously best choice. Following Camerer, I treat that as too much to expect even of sophisticated and alert players. But if players are alert (if they are not caught by adverse defaulting which prompts them to choose as if they were in a Public Goods game), we would see only "5", "6", or "7" choices. It would not be at all surprising if the median turned out to be "7". And certainly we would not see the mostly middling choices that players caught in the "neither selfish nor exploited" frame (2a) would report.

So we have a stark contrast between mostly middling choices to be expected from players caught by adverse defaulting and responding as if in a Public Goods game, as against players not caught by adverse defaulting whose choices would be tightly clustered at the high end. Table 10.5 shows the results. They look nothing like what we would see from alert choosers even if self-interest alone was motivating responses. And that only becomes more emphatic under the constrained but not negligible NSNX concern for group outcome seen repeatedly in earlier chapters.

As the caption explains, the choices on the right are biased downward. But even in the responses on the left the fraction staying with "7" (5/27) in this Median game is actually smaller than the fraction in the Van Huyck's Minimum game (31/107), though on the logic of the situation the result should go in the opposite direction. Choosing "7" should be more common not less common. But it isn't. We should adjust the numbers on the right upward, making the right column look like the left. But that still leaves us with no evidence of the increase in average choice that should be seen if players are responding to the sharp differences in incentives between the

*Table 10.5* Comparing Median game with Van Huyck's Minimum game.

| Choice | 9 | 9(and 27) |
|---|---|---|
| 7 | 5 | 3 |
| 6 | 3 | 1 |
| 5 | 8 | 7 |
| 4 | 8 | 11 |
| 3 | 3 | 5 |
| 2 | 0 | 0 |
| 1 | 0 | 0 |
| Total | 27 | 27 |

On the left (column 9) are choices from the first three groups of nine in Van Huyck *et al.* (1991). On the right are the second three groups of nine who also had to choose for a simultaneous game where the controlling number would still be the fifth lowest, but among all 27 players in the three groups. In that 27-player context, the chance of a low controlling number of course is increased, and the presence of that low choice in a simultaneous game would bias results downward even in the group of nine game. The numbers show that effect.

Minimum and Median games. Any change is in the wrong direction. Somehow players are not responding to the difference between the Minimum and Median games, but apparently only to the most superficial appearance of the matrix.

But if players barely notice the difference between the Minimum game and a Public Goods game, making choices influenced by logically irrelevant salience (such as negative payoffs that a moment's thought would show could not plausibly occur), it is not hard to understand that they would not respond to the difference between the Minimum game and the Median game.

Reviewing the range of very different variants of the Minimum game (the trivialized Valencia game, the Wellesley experiment using Public Goods payoffs in place of the Minimum game payoffs, the auction game, Weber's evolving game, and now the Median game) we see data that are really puzzling in terms of the standard account of why coordination robustly falls to its worst level in the Minimum game. The same results provide a coherent pattern of responses if players are vulnerable to adverse defaulting, as we have seen they are in numerous examples in earlier chapters.

And all this prompts a pair of important questions.

(1) What should we make of the point that observers of this game seem to be as vulnerable to the illusion as players within the game? So far as I have been able to find, nothing in the extensive discussion of the Minimum game questions the standard account, though we have just reviewed a quite overwhelming array of readily available data that suggest that something is seriously wrong with that account. Even as shrewd and careful observer as Camerer, in the comment quoted earlier, is reduced to what almost looks like scolding players for their failure to behave the way he assumes they ought to behave.

But being human, of course we observers of the game might be caught by the adverse defaulting that catches our subjects, as professors are about as easily caught by Monty Hall as students subjects. Few readers would have had trouble seeing that the player responses seen in Chapter 7 are not sensible. Seeing something odd in the subtle but noticeable decline of contributions in the BSM-EX-R game in Chapter 8, and much more grossly with the deficit of normal reciprocity responses in Chapter 9 is not so obvious. But it usually requires no elaborate effort to persuade readers that there is something odd. It seems to be enough just to point to what players were doing. Here, though, I have made a pretty elaborate effort to persuade a reader that there is something to be explained and probably fallen well short of complete success anyway.

What accounts for that difference? In the Minimum game, players are getting a terrible result. They robustly sink to their lowest payoffs. That the players are doing badly is noticed in all discussions of the Minimum game. But this is taken to be as much as could be expected given the condition of this game. Attention quickly turns to the success of players in achieving a Nash equilibrium. The result is terrible. But it is often a Nash equilibrium, even if an equilibrium coordinated on the worst possibility. Except for the puzzling absence of an effect of group size on initial choices, the results have been treated as unproblematical, showing rational choice at work. Could this be right?

(2) But perhaps all that these results show is how irrelevant laboratory results are to understanding how people choose outside the lab. Could anything so odd occur in the world beyond the lab? I have more than once indicated that I think such things do occur, and with more important consequences than are easily recognized. What makes the games in this chapter of special interest is that they appear to reveal a *social* illusion. The illusion is widely shared in a situation where even a player who escapes it cannot unilaterally improve the situation. So correcting the illusion becomes difficult indeed, in the way I described early in this chapter, which may make the consequences more serious, with both problems aggravated when there are many interacting agents and complicated and conflicting motivation, as is characteristic of political situations.

# 11 Notes on terrorism

Learning about observations from the theory and learning how to use the theory from work with observations is an interactive enterprise. Beginning in Chapter 7, we have been pursuing that with respect to how a NSNX + cognition view might give insight into what was happening in data from cooperation experiments. But I have often mentioned, because it is essential not to let it out of sight, that what motivates all this concern with the artifactual cooperation games is that that a theory which works well in accounting for experimental data should yield insight into how cooperation works beyond the lab. And translating what can be learned from working with data from the artificial context of laboratory games into something that can be fruitfully applied in natural settings also requires learning by doing. Can situations in the world be found where the theoretical apparatus developed here has some bite? If so, how would that work? This is a large and difficult topic, certainly not to be settled by the few pages I will offer here. But I do hope to open the door on this large topic.

By way of a not-so-academic exercise in using NSNX + cognition, I sketch out a few illustrations tied to the particularly salient (as I write) question of the relation of the war in Iraq with the broader problem of jihadist terrorism.

As used here, *jihadist terrorism* means terrorist tactics aimed broadly at the West and in particular terrorism targeted on American interests. So I set aside here terrorism focused on more local issues within Iraq, or in the Israeli/Palestinian or Turkish/Kurdish conflicts, or in numerous other conflicts even further removed from any plausible connection with 9/11. I write in early 2007, but with some confidence that what happens between when this is written and when it is read is unlikely to make it out of date for the purpose at hand, which is to explore how the NSNX + cognition argument might be put to work.

Since comment on this topic is vast, saying something no one has said (and that has any serious prospect of turning out to be right) may be impossible. But it is useful in general, and especially so dealing with a novel kind of account, to manage to say something that is only novel in the limited sense that seeing a point from the novel perspective brings some aspects of an insight more sharply into focus. And I will try to get at least a little beyond that.

The key issue for us concerns the persistently proclaimed view by supporters of the Bush policy in Iraq (as I write) that the war diverts jihadist effort into Iraq to American advantage since we get to destroy jihadist resources sent there to oppose us, rather than have those resources used against us, perhaps in some repeat of 9/11. The overwhelming view among people seriously immersed in work on terrorism from early on has been that on the contrary, the war in Iraq fuels recruitment to jihadism worldwide that by a wide measure exceeds any attrition that can be claimed in Iraq. I will reach that usual conclusion, by way of a discussion in terms of NSNX. By that route I also reach a conjecture – it would too strong to say a conclusion – on how the Bush Administration could have performed so badly. That the war has been handled badly is a point that no longer seems in much dispute even among supporters of the Administration. But the conjecture about how this could have happened is unconventional, hence certainly might be wrong. But if correct, it has consequences worth noting.

From the earlier chapters we have four main points to work with.

1   The basic NSNX equilibrium developed in Chapter 1, turning on the pair of NSNX rules governing how an agent finds a balance between competing propensities favoring self-interest and group-interest. This yields the NSNX equilibrium condition, $W = G'/S'$. W is weight to self-interest, which goes up as an agent perceives himself as sacrificing more for a cause than other people in his situation. $G'$ is the perception of social value (utility), $S'$ of the private value (utility) that must be traded-off in a choice. $W > G'/S'$ favors self-interested choice, $W < G'/S'$ favors group-interested choice. An agent favors the choice that gets closer to equilibrium.

2   The S-diagram developed in Chapters 4 and 5 captures implications for *social* equilibrium of the *individual* equilibrium condition in (1). The logic which leads from the NSNX individual equilibrium condition to the S-diagram points to the characteristics and importance of an initiating seed, of tipping point effects, and of a set of tactics available to agents motivated to tip a social situation to a different equilibrium.

3   What I have called *neglect* defaulting was developed in Chapter 6. A human being could not get through the day unless she neglected the vast bulk of what comes within the range of detailed attention. In familiar settings we are very good at choosing what to attend to (we don't *choose* to ignore anything: that is the default). In unfamiliar settings that reliability must begin to fade, which has consequences for choices outside the range of familiar experience, and which also effects how NSNX interacts with context.

4   The NSNX cascade developed in Chapter 7 (repeated as Fig. 11.1) here concerns the subjective frames which might guide intuition in a social interaction. Some social interactions are competitive, some cooperative. Of competitive contexts, some are zero-sum, others payoff-maximizing. Of cooperative contexts, some are pure coordination, others subject to

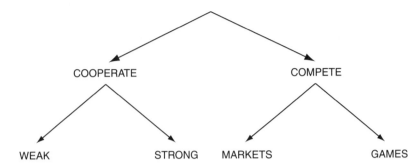

*Figure 11.1* The NSNX cascade

free-rider risk. The frame that (usually covertly) guides intuition in a context governs what sort of choices seem sensible to an agent. But an extension of (3) points to the possibility of adverse defaulting within the cascade, where an agent sees a context of social interaction from a frame that on reflection she would regard as mistaken. At the extreme, a situation which is actually zero-sum may be somehow framed as a problem of coordination, or the reverse, but in either case yielding a result the chooser would on reflection see as a blunder. So analysis in terms of NSNX of choices in a context that is complicated, conflicted, and out of the range of familiar experience needs to allow for difficulties due to what I have labeled *adverse defaulting*, leaving a person blind to important information that is plainly in sight, or leaving a person with a sense of the kind of social context he is in that does not fit the situation he is actually in.

In sum, the S-diagram (2) and framing within the NSNX cascade (4) follow from the basic NSNX logic (1). And in cognitively difficult conditions, how they work will be complicated by the vulnerability of agents to adverse defaulting (3). Earlier chapters have taken up a number of what seem to me downright startling examples of experimental results that diverge from what standard theory and often also from what common sense would expect, but in ways that invite an explanation in terms of NSNX + cognition. In the experiments there is no real complexity, but also no rich context of the sort routinely available to guide intuition in natural situations. But when we turn to natural situations that are novel, and conflicted, and complex, and out-of-scale with everyday choices – which describes many contexts of large-scale cooperation (or failures of cooperation) – that is not at all an unusual situation.

Directly from the NSNX equilibrium condition (1), making $G'/S'$ larger (or smaller), or making W smaller (or larger), would increase (decrease) any propensity to favor what the agent sees as group-interest. We want to consider what would move things one way or the other. We also want to consider what would diminish support even though $G'/S'$ for commitment to jihadist terrorism is not changed. That possibility arises mainly because a person who sees social value in jihadism very likely also sees social value in any number of other cleavages (Sunni/Shiite, Arab/Persian, and others) that might compete with his sense of G′ with respect to supporting violent attacks against American or friendly-to-America targets. And if the salient focus of concern shifts (in NSNX terms, if the most promising outlet for group-interested choice changes), the agent's sense of the relevant "people like me" governing W would also change. This competition among alternatives for what is salient as group-interest is like the mundane competition of items on a menu: you are not going to have room for everything. And another way there might be competition is in the sense that a side-effect of attacking Americans might have an adverse effect on another cleavage an individual cares about. Or a person might see the two concerns as complimentary, not competitive, and either way parallel to the analogous point in a mundane context of consumer choice.

Another dimension is the scale of the political goals, which range from pathological (the world is evil so destruction is good), to grandiose (re-establishment of the caliphate), to highly ambitious (forcing US and European withdrawal from any influence in the Middle East) to relatively modest (forcing the US to pressure Israel to make major concessions to the Palestinians or move away from intervention in support of pro-American governments in the area). The possibilities are complicated, and the first is entirely beyond the reach of rational analysis and also beyond the scope of these notes. For the rest, grandiose goals attract some supporters and alienate others, but if treated as long-range aspirations in some contexts and heralding imminent return of the Prophet in others a jihadist might hope to keep both utopians and realists in hand, while enemies on the right (opposing jihadism) and on the left (radical splinters) would try to make that difficult. But to the extent that G′ for attacking the US seems overwhelmingly high across the spectrum, the problem of papering over cracks in the jihadist platform of course must be eased.

The possibility of adverse neglect defaulting is relevant here (and at several later points). Recalling the distinction in Chapter 3 between aspirational and pragmatic norms, here observers lacking an intimate familiarity with the context will easily miss distinctions between aspirational and pragmatic goals that are easy to see from inside. Without the visceral prompts that make an insider quick to notice distinctions, an outsider can miss what is logically plainly on view, as in a number of examples in the experimental games of earlier chapters. Misjudgments can follow of either a hawkish or dovish form. A hawk inclined to see the adversary as intransigent (so it is a mistake to encourage him by concessions) may not register good evidence that a goal is aspirational, while a dove fails to register good evidence that an entirely intolerable goal is actually seen as pragmatic, not merely aspirational. And misframing within the NSNX cascade could then follow, with a hawk seeing a situation as zero-sum when payoff-maximizing would be more sensible even from his hard-line perspective while the dove might see a coordination problem where the more prudent framing would be one of very risky cooperation.

But jihadism of course is not just another outlet for group-interested motivation. The targets are civilians. Inhibitions have to be overcome. What is needed is evidence and argument that provokes a severe visceral sense of outrage. And arguments that make sense to potential supporters, justifying extreme actions, are needed to lock down what has been put in place by visceral responses. Sheer anger and outrage cannot be at hand continually, so argument is needed to keep conviction alive, ready to be stoked into passion again by new evidence of outrageous behavior. Extreme actions incite visceral responses from the other side. Each side attends to what inflames passions ready to ignite and easily neglects what ignites passions on the other side. But since contemporary people in the West do not feel they have been subject to humiliation and domination by Muslims, there will be a very large asymmetry in readiness to be provoked. In terms of the neglect defaulting introduced in Chapter 6 (and recalled in the previous paragraph), consequently, it would be hard for someone in America to notice how outrageous in Middle Eastern eyes images might be of American troops kicking in doors, perfectly routine and appropriate military behavior as it may be, and mild as the abuse may be relative to what is commonplace in that part of the world. And of course there are many more provocative images commonly on view.

Reducing the occasions for sparking fresh ignitions lets $G'$ (for jihadism) cool down. Since it is impossible to be impassioned in two directions at once, competition between opportunities for group-interested choice will be inevitable. Sometimes passions will be diverted from outrage at the West to outrage dividing the Muslim community. Passions directed one way might be eventually judged a diversion from more important interests, or more effectively pursued interests. Outrage is not the only element in choice. But passions, being passions, are not easily set aside to allow reflection. Arguments might make violent attacks seem unlikely to be effective, or misdirected, or likely to provoke painful retaliation, but effective arguments might be hard to find. All sides would warn against expecting immediate results and point to historical examples of the success of sustained campaigns.

So there will be many ways in which terrorists and counter-terrorists will seek to inflame or moderate passions, communicate arguments, sustain commitment, impose costs, offer rewards that will move the NSNX value ratio ($G'/S'$) of agents they would want to deter or to encourage. Well-chosen concessions, for example, reduce $G'$ both by making extreme tactics less urgently justified and by making the extreme tactics less likely to succeed (what is left after the concessions is what those who offered the concessions will fight harder to keep). Badly chosen concessions, on the other hand, can backfire by making it seem that the adversary is in retreat. And, returning to a point already introduced, a campaign of extreme violence profits from actions (or purported actions, or portrayed actions) that put people in a frame of mind where nothing seems too outrageous in the face of the outrage being imposed. Among other difficulties, this creates temptation to provocateurs.

So there are many possibilities, sometimes conflicting, to consider with respect to $G'$, but as will be seen reasonably secure judgments can sometimes be made anyway.

For $S'$ things are simpler though not simple. Private wealth of course makes it easier to provide any given level of support to whatever an agent sees as socially good, which extends to jihad, and especially if no personal risk is involved. The more wealth the less severe the bite ($S'$) from whatever private value is sacrificed, making $G'/S'$ larger. Since $S'$ is cost *net* of any loss or gain from side effects, criminality of a sort which complements the jihadist needs for such things as forged documents offsets, or perhaps more than offsets its direct private cost. Most commonly, $S'$ is small because the person is not doing much, recalling (from Chapter 1) that $S'$ and $G'$ capture the differential private cost and social benefit of a finite choice, not the marginal cost and benefit of an arbitrarily small increment of resources. Neither a small value of $S'$ nor a large value of $G'$ of itself implies substantial participation. $S'$ may be small merely because the choice being considered would not entail much of a private cost even for someone not particularly well off, in which case $G'$ can also be small and still allow a high value of $G'/S'$. The significance of this point will become clearer when we move on to considering implications of the S-diagram (item 2 in the earlier listing). But we can note that how far the public is sympathetic even though most are not doing very much is not a small element, since in the aggregate modest but low cost participation by many people will not be negligible compared to large cost participation by a dedicated few. The large cost activity by a dedicated few may be substantially enabled by the low-cost participation of many mild sympathizers.

For the special case of criminal activity complementary to jihadist effort, cooperation with jihadists may have a negative cost ($S' < 0$). It is profitable to self-interest not a sacrifice of self-interest. We would then get (for that special case) cooperation even if $G'$ is negligibly small, as discussed in more general terms in Chapter 1 (p. 6). And net $S'$ will be small for a person in a social context where failing to be sympathetic to jihadism would be socially costly or even dangerous (because you are part of a community where that is seen as what any decent person would be). Social costs (or social rewards) affecting ordinary people in a community will be contingent on how far the terrorist campaign has general support. And there would be individual threats from activists to individuals seen as harming the effort, or even merely insufficiently enthusiastic. That would be most significant in contexts where individual threats complement rather than run against general sentiment in the community. So general support may enable threats to individuals which might otherwise risk alienating too many people.

How would improving economic conditions affect terrorist propensities?[1] In terms of $G'$, economic improvement would reduce anger and frustration in the community, hence reduce $G'$ for drastic and risky measures which might harm the community. And the opportunity cost to individuals of jihadism increases if opportunities for pursuing a "normal" career improve: a potential especially likely to be important in a context of severe unemployment rates. On the other hand, both effects would be at least partly offset by increasing the number of people who can afford to devote time and resources to a social cause. Within a community the effects would be mixed, especially to the extent the improving community is one that supplies funds and other sorts of support for terrorist operations elsewhere (perhaps even within the same country). So a mix of effects should be expected, some alleviating terrorist dangers, some the converse, with much depending on the details of the situation.

The final element of the NSNX equilibrium, W, turns on how far an individual seems to be exceeding, or just matching, or falling short of what others "like me" are doing. In the Darwinian story in Chapter 1 this was simple. Others "like me" might not be anyone I know (there would be differentiation by sex or age) but still would be drawn from my immediate living group of perhaps a few dozen people I am with essentially all the time. But we are now vastly removed from that hunter-gatherer context. What counts in a particular context as people "like me," hence governs where I stand with response to the NSNX "neither selfish nor exploited" balance, may be people very remote than my immediate companions. This is not entirely new. There have always been isolated individuals whose sense of mission was vastly out of scale with that of anyone else they might have been expected to sense as "like me." But with the coming of vivid, responsive, immediate communication worldwide, including imagery and sound as well as text, it has become far more likely that perfectly ordinary people might find themselves marching to the beat of a distant drummer.

And now the internet has vastly extended such possibilities, which have multiple consequences in terms of NSNX effects. Relative to a world without the internet, it becomes easy to communicate, easy to get and share information, easy to find and establish a working relationship with like-minded people, and all in ways that involve very little risk of detection. An image can be concealed in another image, a message sent from a one-time location (a few minutes in an internet café) to a one-time use free email address, and so on. Even elaborate exchanges of information would be hard to observe. The main risk to either party would seem to be the risk that the other party is an agent for the opposition, and in various ways that risk can be reduced as well. And easily available postings on the internet will tell you how to do all this.

We can consequently expect a great expansion of the sense of people "like me" that governs W to allow for a reference set which includes people I have never met and even never could meet. Not long ago, that would have to be because I infer that they would behave like me and have interests like me. But with the coming of the internet, a much stronger sense that we are on the same team becomes available, because we can be active, interacting, cooperators.

We can notice multiple bases which might guide a person's sense of what "people like me" are doing for a cause, hence what will guide the "neither selfish nor exploited" sense of equilibrium. At a critical moment what is crucial for terrorists, as on a great many other things, and very well documented in military matters, is "unit cohesion." People develop intense loyalty to their local unit and judge their appropriate level of commitment by comparison with the comrades in the unit. But what makes a person a willing candidate for such a unit? There has to be a prior stage where willingness to commit goes beyond what is common. On a wider scale, elite units in any country's armed forces judge themselves by comparison with others in the elite forces (airborne, marines, rangers). On a much wider scale, individuals see their effort in comparison to admired leaders who could be leading completely comfortable lives but commit themselves to the cause, here the wealthy Bin Laden choosing to live a rough life for a cause. But all such effects are magnified by the new opportunities for cooperation offered by the internet, which offer opportunities to enter a path which may lead to life-sacrificing commitment, on a front far removed from a person's own neighborhood (hence going beyond the usual situation for suicide bombers with local targets, who are not the focus of attention in this discussion of jihadism).

Setting aside jihadist terrorism for a moment, what has emerged with the internet has proved to be downright astonishing. Collaborative work on (most remarkably) FOSS – free-and-open-source-software – has yielded exceedingly complex projects in a way that certainly would have been predicted to be hopelessly vulnerable to free-riding and multiple other difficulties until actually demonstrated to be workable. A computer operating system and a large suite of subsidiary programs able to compete on reasonably equal terms with Microsoft Windows has been created largely out of voluntary cooperation among people who have never met. For a survey and references, see http://en.wikipedia.org/wiki/Free_and_open-source_software, where the Wikipedia free encyclopedia providing this URL is itself another example of voluntary cooperation on the web, but not so completely astonishing as the ability to create something as complex as a computer operating system able to rival Windows. As both standard theory and NSNX would expect, a closer look reveals various sorts of returns to self-interest in participating. But on the standard theory it is obvious that these cannot possibly add up to enough to allow this utopian project to fly. But it soars! NSNX can make sense of this, but I freely allow, only in hindsight. That is not the story here, however, where the relevance of FOSS is only to alert us to potential of the terrorist dark side of cooperation on the internet. What FOSS can manage, terrorists and aspiring terrorists can notice and hope to emulate. Consequently, a new element of social comparison appears, which is being "neither selfish nor exploited" relative to others engaged in internet cooperation intended to support jihad.

And without extending this quick survey, we now have enough of the table to prompt some general remarks bearing on the substantive question at hand.

It is easy to see how from the jihadist perspective it would make sense to promote the war in Iraq as (with a suitable change in labeling) "the central front in the war on terror," but not clear at all why Americans would promote that idea. Huge costs are being imposed on the Americans. Propoganda victories are unending with each day's televised reports on what can be portrayed as American atrocities against Muslims. Every helicopter shot down or tank destroyed is a victory. Chaos reigns. So long as the war goes on, the jihadists can point to a war aim of ending the American occupation that commands wide support; and if the Americans leave they will claim victory. There has rarely been so clear a "heads we win, tails you lose" situation.

G' for jihadist activity must be partly contingent on sympathy in the Muslim world for claims that striking at America is in the interest of the worldwide Muslim community, and partly on the credibility of claims that jihadist tactics get results. S' is substantially contingent on how far, in Mao's famous phrase, the jihadists are able to swim in a sea of sympathizers. And W decreases as others are seen to be active, but if G' is nudged up and S' nudged down by effects of the war in Iraq, then participation in jihadist activity increases and this feeds back on W, nudging it down, aggravating the problem by the feedback described in Chapter 1. So one might think that shrewd American policy would be minimize the importance of Al Qaeda in Iraq, and seek to minimize not endorse claims that moving towards American disengagement would be a victory for Al Qaeda.

Given the multiplicity of cleavages within the Muslim community (not only Sunni versus Shia, but in several combinations among Arabs, Persians, Kurds, Turks, and within these categories between Bedouins and Palestinians, and more, and at a yet more detailed level tribal rivalries within these communities), the last thing American policy would want to do is to facilitate uniting all the passions of these divisions on America as the root of all problems in the Muslim world. So there would appear to be a considerable burden on claims that disengagement from Iraq would make the problem of jihadist terrorism worse.

But turn now to the S-diagram (p. 72). The NSNX equilibrium is presented as $WS' = G'$ (instead of $W = G'/S'$), with one curve in the figure showing $WS'$ as it varies with the fraction of a community participating, and the other showing $G'$. Where $WS'$ is above $G'$ the marginal person will avoid contributing to the cause at issue (here jihadism), and the opposite where $G'$ is above $WS'$. The pair of NSNX rules introduced in Chapter 1 follow from a simple Darwinian argument. The NSNX equilibrium condition follows from the pair of rules. The S-diagram follows from the NSNX equilibrium. I will come to cognitive effects as those interact with NSNX in the next section. But the logic of the S-diagram is not contingent on any such effects. And that logic will motivate what in (Chapter 5) I introduced as *vertical* and *horizontal* tactics implicit in the diagram. Vertical tactics operate by changing the vertical relation between the curves. Horizontal tactics operate by shifting the anticipated level of participation along the horizontal axis, probably in conjunction with vertical tactics, to the right of the tipping point, with both calibrated to exploit exogenous shocks to the system.

The argument in Chapter 4 explains why the curves shown on p. 72 will have the characteristic shapes shown here, with a low equilibrium at $Q^-$, where few people are active (the *seed*) and a high equilibrium at $Q^+$ where many are participating, and a tipping point at $t$. Agents in the seed will want to find some way to shift expected participation as far as $t$, beyond which the social situation will tip to a high participation equilibrium at $Q^+$. The logic of the diagram captures the incentive of agents in the seed to seek to push the WS′ down or the G′ curve up and the opposing interest of agents who want to discourage whatever sort of cooperation is at issue. I have tried to give some sense of the dynamics by the contrast between Figures 5.1. and 5.2 (p. 72), where you can see what happens if indeed the WS′ curve could be shifted down relative to the G′ curve. The seed (core of committed supporters) at the left of $Q^-$ would expand, the *hump* that must be overcome to reach the tipping point would be deflated, the tipping point would move to the left, the *cushion* that would secure a new social equilibrium at $Q^+$ would fatten.

In Chapter 5, and then in the prior discussion here in the particular context of jihadism, I sketched something of what activists would want to do to shift W, or G′ or S′ in ways they would wish (vertical tactics). Now consider the three horizontal tactics identified in Chapter 5, which were *top-down*, *segment & coalesce*, and *intensity/prevalence tradeoffs*.

If the status quo can be moved to any point beyond the tipping point, movement all the way to the high participation equilibrium then follows. So if a credible voice can be found to assert that we are beyond the tipping point that becomes a self-fulfilling assertion. A simple example is when we are told that as of 2 am tonight we will be on daylight saving time. Even if you happen to object to daylight saving time, it is extremely likely that you will conform anyway. A grand historical example was when Constantine announced that his empire was Christian. A vastly smaller but important example was the Montgomery bus boycott, where timing of the announcement of a boycott was shrewdly judged and consequences obtained out of all proportion with the scale but not the aspirations of this peaceful insurrection. Constantine could threaten terrible consequences for anyone who defied his edict. The black leaders in Montgomery could overtly threaten no one. But the ability to coordinate by a credible announcement of what was to happen was powerful.

And the internet allows worldwide announcement and worldwide publication of specifics of what is to happen. In circumstances more dire than any currently in sight, it could be an important possibility, and adds weight to risks entailed (or reduced) by US choices that magnify or reduce adverse perceptions of American actions and policies. Attention has been focused on risks of major terrorist attacks, which require careful planning and coordination across a dedicated group. But another tactic certainly capable of killing many Americans in a spectacular way requires only random murder of

Americans around the world in some identifiable way, coordinated by inter-net instruction of what to do (including how to reduce risk to self, S′) and when to act, broadcast to potential self-appointed agents worldwide. Percep-tions of the social value (G′) of punishing Americans would make the differ-ence between such a call to action being self-defeating or appallingly successful.

*Segment & coalesce* arises as a tactic because a tipping point that is wholly out of reach on a large scale might not be out of reach on a small scale in a particularly favorable context. Indeed the Montgomery bus boycott which just provided an example of *top-down* tactics on its local scale also provides an example of *segment & coalesce* tactics on a national scale. The S-diagram for the large-scale context would have a tiny seed and a huge hump, but in a favorable small-scale context there may be no insurmountable problem in reaching an effective level of cooperation. Examples used in Chapter 5 were the origins of national labor unions (from especially favorable local situ-ations) or spread of a new religion (where Constantine's *top-down* choice could only come after considerable Christian success with *segment & coalesce* tactics). New norms or social practice usually follow that route, with recent examples being recycling and smoking bans in restaurants. Successful local ventures become mutually reinforcing, provide advice and perhaps resources and an example of success to other local situations, and eventually may coalesce into larger scale cooperation. This is obviously happening for terror-ist cells, commonly discussed under the label of "franchising," but mislead-ingly since there need be no central entity organizing or sanctioning the "franchises." Indeed, from the chilling discussion in Bruce Hoffman's (2006) analysis of "religion and terrorism," we no doubt would find some sorts of cooperation via the internet that engage groups whose aims are not merely orthogonal but violently incompatible. People who would kill each other had they the opportunity may be cooperating to kill other people, and the cooperation need not even always be unwitting.

*Prevalence/intensity tradeoffs*: the S-diagram is not fixed even within a given context, since the diagram treats the commitment required of a cooperator as given. But clearly that is not so. Cooperators can be asked to do a lot or asked to do very little. A situation in which an impossible hump must be traversed to secure a basic shift in the social equilibrium may be transformed into a manageable context if the commitment required of cooperators is made smaller. As shown in Chapter 5, G′/S′ will typically increase as S′ is reduced even though in order to reduce S′, G′ (the social valued increment obtained from a cooperator's private sacrifice) also must be reduced. Cutting the material private cost in half will typically cut the private utility cost by more than half. The situation motivating attention to the *prevalence/intensity tradeoffs* in Chapter 5 was that of getting past a tipping point by making cooperation easy and then increasing what was being asked of cooperators in that far more favorable context. With a high level of participation in place, social conformity and other considerations spelled out in Chapter 5 would favor rather than inhibit cooperation. The term most likely to be used by activists is "consciousness-raising" or some equivalent, which engages widespread participation at a minimal level and gradually escalates the commitment. Even without ever reaching a very high level, that may nevertheless provide the level of background support needed for Mao's sea to swim in.

But the *prevalence/intensity tradeoff* is also very relevant to the recruitment process of deeply engaged terrorists, who may find recruits who are willing volunteers without this sort of transitioning too untested, unstable, untrustworthy, or unskilled to be the people really needed.

Heterogeneity across people who might be sympathetic to jihadism complicates matters for both terrorists and counter-terrorists. Across vast numbers of people there will be many individuals for whom what seems to be low risk collaboration is a consumption good, allowing participation in some large, mysterious, or otherwise intriguing secret life, perhaps far more interesting than their routine existence. $S'$ is then negative, so that minimally positive $G'$ is enough to attract their interest. Indeed, such a person has positive motivation to come to believe what if believed opens this new dimension to him. On the other hand, the hard to detect character of communication on the internet should make it possible to recruit some such people into counter-terrorist surveillance if $G'$ for jihadist activity seemed even minimally negative, as might occur in very different ways, in particular from revulsion against extreme tactics or due to splintering and rivalries within the terrorist camp.

And here is a concluding conjecture on a related topic. A real puzzle exists about how the Bush Administration could have so absolutely misjudged the difficulty of the Iraq campaign. Pre-war planning at the highest level, a small library of accounts by now makes clear, prepared for essentially *nothing*! It assumed a smooth transition to a pro-American, American-style democracy. Iraq would be like conquered Germany and Japan, which indeed became pro-American democracies. And a leader in exile would come from London and be accepted as the natural leader of the country.

These are staggering things to assume with such confidence as to simply neglect contrary considerations. But in earlier chapters we considered an argument about how what I labeled adverse defaulting might account for neglecting what it would logically seem nonsensical to neglect. An then we repeatedly saw laboratory games in which intelligent subjects indeed neglected essential information that is right in front of them. Highly intelligent subjects looking right at information relevant to their choice sometimes act as if they do not see it, as the most senior officials in this case act as if unaware that the Sunnis, Shiites, and Kurds in Iraq might have difficulty cooperating, or as if the model of post-war Germany and Japan were unproblematical and the very different case of post-Tito Yugoslavia were irrelevant, or as if Ahmed Chalabi's standing in Iraq in 2003 would be like De Gaulle's standing in France in 1945. Any sign that the key decision-makers were troubled by potential difficulties seems to be invisible.

A point of agreement across all accounts of the matter is that there was, at the heart of American policy, essentially no post-war planning at all, generating accounts with titles like Ricks' *Fiasco* (2006) and Isikoff and Corn's *Hubris* (2006). There is nothing that seriously challenges the appalling lack of foresight these authors and many others have reported. The State Department engaged in elaborate planning exercises, but the Defense Department was put entirely in charge and ignored anything the State Department had to offer. Yet the most senior officials who did this all knew something about Iraq from close connections to the White House at the time of the first Gulf War. Indeed, Vice-President Cheney had been Secretary of Defense. It was as if the critical figures (Bush, Cheney, Rumsfeld) neglected to notice what might cause difficulties though many people were warning of that, including the Secretary of State. It is hard to find any evidence that the possibility of difficulties was ever treated seriously, so that even if a risky venture was judged worth the gamble, precautions would have been put in place to ease the gamble. But there seems to have been nothing. The results have been terrible, including terrible results for the Bush presidency. How could that possibly happen?

In terms of the NSNX cascade interacting with neglect defaults (points 3 and 4 of this chapter's opening discussion) it as if the situation was framed as an easy matter of coordination rather than as a very difficult case of risky cooperation.

All this is hard to believe. But it happened. Absent the now extensive indications that it happened, no one would believe that the post-war dangers in Iraq could have been so completely neglected. But there are historical parallels, such as Stalin's utter neglect of repeated warnings of Hitler's impending attack. There is a much closer parallel as well. How could Saddam remain confident that the invasion so clearly on the horizon would not come? Saddam's explanation (to Charles Duelfer, who headed the US post-war search for Saddam's terror weapons) of why he wanted to leave people thinking he had the weapons is convincing.[2] But it becomes incredible that he would continue to hold to that as indications that the invasion was coming became unmistakable to, apparently, everyone in the world except Saddam.

The circumstances under which such an extreme case of neglect defaulting can occur warrant attention, since it is hard to deny that what has actually occurred in the past could possibly occur again. So it would be worth some effort to look carefully into the record with this outlandish possibility in mind. Note especially that the puzzle is not that the key figures, determined to proceed, did not want complications that might interfere put in their way. That would imply that they were aware of what was readily in sight but as a matter of tactics did not want to acknowledge it. But if that was the situation they would have wanted care to be taken about minimizing a risk, even if they did not want that risk visibly on the table. But on the record they did not see the risk, however clearly the logic of the situation should have alerted them.

And an element worth flagging is tied to the issue of social illusions developed in Chapter 10. What about the choices of subordinates who lacked the zeal of the principals? At least some such people must have found the process disturbing. But they might have assumed that their concerns were certainly getting attention elsewhere, and anyway what could they do alone that would turn the process another way, and at what cost to their standing within the Administration? But, to make one final use of the NSNX formalism, if others might already be onto the difficulties (so perhaps your voice was not needed), or making noise was not likely to do any good (so your voice would make no difference), and in either case at considerable career risk, then G′ for raising the warning flag would be reduced and S′ for annoying superiors might be high, and noticing that no one else was speaking out would make W higher, so that just quietly hoping for the best might seem as much as a prudent person would do.

The case cries out for the sort of post mortem Richard Neustadt (1983, 1999) provided to Kennedy for the Skybolt fiasco and to Johnson on the Swine Flu fiascos, neither remotely so damaging as this case has proved to be.

# Appendix 1: Notes on the template

To handle the data solicited from experimenters, I gradually built up a "template" for storing the characteristics and results of experiments and for running across-experiments analysis. A routine called "takedata" extracts, codes and compactly stores the experiment characteristics, parameters and results. The software is intended to then search across datasets stored to find suitable experiments for a test, then searches within the chosen datasets for particular situations which may be of interest. But since I was motivated to do only as much as I needed for my own project, things are in an incomplete state. But enough is in hand to show an interested reader how all that can work.

The tests currently coded are prompted by the NSNX model of choice which is the focus of my own interest. But the template is not intrinsically tied to NSNX. It always starts by retrieving a stored vector which codes for the type of experiment and for the particular parameters in play. It then can compile the relevant data into several multi-dimensional abstract arrays. A user with the modest familiarity with coding required to write simple nested loops will then be able define routines which will run through the arrays to test whatever theories they wish to explore.

For a single experiment the basic array is 4-dimensional (GRP × RD × ID × TESTDATA). In its current state, the final dimension of the 4D array contains: (a) the choice for that GRP × RD × ID, (b) the ratio between the choice and the average of others choices for that GRP × RD, and (c) the ratio of player's payoff to her starting endowment for that round. A supplementary 3D array contains (in its third dimension) the pool and the standard deviation for each GRP × RD. For particular tests these basic arrays can be extended to hold additional numbers in their final dimension, such as penalties imposed by some players on others. Tests that run across multiple experiments require a fifth dimension (XP × GRP × RD × ID × TESTDATA). For a 4D array it is easy to envision the array as a 3D grid with a sequence of numbers within each 3D cell. For fifth or higher order arrays this intuition is lost, but of course the mechanics of handling the data remain trivial for the computer.

A minor but significant use for the template is simply to be able to efficiently locate within what could gradually become a very large repertoire of stored datasets an experiment or two that have some characteristic(s) a person finds reason to want to examine closely, for example in preparation for running an experiment on similar or related lines, or that a person recalls but not with enough specificity to easily locate it.

But the *template* has a more ambitious potential for creating what I'll call "pseudo-natural experiments": so-called because the raw material for the experiments I have in mind arises not in actual natural settings but fortuitously in the course of experiments. The template will be able to scan quickly over a large repertoire of raw data from many experiments, picking out situations which only occasionally and unpredictably arise in an actual experiment, but which are bound to be found many times in a large repertoire of datasets. So we have a statistically meaningful basis for distinguishing (to mention a salient example) situations which strongly prompt reciprocal behavior from others – within the same or interestingly related sorts of experiments – where reciprocity falls far short of what common experience and systematic study by social psychologists would lead us to expect. And if we are exploring a model with some analytical bite – of course that is what I want to claim for NSNX but also what people interested in other models must want to claim as well – we will be prompted by the model as to what sorts of comparison situations are likely to prove especially fruitful, or especially challenging or both.

As with the "reciprocity" issue, many other questions are currently in sight (the stability of "types", the conditions for pareto-damaging indifference aversion, the conditions for marked inequality indifference or the lack of it, conditions which make "cheap talk" highly effective or not so, and so on). And no doubt as these issues are clarified, deeper or less transparent questions will surface.

An important, not controversial but often neglected point here turns on the striking propensity *and* also the striking ability of human beings to concoct some sort of story to justify not believing unwelcome evidence and uncritically accepting agreeable evidence. Overcoming the tendency in either direction usually requires finding an effect repeatedly in different places, in different ways. Single pieces of evidence blunt enough and reliable enough to persuade are rare. What is usually needed is multiple pieces of evidence supporting the same inference . . . as indeed it ought to be, since any single piece of evidence might prove to be misleading. A great merit, I think, of the *template* is that it will greatly facilitate constructing tests that reinforce sound claims and embarrass faulty claims.

Since the NSNX account I am exploring is out of the mainstream, the need for multiple evidence is especially acute for me. That is probably why I was especially motivated to work up this kind of software. But from the absence (so far as I know) of any papers that survey *data* across more than a handful of experiments (*not* just results, as in most literature reviews), apparently software of the sort I have been constructing has not been worked on by others. But it ought to be.

Developing the template on a lone wolf basis would hardly be sensible. Readers here are unlikely to need instruction on the interactions of individual incentives and public goods. The template as it stands can quickly take up and compactly store data, parameters and subsidiary features of experimental data (rewards, exclusion, heterogeneous endowments, etc.), and then search across its repertoire to compile test arrays meeting prescribed conditions. It provides a running start for developing things further, either from this start in hand or perhaps starting from scratch but with a trial run at hand.

My coding is in VBA/Excel which would need to be made compatible with Z-tree software.

But the template as it stands is organized to set up a very small number (perhaps just one) multi-dimensional array on which some test is run. Running a search requires only responses to ordinary language pop-up prompts.

The (usually 5-dimensional) VBA test array can be saved as a one-dimensional CSV (comma-separated-variables) file, then directly operated on by whatever machinery the user customarily uses, given that the row of numbers in the CSV is organized in a predetermined way, so that serial position in the row implies whatever else the user needs to know.

On the FOSS model, perhaps there need be no centralized entity doing this.

The most obvious things that need to be done seem to be: (1) editing of my surely idiosyncratic and amateurish coding by someone with real competence at this sort of thing; (2) extension of my notes and comments within the coding to an adequate User's Guide; (3) extension of the "takedata" coding to intermesh easily with the Z-tree software commonly used to run choice experiments. This last is what is needed to make the template really useful and really easily used. It could not be difficult to do. But it requires participation by one or more people interested in the project and intimately familiar with the Z-tree coding.

A reader interested in exploring what use she might make of the template can download a copy (which would include a "starter" set of data from nearly 100 experiments) from the Harris School website, or download the Working Paper version of this Appendix, which provides a printout of the coding.

# Appendix 2: QRE and NSNX

*While this book was in press the American Political Science Review published an account of turnout in large elections as explained by a tremble (quantal response) which prompts "highly but not perfectly" rational voters away from abstention even if millions of others are voting (Levine and Palfrey 2007 [LP]). This relates directly to the "rationality of voting" issue taken up here in Chapter 2, and in a broader way to the more fundamental question of whether a departure from standard theory as marked as the NSNX dual utilities is warranted. For while this prominently-discussed quantal response equilibrium (QRE) looks more like the standard model than does NSNX, it requires at least as radical a departure. Agents responding in this way are no longer maximizing utility, even after allowing for known behavioral departures from strict rational choice. I note several reasons to doubt that the extrapolation from apparently quantal responses in the LP voting experiment to millions of voters could be right. But the extrapolation raises the more general issue of how far the success of QRE, in often achieving better fits to data than Nash, in fact goes deeper than achieving, ex post, a better fit. In particular, I note why the basic QRE equation would substantially mirror departures from Nash under various recognizable conditions—of which the most important would be the mirroring of NSNX choice in a context that might elicit cooperative behavior. I specify an experiment which would cleanly distinguish between actual QRE effects and NSNX effects in a variant of the LP voting game.*

Even a very generous estimate of the private value of changing the outcome of a large election, discounted by even a generous estimate of the probability that one vote will change the outcome, makes the expected private value of bothering to vote some small fraction of a penny. So it is a puzzle, discussed at least since Downs (1957), to account for why a large fraction of the electorate (commonly upward of 50 percent) bothers to vote. On standard rational choice modeling, the fraction should be close to zero.

Nor, as already discussed in Chapter 2, does the puzzle disappear merely by allowing for more than the private value. We can postulate a duty to vote, or a consumption value in voting, and assume that sufficient to make the net cost of voting 0 or even less than 0. That very simply solves the formal problem, but not in a way that many have found satisfying. Rather, as Levine and Palfrey stress in the article which prompts this note, it looks like just an ad hoc rationalization. Or we could suppose that voters respond not just to the private value of changing the outcome but to their sense of the social value. Now the effect can be really large – quite easily billions rather than (at most) thousands of dollars. But if we make plausible estimates of how much voters would ordinarily be personally willing to pay to secure those huge social gains (but discount that by the chance of being pivotal) then, even if the standard model is enlarged to allow for social motivation, the numbers again fall far short of what is needed to account for half or more of potential voters taking the trouble to vote in a very large election. All this reviews the discussion earlier in Chapter 2.

LP offer a surprising resolution, turning on a particular account (quantal response equilibrium: QRE) of what can happen if voters are very rational but not perfectly rational. On their account the cost of voting is indeed much larger than the private gain discounted by the chance the vote will be pivotal, and voters know that. Voters do not greatly overestimate either their chance of being pivotal, or the private value they would gain if that happened. But on the LP account about half will vote anyway. Voters respond with a sort of tremble, as if choosing between identical candy bars for $2 or $1 they would sometimes – perhaps almost half the time – pay $2. So Levine and Palfrey follow the standard view that if citizens were *perfectly* rational, turnout in an election with millions of potential voters would be close to zero. But they conclude that citizens who are highly but not *perfectly* rational might be about as likely as not to tremble and vote anyway. "QRE effectively resolves the 'paradox'," they write, "without the addition of utility terms such as citizen duty or other ad hoc rationalizations. That is, *substantial turnout in large elections is consistent with equilibrium behavior of highly (but not perfectly) rational voters*". [LP, p. 155, their emphasis]. This is either a very remarkable counter-intuitive result or a demonstration that something is awry in the QRE analysis.

QRE has received a good deal of attention since it was introduced by McKelvey and Palfrey (1995), and the paradox of rational voting is easily the most extensively-discussed puzzle in rational choice theory. So the claim warrants attention. I have the extra motivation that if other-regarding motivation comes in the particular form I have labeled NSNX, it is not hard at all to account for the propensity to vote in a large election, as discussed in Chapter 2. So QRE and NSNX provide alternative resolutions of this long-standing puzzle. In a sense NSNX and QRE are on the same page here. It is hard to accept the NSNX dual-utilities. But it is also hard to accept that plausibly rational citizens choose to vote not because their preferences are such that they see that as a sensible choice but because of some ungovernable tremble.

In the Levine and Palfrey voting game, a player learns whether she is in the majority or minority party for the upcoming round, and she is also assigned a cost of voting in this round in the form of a bonus which she gets if she does *not* vote. The bonus is randomly chosen from the integers [0,1,2, . . . 55]. A player knows how many majority and minority players are in the game. But she does not know the random assignment of cost to anyone but herself. If she votes, she forfeits her bonus but gains a chance to change the result of the vote. So she faces competing incentives. Each member of the winning side in the vote gets 105 and each loser gets 5. If there is a tie, everyone gets 55. So a pivotal vote (turning a 1-vote loss into a tie, or a tie into a 1-vote win) gains 50. But unless the situation without her vote is pivotal (her party is one vote behind or both parties are tied) then she has forfeited her bonus for no gain.

If the number of other players who in fact vote were known, then a voter would know which of these possibilities (make a tie or break a tie) is actually a possibility in the current round. But either way, a pivot offers the same 50-point gain. A risk-neutral, self-interested player who knows the probability of being pivotal (p), has an incentive to vote only if 50p exceed his bonus for this round. Maximizing own-payoff turns on correctly balancing the sure cost of voting (forfeit of the bonus) against the player's judgment of the chance of being pivotal. LP ran variants of this game with 3, 9, 27 and 51 players, divided (except for N = 3 where there is no difference) either as equally as possible or giving one side a 2–1 advantage. A player faces 50 trials of one of these games with a bare majority, and also (except for N = 3) 50 trials in the same group size but with a 2–1 majority, always with a new random assignment in each round to majority or minority and a new randomly assigned bonus for not voting.

Even in the smallest (three-player) game, assessing $\pi$ would be complicated. A player must judge that without knowing the bonus assignments to other players, and contingent on how far others might be risk-neutral and self-interested choosers or something else. A reader of this note will be far better prepared to assess the situation than a typical subject. Unless you find this pretty easy to do, you should expect subjects to make many errors (even for the simplest N = 3 case) relative to ideal rational actors with unlimited computational resource, as indeed they do. But some 30,000 individual choices were accumulated, and while individual play is erratic, LP found that averaged across players, the Nash comparative statics inferences were very nicely matched by the data. But as will be considered in more detail in a moment, there are striking quantitative discrepancies even though (as LP stress) the comparative statics inferences across conditions almost always come out as they should.

LP then re-analyze the data in terms of the quantal response equilibrium (QRE) introduced by McKelvey and Palfrey (1995). QRE has an impressive record of improving on Nash equilibrium results where Nash goes astray (Goeree and Holt 2005), and it does so again in the voting game. See Table A1, where QRE improves on Nash in 12 cases out of 14. But the significance of the improved fit as against a conventional treatment is difficult to assess (Haile *et al.* 2006). This is partly because QRE uses projections fit to a parameter ($\lambda$) which is derived from the data. But difficulty in interpreting the improved fit also comes for other reasons which I will come to. Nevertheless, as Goeree and Holt (2005) show, it is clear across a range of experimental games that QRE does better, and sometimes very impressively better, than standard Nash. QRE often does well when Nash fails catastrophically.

Following LP, set c = (cost of voting)/(gain if pivotal) and $\pi$ = pivot probability. On a standard choice model, a player would want to vote if $c/\pi > 1$. But QRE choice introduces the propensity to tremble governed by the QRE parameter $\lambda$. The probability of voting (from LP (2007), p. 154) is given by:

$$p(c, \pi, \lambda) = \frac{1}{1 + e^{\lambda(c - \pi)}} \tag{1}$$

where within the experiment $c$ is the player's normalized cost in the current round (cost divided by 50, giving the ratio between the bonus forgone if she votes and the gain if she votes and her vote turns out to be pivotal). The voter knows this ratio. But $\pi$ is a voter's subjective assessment of the pivot probability in this round, about which she can do no better than to make a partially informed guess. $\lambda$ is the parameter aggregated from all the data by the experimenters, which is wholly unknown to a player but taken to be a common influence on all players.

From the equation you can see that in the limiting case of $\lambda = 0$, p is always 0.5. For $\lambda = \infty$, p = 1 if c − $\pi$ is negative and p = 0 if c − $\pi$ is positive. At this extreme, QRE yields the same result as a simple expected value response. But in between QRE makes a difference. LP take the improved fit of the equation to the experimental data (Table A.1) to warrant extrapolating the quantal responses to choice in large elections. Then, unless $\lambda$ is very radically different for the large election case, the LP resolution of the paradox of voting follows immediately. In a very large election c must be very small, but $\pi$ is far smaller yet, so that c − $\pi \approx$ c. But unless $\lambda$ is vastly higher than in their experiment (they propose 100 as about as high as it could credibly be), then the QRE equation yields a probability of voting that moves arbitrarily close to 0.5 as c − $\pi$ remains positive but grows arbitrarily small.

*Table A.1* Participation (Levine and Palfrey (2007), Table 3)

| N | Min. | Data | Nash | QRE | Maj. | Data | Nash | QRE |
|---|---|---|---|---|---|---|---|---|
| 3 | 1 | 0.530 | 0.537 | 0.549 | 2 | 0.593 | 0.640 | 0.616 |
| 9 | 3 | 0.436 | 0.413 | 0.421 | 6 | 0.398 | 0.375 | 0.395 |
| 9 | 4 | 0.479 | 0.460 | 0.468 | 5 | 0.451 | 0.452 | 0.463 |
| 27 | 9 | 0.377 | 0.270 | 0.297 | 18 | 0.282 | 0.228 | 0.275 |
| 27 | 13 | 0.385 | 0.302 | 0.348 | 14 | 0.356 | 0.297 | 0.345 |
| 51 | 17 | 0.333 | 0.205 | 0.245 | 34 | 0.266 | 0.171 | 0.230 |
| 51 | 25 | 0.390 | 0.238 | 0.301 | 26 | 0.362 | 0.235 | 0.300 |

However, this extrapolation looks implausible. In the game, whether voting or abstaining would be the better choice is often a close question. With a random cost from [0,1,2, . . . 55] the average cost is 27.5, the gain-if-pivotal is always 50, and with the LP electorates of 3, 9, 27 or at most 51 the chance that a vote would turn out to be pivotal is never trivial. Indeed for N = 3, at least one player will be pivotal over 80 percent of the time, since the only N = 3 case where no player is pivotal would be when both majority players vote and the single minority player abstains. But with the cost of voting changing from round to round and the other complications mentioned earlier, even a player who was an accomplished game theorist, and even for the simples (N = 3) case, but here needing to make choices quickly (a player has to get though 100 rounds in about 30 minutes of decision time) would often be uncertain about what to do. The individual choice data, which is very noisy, reflects that.

In a very large actual election, however, while both c and π would be far smaller than in this game, they would not be at all comparably smaller. For plausible values (LP agree with the usual view here) π, which can easily be comparable to c in the game, would become far smaller than c. In their extrapolation, LP themselves, consistent with that usual view, treat c − π ≈ c. Hence unless λ is *very* much larger than the "7" LP estimate from their data, λ·c will be very small, hence $e^{\lambda c}$ would be very close to 1, making the probability of voting close to 0.5. The size of the electorate becomes irrelevant. Millions of voters give essentially the same result as billions or trillions. LP's "highly (but not perfectly) rational voters" behave about the same as completely irrational voters who just choose at random whether or not to vote.

So this is the LP result. Mathematically it could hardly be simpler. But pragmatically it could hardly be more surprising, since why would we believe that error patterns that describe the computationally difficult choices in the experiment would also be characteristic of errors in a very large election, where the choice for someone concerned only to maximize own-payoff is starkly obvious? We are moving from a context where seeing what choice would be optimal is really difficult (LP themselves can only locate equilibrium responses with extensive computer assistance) to a context in which everyone who thinks about the issue for a moment sees that the private payoff, once discounted by the probability of being pivotal, is inconsequential. In the game there is extensive overlap between the cost of a vote and its expected value, as against a large election where even a tiny cost of voting could not get anywhere near the expected private value. LP do not disagree. As already mentioned, in their large election extrapolation (LP, equation 11, p. 155) they set c − π = c.

Elaborating on this result leads to further puzzles. On the QRE account, voters see that this is a choice with negative expectation but half the electorate nevertheless are caught by a random tremble which makes them vote anyway. If this were so, a citizen who trembles into voting today would not be particularly likely to tremble the same way in the next election. So there would be little serial correlation of who votes across elections. But such serial correlation is perhaps the least disputed point about voter behavior. On the other hand, if the tremble was *not* random across voters but systematic, then we presumably would find that it is more sophisticated voters who are less likely to be caught by the tremble. This suggests that well-educated citizens should be less likely to vote than poorly educated, which is also unambiguously false.

More simply, if the QRE equation captured actual voter choice there would be a strict upper bound on voter participation of 0.5. But on the QRE logic what is relevant is not the total number of legally qualified voters, but the number of possible voters on election day: i.e., registered voters. In 2004, the U.S. Census Bureau reports (www.census.gov/prod/2006pubs/p20-556.pdf), almost 90 percent of registered voters voted. And similar or higher numbers can be found in other countries. In the 2007 French presidential election 84 percent of all eligible citizens voted. So the QRE upper bound is often exceeded in actual elections, and by a large amount. Turnout is often closer to 100 percent of potential voters than to the QRE upper bound.

But return to the question of what to make of the well-documented success of QRE in accounting for the major discrepancies which frequently occur between data from experimental games and Nash equilibrium. In the voting game at hand, how strong is the case that quantal responses are in fact governing choices, which is the foundation for the bolder result about actual elections? No one supposes that subjects in the game are somehow intuiting the correct Nash equilibrium response and then responding with a random tremble away from that, and even less that subjects are intuiting a quantal response equilibrium and trembling away from *that*. Rather, everyone will agree, indeed Nash himself remarked in his original work half a century ago, we should be thinking of some behavioral account which, over the sequence of choices in the experiment, yields data that on average are closer to QRE than to Nash. So there is a question of what QRE adds to a behavioral account, and also a question of how that works.

The simplest behavioral account of the voting game would be that subjects start from a sense of "just guess," with implicit $p \approx 0.5$, and adjust from this anchor in commonsense ways. As the number of players grows, everyday intuitions about the chance of a tie vote must decline, as would a formal calculation (e.g., Margolis 1977), increasing the incentive to abstain. Even more obviously, as the cost of voting goes up, abstention must go up. And player responses will be influenced by the tendency to start from the simplest assumption about participation, which would be that minority and majority players vote with equal probability. But the chance that you will be pivotal because your party would otherwise lose by one vote is not quite the same. If participation were the same for both parties, the minority party is more likely to find itself one vote short than the majority. So the chance that the count will end up with your side one vote behind will be more salient if you are in the minority, which would increase the relative propensity to vote within the underdog party. The two certain points plus the weaker third point would yield the comparative statics results LP report.

With trial and error learning over 100 rounds of a pair of very similar games, the Nash fit to the comparative statics results does not appear to be better than what someone who had never heard of Nash equilibrium would be likely to guess from the "anchor and adjust" behavioral model. Nevertheless, the Nash calculations in Table A1 give us numbers which can tells us important things, and they can do that even when they do not agree with observations, as calculations of how prices and quantities would vary in perfect markets contribute to understanding what might be influencing sometimes very different results in an actual market.

The qualitative success of Nash is almost complete, but the quantitative misses are also striking. Nash calculations yield projected participation which is very nearly right for the minority in the N = 3 case (Table A1), but not for the majority with N = 3, where participation is clearly below the Nash projection. For the largest LP cases, Nash misses in the other direction, and more severely. For both majority and minority parties in the N = 27 cases Nash is clearly too low. And Nash misses quite dramatically on the low side for the N = 51 cases.

Another puzzle concerns the "underdog" effect. For the closely-divided cases, this effect should be slight for N = 9, very slight for N = 27, and almost invisible for N = 51. Both Nash and QRE project it that way. But the data fail to obey, keeping to a roughly constant and never trivial difference as we move from N = 9 to 27 to 51.

But whatever the resolution of these quantitative puzzles, from Table A1 it is clear that QRE alters equilibrium participation in these games in ways that almost always improves on Nash. How that happens warrants attention. QRE was designed by psychologists exploring how perceptual accuracy degrades as lighting fades, noise increases, and so on. Extending this to contexts where the signal is unambiguous but choice is difficult due to strategic uncertainty is a bold move, but as mentioned earlier, QRE has in fact repeatedly shown marked improvements over Nash. Given an additional free parameter it is not surprising that QRE yields something of a better fit to data than without it. But QRE clearly does more than can be explained solely by the advantage of the free parameter. How QRE does this is puzzling, since taken as a description of what players are really doing, QRE requires responses governed by a parameter derived ex post from the data, anchored on the equilibrium choices that would occur if everyone knew that everyone else was trembling in that way and could anticipate what equilibrium behavior would result. And then, having somehow intuited this, each player then herself trembles *away* from her payoff-maximizing response. If this is what is happening it seems a mystery how it could be happening and also a mystery why it would be happening even if it could.

So to take QRE as a literal description of what players are doing is hard, and its advocates have never claimed that. Even for Nash, no one supposes that players are performing some functional equivalent of Nash calculations. But over a sequence of trials, and averaging across many players, it is not hard to believe that the anchor-and-adjust behavioral model leads toward Nash . . . or would lead that way unless something other than own-payoff maximizing was shaping preferences. But QRE looks a good deal more difficult. Players choose as if they are smart or sensitive or intuitive enough to sense the QRE choices of other players and how those choices would interact, but then tremble away from payoff-maximizing responses to that. How could that happen? Although it is not generally true that QRE earnings are lower than if players could control their trembles (I will shortly introduce two examples where players profit if they *mutually* follow QRE rather than Nash), in the LP voting games they mostly get worse payoffs than Nash implies rational players would get either individually or collectively, so that learning over the 100 rounds would not explain how QRE gets its result. LP found payoff-improving learning over their many trials, but it falls well short of enough to characterize play as payoff-maximizing.

So, again, we have the question of why does QRE work? In any game where choice is subject to uncertainty but risk is asymmetrical, it is easy to see why QRE, which biases noisy choice in favor of less risky own-payoff, should do better than unadorned Nash, though not necessarily significantly better than Nash allowing for an asymmetrical error term. But QRE has also yielded projections "as if" QRE were in play even when own-payoff asymmetry is not at hand. Through the $\lambda$ term in the exponential in Equation 1, the QRE tremble has a social character. If there is asymmetrical risk this shared propensity would be present even in a context with no strategic interactions. If we are playing a golf hole with a lateral hazard on the left, everyone will play a little to the right. Nash, if it neglected this detail would recommend aiming right at the hole, and in this artificial example QRE would improve on naïve Nash (Nash that neglects to notice that players have an incentive to aim to the right of the hole) by building in a propensity for errors to lean to the right. Everyone trembles, $\lambda$ in Equation 1 governs how much, and the cost variable ($c - \pi$ in Equation 1) will bias the tremble in the sensible direction if the risk is asymmetric. And if all the players were about equally good, a single value of $\lambda$ for all players would work well.

But QRE has also been used, as in the LP context here, where "errors" (I hope it is apparent why I have begun to use scare quotes) might have a more clearly *social* character. This occurs when the situation is one where everyone would be better off if everyone would "err" (relative to standard Nash) in the direction that yields a better social outcome. Every chooser trembles, though each chooser could do better (given what others are choosing) by not trembling. In that sort of context $\lambda$ might be social not just in the sense that it can be taken as common to all players (as in the golf example) but in the deeper sense that it is capturing a propensity for conditional cooperation. The social component intrinsic to QRE need not be socially benign. It might be socially neutral and just a shared propensity shaped by purely individual motives in the context. In some contexts it might be socially perverse, making everyone worse off by some important measure, as in a zero-sum or wartime context. But it ordinarily cannot go against the actual tendency of the subjects since it is tuned to the data.

If the structure of the game is one that leads players to collectively undermine their own interests, QRE can reflect that. But in a context where it would be collectively advantageous to tremble, even if individually not so, λ provides a shared tendency favoring a better social outcome. But the response to own-payoff in the QRE equation reduces that propensity as the cost of cooperating increases. Together we have the tension between self-interested and cooperative choice that defines a viable model of conditionally cooperative choice. NSNX agents, in particular, lean toward choices good for the group, but subject to a "neither selfish nor exploited" equilibrium condition. These conditionally cooperative agents, in a context that evokes social cooperation, but also subject to the risk of being exploited by free-riders, might yield data which moves away from Nash in the direction that QRE will match.

Since the point is central, let me restate it. QRE treats agents as subject to a shared propensity to error relative to pure Nash. This could occur in a variety of ways. But in contexts where a propensity to cooperation would be relevant, a component of the "error" (relative to own-payoff maximizing) might not be error at all, but a reflection of real preferences by conditionally cooperative agents who respond to their sense of social value as well as self-interest. The QRE error function varies with λ, which is intrinsically social, a characteristic of the group, not of any individual within the group. But it also varies with the private cost of departing from strict self-interest. Both elements would affect the choices of NSNX agents, where the extent of a shared propensity to "err" in the cooperative direction would affect W, the value that could be achieved by enhanced cooperation would affect $G'$, and the private cost of departing from own-payoff maximizing would effect $S'$, and all jointly influencing the NSNX equilibrium at $W = G'/S'$. So in addition to cases of asymmetric risk (and sometimes overlapping them) in some perhaps fairly wide set of cases QRE might improve on Nash because QRE responses would be correlated with NSNX responses.

How does this work across a range of cases?

A generalized matching pennies game provides an example often used in discussions of QRE, but it is not easy to see how QRE does more than coincide with what would be expected without it. Call the player who wins on a match P and the player who wins on a mismatch $P'$. But the game is asymmetric. P wins 9 if both players show heads (HH), but P gets only 1 if the match is TT. $P'$ gets 0 in either case. And on either mismatch (TH or HT), $P'$ gets 1 and P gets 0, where the first choice listed is by P and the second by $P'$. In a simple matching pennies game Nash has each choosing H or T with probability 0.5, since the game is zero-sum, and if P favors heads, $P'$ will be able to exploit that by always playing tails, and the converse. The only equilibrium is where P and P′ both randomize, as by actually tossing a coin to determine the choice. But that is for the symmetric game. The game at hand is asymmetric and no longer zero-sum. But Nash equilibrium is still for P to choose H only with probability 0.5, even though he wins 9 on a match with heads and only 1 on a match with tails. For it remains the case that if P favors H, P′ can exploit that by always choosing T, and P would never see his fine result at HH.

Typical results, however, are that P favors H anyway, as QRE would predict, choosing it about 60 percent of the time, and he can do this because P′ only punishes this behavior with restraint, choosing T about 75 percent, though he would do much better if he would respond to P's propensity to mostly choose H by always choosing T. QRE anticipates that result. P trembles away from Nash. So does P′. Each player trembles, and QRE can backtrack from the data to choose λ such that a quantal response equilibrium will do well as a match with what happens.

But NSNX can give an entirely different but equivalent reading. If the players could bargain, they could do far better than Nash. P should always play H conditional on P′ agreeing to limit his exploitation of that (or, reaching the same result, P′ could always play H but P compensates P′ by sufficiently often choosing T). Either way, the socially inefficient TT combination would never occur. But here play is between anonymous subjects randomly matched from round to round with no communication or side-payments allowed. Each player can see that it is in group-interest and in each player's self-interest to settle on some tacit bargain where neither side moves too aggressively to exploit the other. For repeated trials against the same opponent strictly self-interested but sensible players would reach some rough, tacit, but mutually profitable accommodation. But since the games here involve random matching of players from round to round even modestly profitably tacit coordination requires some tendency, on average, for players to lean a bit in the direction of enlarging group-payoff. Mainstream models of other-regarding choice have difficulty managing that. But if NSNX holds, S′ would be a player's subjective sense of what it is likely to cost in own-payoff to shade responses towards a mutually advantageous departure from Nash. G′ would be the joint gain. Risk is small – indeed a player might judge (correctly) that the cost of a small departure from Nash is almost certain to favor both self-interest (he will earn more) and also group-interest (the other player will also make more). We would have S′ negative (the cost of a socially positive move is actually a gain), and G′ positive, so that since W is always positive, we must have W > G′/S′, favoring self-interest. But in this case (as discussed in Chapter 1), there is no conflict between self-interest and group-interest. Both favor departing from Nash in the same direction. As the departure grows larger, however, this will change (differently for P and P′ but an interested reader could easily work through the details), so that eventually one player or the other will back off, well short of the Pareto optimal solution they could choose if communication were allowed.

So either QRE or NSNX can account for the limited departures from Nash towards a more cooperative outcome that is the robust result in this game. But if QRE is right, subjects blunder into cooperation that as rationally self-interested choosers they would destroy if they could control their trembling. A reader might find it easier to believe that human agents exhibit NSNX propensities to "neither selfish nor exploited" cooperation than that they somehow achieve a measure of cooperation through QRE, since they are not rational enough to avoid it.

Traveler's Dilemma (Basu 1994, Capra *et al*. 1999) provides a more intricate example where again either QRE or NSNX can account for what in this case is a very sharp divergence from Nash. Here again two players interacting anonymously with different partners simultaneously make choices that jointly determine payoffs, but now in a context with a much more obvious cooperative aspect. Each player chooses a number between 80 and 200. Each receives a payoff (say in pennies) equal to the lower number chosen. But the lower choice wins a bonus which is subtracted from the higher chooser's payoff. This leads to a bizarre result for players known to be unwaveringly committed to maximizing own-payoff. No one would pick 200 since that is dominated by picking 199. But if 199 is the highest that could be picked, that would be dominated by 198, starting down a backward induction ladder which has no end short of 80, no matter how small the bonus is made. The bottom of the ladder is then the Nash equilibrium. No one is surprised that in experiments where the bonus is small players come close to the top of the payoff range, not descend to the bottom as Nash projects. But how do players escape the perverse result? Why aren't they trapped by the backwards induction logic?

QRE does very well here. With the bonus small, it costs very little to "err" relative to Nash, reporting a high number. If the other player is lower, you lose the bonus, but since the other's lower choice might be much higher than the safe Nash choice of 80, a player who chooses high and loses the bonus can easily be better off than if he had chosen low and won the bonus. So QRE correctly expects players to tremble in the direction of higher choices and obtain some high level of payoff. QRE does better than Nash in accounting for what happens, and by a wide margin.

But it is easy to give both a NSNX account, and also a behavioral account limited to maximizing own-payoff. Anyone can see that it may not make sense to risk sacrificing 120 (by choosing at the low end) to avoid the risk or even the likelihood of paying the small bonus. Sensibly choosing low really requires believing it is *almost certain* the other player will choose very low. But a player subject to bounded rationality could decide that choosing low is stupid without wrestling with how to logically avoid it. He can be very comfortable in not troubling himself trying to see if there is a way to escape the backward induction dilemma. He can cut that short at very low cost by just deciding it is not worthwhile to worry about the tiny bonus. He can write it off, choose very high, and get a very good payoff. Indeed, given the severe asymmetry in this game (choosing too low can cost a lot and never gain much, choosing high can gain a lot and never lose much) allowing some prospect for just such a behavioral departure from classical rational choice becomes the sensible choice even for a player himself immune to such effects. If the other player is even modestly likely to take the short cut, it becomes rational for both to follow it.

This is so conspicuously so that it is perhaps a small thing that NSNX motivation easily resolves the logical dilemma. G' is clearly big. S' is small even for a very high choice though there is a risk – non-trivial in this artificial context of a laboratory game – that the other player in this round could be intent on playing as if the game were zero-sum competitive: he may want to *win* even if it costs payoff to do it, as discussed in connection with the NSNX *cascade* introduced in Chapter 7. But unless a player judges such behavior to be common, the G'/S' ratio remains lop-sidedly favorable to anchoring on the maximum and even after some possible adjustment still choosing high.

But that is so in part because if NSNX governs intuition, everyone sees that everyone (or almost everyone, allowing for the atypical strictly competitive player) will lean towards the socially sensible choice of choosing high. Choosing quite high looks best for self-interest, and NSNX inclination would be to go at least a bit further to enhance group-interest. Hence allowing for conditionally cooperative, and specifically for NSNX preferences strengthens the behavioral model and in fact turns it into a formally as well as pragmatically sound account of what happens in this game. This is not merely redundant. For where does the compelling intuition that playing Nash would be foolish come from? This is fully shared even by experts in game theory, who know the backwards induction argument very well, and even when playing against other experts, so that the Nash equilibrium is truly common knowledge. But if human beings, pathological cases aside, are intrinsically conditional cooperators, as NSNX requires, then so are the subset of human beings who are game theorists. However devoted to the formal theory, they cannot easily escape the intuition that in this game, where following Nash yields a socially absurd result, that it is just not sensible to follow Nash.

But so far we have different but about equally valid (with respect to the data) QRE and NSNX accounts. Is there any reason to regard the NSNX account as *better* than QRE? In fact there is, and for a reason beyond the plausibility argument that concluded the discussion of matching pennies. QRE, tuned ex post to the data, yields a good fit to the, average player's response. But there is no average player. The average player is a mathematical fiction. And in this game we can see a distribution of choices not available in matching pennies where the choice is just H or T. That distribution of choices fits NSNX not QRE. QRE logic implies that players share a common tendency to tremble, which should show a decline in the probability of choosing a number as it gets sufficiently distant from the Nash choice of 80. NSNX, on the other hand, would expect very high choices other than by a minority of players caught by a competitive gestalt in this game with a cooperative aspect (a chance to gain 180 extra pennies each) that is huge compared to its competitive aspect (a chance to gain 5). Even the occasional player caught by the competitive gestalt introduced in Chapter 7 would be drawn upward as rounds proceed and it becomes obvious that he will gain from that.

Given this combination of effects, NSNX would then not differ sharply from QRE in how the average would behave. But the two accounts do differ sharply in what to expect in the individual data. If QRE was substantively correct actual players would mostly behave much like the average player. If NSNX were correct there would be a few competitive players (in this conspicuously favorable for cooperation context) who start well below 200 while most make choices close to 200 from the start. And what the individual data show across many replications is that a substantial fraction of players choose either 199 or 200 from the start, most others are close to that, with the average brought down by a small fraction of players who choose much lower. The resulting far from normal distribution of choices should not happen if QRE were correctly describing individual choice. For a survey across many replications see Basu (2007).

So in the way already reviewed in connection with the LP extrapolation to large elections, QRE may mimic conditionally cooperative choice at the level of aggregate results, but since it is not describing what actually governs individual choice it easily yields serious discrepancies when further inferences are drawn. That happens in the individual data here, in the large election context discussed earlier, in the very robust restart effect in Public Goods games, and in a variety of other examples that can be gleaned from the earlier discussion.

But now turn back to the voting games studied by Levine and Palfrey. As has often been noticed, results in experimental games often show the effect of life beyond the lab on behavior within the lab, even when the formal logic of the experimental game conflicts with that. In the phrase of a stalwart of mainstream game theory (Ken Binmore), players are influenced by the "game of life." Players do not leave their experience in the world behind when they enter the lab. Rather, in the artificial, unfamiliar, impoverished environment of an experimental game, there can often be important effects imported from habitual experience in the world. Here responding in a more or less literal way to the lab game is likely when there are just three players, as in many parlor games, and not so easy for nine players, and perhaps not easy at all once the LP groups involve 27 or 51 players. It would become increasingly likely as the group of potential voters grows beyond anything encountered in a parlor game that player intuitions are guided by experience in dealing with actual elections in the world rather than with the payoff-maximizing play usually appropriate for a parlor game. And if so, then as with very large elections, social motivation would sustain participation as numbers grow since although the chance of a pivotal situation is going down the social value (here the number of own-party members who will benefit) is going up.

The grossest departure of the data from Nash, which is meliorated but not reversed by QRE, then has an immediate explanation. Going from N = 27 to N = 51, participation for the closely-divided LP groups actually goes opposite to the sharp decrease that players motivated only by own-payoff should reveal. Nash calculations miss that completely. QRE calculations also miss it but not by as much. LP comment that the difference between N = 27 and N = 51 participation is only insignificantly in the wrong direction. But the expected change in the predicted direction fails by some 10 standard deviations.

The LP instructions, if taken fully to heart, make socially-modulated responses inappropriate. Players are told they are randomly assigned in each round to parties (A or B), where A is always the majority, B the minority party. Logically there is no reason for loyalty to others in your group when the groups are reshuffled every round, so that anyone who happens to be voting your way in this round is as likely as not to be voting against you in the next round. But in Binmore's "game of life" that is not what happens. Party switches are rare. What is common is that our own party looks to be in the majority in some elections and in the minority in others. So players might easily miss the literal meaning of their instructions and respond to party loyalty, as they certainly do in real elections.

Choice when in the N = 3 majority invokes a social component of motivation in a different way. Now the game really looks like the parlor game it is, not a simulation of an actual election. A majority player has one partner, who is randomly changing from round to round. But for most configurations of own-choice and observed payoff it is apparent whether the partner voted. Players know the distribution of bonuses but not their partner's bonus in this round, nor the identity of the partner in this round. This makes efficient coordination hard, especially for risk averse players who respond to concern about being exploited by a free-riding partner. The two-player majority party in the N = 3 case would then easily jointly fall short of the participation that would be payoff-maximizing, which is what the data show.

Are voters in these games mostly risk averse, hence hesitant to trade a sure thing (the bonus) for the chance of being pivotal when the expected gain is small? Data from experiments routinely reveal predominant risk-aversion. But here we can directly see it, since the players who are in the majority twosomes in most N = 3 rounds are the single minority player in the remaining rounds. Their participation as single minority players is not far from the Nash projection in Table A1. But for payoff maximizers, that is too low given that the majority participation is decidedly too low. The single minority player has no group to benefit, no partner to reciprocate, hence no reason to vary from own-payoff maximizing. The single player is also always pivotal except when both majority players vote. From Table A1 you can see this chance, given actual majority participation, which is what she observes, will be almost 2/3, which against a pivotal gain of 50 implies a cutpoint of 33. With costs drawn randomly from [0,1,2, ... 55] this chance is 34/56 = 0.61. But minority participation is only 0.53, revealing significant risk-aversion.

Consequently, the decidedly big overvote (relative to Nash) in N = 27 and even greater overvote in N = 51 is especially striking. It is so strong that it overrides the risk-aversion that is apparent in the one case (the singleton party in N = 3) where it is easy to see it in this subject pool.

But odd situations aside (the "lumpy" N = 3 case here), if risk is symmetrical QRE must move participation towards 0.5, as can be seen in Table A1 for all cases except the singleton party in N = 3. With the qualification, QRE must move predicted participation up for Nash <0.5 and down for Nash >0.5, since the direct effect of Equation 1 is to take a slice of each Nash choice and move it to the alternative choice. So if the context is symmetrical (which holds here) and participation is less than 0.5, there are more "exit" than "enter" Nash votes, hence a bigger aggregate slice to be transferred away from exit (abstain) to enter (vote) than the converse. After the QRE adjustment the votes of both parties, and whether participation for either is more or less than 0.5, will tend to be closer to 0.5. A change in pivot probability changes the expected value of voting ($c - \pi$) proportionately. But the indirect effect through the change in pivot probability due to the interaction with the QRE shift in participation is ordinarily stifled before it can fully offset the direct effect.

Overall the QRE effects plainly move in the right direction in the LP experiment. But is there any causation in this correlation?

Start from a simpler case where there is a clear QRE effect but no possibility it can be attributed to incidental QRE mirroring of conditionally cooperative propensities. This is provided by a market entry game discussed in Goeree and Holt (2005). The context (Sundali *et al.* 1995) is a sharply competitive one where cooperative inclinations would be irrelevant even from players inclined to cooperation. We have a game where we should not expect players to qualify own-payoff maximizing to help the group.

But players on average make choices that depart systematically from their own-payoff best responses. The departures from Nash are slight, and indeed the game provides a case where the power of Nash projections is quite startling. But for parameter values that yield a Nash entry projection of less than 0.5, average entry slightly exceeds Nash in every case. Where the Nash projection is for entry above 5, average entry falls slightly below Nash in every case.

Goeree and Holt demonstrate (their Proposition 2) why this is what is required if QRE in fact is governing player responses in an entry game. And like the Sundali *et al.* game, the LP voting games are a variety of entry game. A player can take a guaranteed payoff (exit) or risk that payoff on the chance of gaining a bigger payoff (enter). We might, consequently, gain some insight into the how QRE is working in the LP voting games by first considering whether an interpretation of the Sundali *et al.* game is available which can account for QRE-like results even if there no actual quantal responses, and even though in this game (in contrast to LP) there is no occasion for social effects.

In Sundali, as in the Traveler's Dilemma game and matching pennies games discussed earlier, there is indeed a salient behavioral explanation of why QRE would improve on Nash. Typically about half the players in experimental games are risk-averse, about a quarter risk-neutral, and a quarter risk-loving. The presence of significant risk-prone choice in Sundali is enhanced, since the game is a lottery where the entry cost is just 15 cents at each choice. It is easy to gamble just for the fun of it if you are so inclined. The game offers a winner-take-all prize to be given to a randomly-chosen entrant. So when the prize is high, it is tempting to enter even though there could be many entrants. But at low values players would find entry unattractive even if not risk-averse. So at low values, risk aversion would be hard to see since even risk neutral players would tend to stay out. In this range, the chance for risk lovers to disproportionately affect the result is enhanced. And the converse holds for high market values, where risk averters would be atypically salient since at high payoff levels it is conspicuously risk-averters who would be likely to stay away from a tempting gamble. Together this yields effects that coincide with what would happen under QRE – for participation <0.5, QRE adjusts Nash up a bit, for participation >0.5 it goes down a bit – but for reasons which have nothing at all to do with quantal responses.

Fischbacher and Thoni (2006) report results from another entry game which provides a test of how far QRE might be capturing some subtle property of choice as against mechanically moving choices in an entry game towards 0.5. In Sundali a single winner is drawn from all entrants, with a prize that varies across rounds but is fixed within a round. In Fischbacher and Thoni, the prize increases with each entrant but at a decreasing rate, and then is divided equally among entrants. After a certain expected number (set to be about 3.5) it no longer pays to enter since the entrant's expectation is less than his expectation from just exiting. With two group sizes, 7 and 11, therefore Nash is about equal to 0.5 in the smaller group and about 0.3 in the larger. Observations are clearly above Nash for both groups. QRE succeeds with the larger group, where Nash participation is <0.5, but fails to move predicted participation towards observed participation with the smaller group, where Nash participation is already about 0.5. But that means that QRE does nothing in this game. It improves on Nash when Nash is less than 0.5 but fails to improve on Nash in the converse case, as would be expected merely from its mechanical tendency to move towards 0.5.

This point generalizes to show how clear tests can be arranged to distinguish between QRE as merely correlating with other effects under favorable conditions, as against QRE as revealing a hitherto unrecognized behavioral regularity. By selecting appropriate parameters it should be possible to design cases in which QRE would move projections away from both Nash and observations, while an alternative account predicts movement away from Nash towards observations. Here is an example that suggests a stark test of QRE versus NSNX based on a slight variant of the LP voting games. Set N = 50, with parties of equal size. Set costs that run 0 to 19 instead of 0 to 55.

Nash equilibrium with these parameters will be at 0.6. Using the LP $\lambda$ of 7, the QRE prediction will be about 0.55. From the discussion of the LP $N = 51$ game, a NSNX prediction must be clearly above Nash, perhaps 0.65. QRE and NSNX inferences cleanly separate.

# Notes

## Introduction

1 For a survey from the 1970s, see David Collard's *Altruism and Economics* (Oxford University Press, 1978).
2 On the distinction intended here between other-regarding and norm-obeying, see the set of papers from Gintis, Seabright, Ross and Binmore in *Politics, Philosophy and Economics* (2006). This also provides extended discussion of Darwinian accounts of choice beyond narrow self-interest, different from the one I will be providing here.

## Chapter 1: The NSNX model

1 For a survey, see Wilson and Sober (1998).
2 The issue here concerns actual self-interested effects on the agent making the choice, as distinguished from a fossil self-interest which might have been inherited from selection pressures relevant to life under conditions that existed many thousands of years in the past. That seems likely enough to be a component of how the social motivation of Darwin's argument could become entrenched despite the constant within-group selection favoring self-interest. But it complements rather than refutes the Darwinian argument. I provide some more detailed comments in Margolis (1998).
3 $S'$ is the finite private cost of participating, $G'$ the finite social value of the participation (each as seen by the chooser). So $G'/S'$ might be better characterized as a ratio of differentials not a derivative.
4 Suppose A might bid 300. B's best choice would then be 299. So B might gain and cannot lose by bidding 299 rather than 300. A sees this too, so that 299 is the highest either will bid. But if so, neither can lose and might gain by bidding at most 298 rather than 299. And so on.

## Chapter 5: Using the S-diagram

1 Without denying a political aspect to science, the deliberate manipulation and tactics characteristic of a political episode are not likely to come close to being matched in a scientific revolution, for reasons already reviewed in the closing discussion of Chapter 3. In science vastly more than in politics it may be possible to eventually win over rather than only defeat opponents. Even more important, no decisive choice binding on everyone needs to be sought, and in particular does not need to be decisive right now. A scientific revolution that is succeeding can usually ignore those who are not persuaded. They eventually die out. And even while active and prominent, opposition to the new idea may be negligible as a burden on those who are converted. Opposition does not need to be eliminated. But in politics

choices have to be made for everyone, there are windows of opportunity that soon can close, and holdouts unless sequestered can cause great difficulty.

Drawing on the account developed in much more detail in my 2002 book on the Scientific Revolution, the Copernican discovery, like the very earliest beginnings of a political movement, is idiosyncratic, turning on a special set of circumstances that put Copernicus in a position to see what had been logically easily available for 1400 years (since Ptolemy) but that no one before him had noticed. Copernicus' early readers praised (and used) his technical work but with few exceptions ignored the heliocentric framing. For the next generation (following the usual pattern noted in the Introduction here) that "absurd" (as Copernicus himself called it) idea had become only wrong, not crazy, leading converts for a while mostly to a compromise (the Tychonic system) which looks Copernican but without actually throwing the Earth into the heavens. But eventually, after half a century, we reach a generation of students who become familiar with the Copernican idea before they could be solidly socialized in the traditional view, and learn it from teachers who themselves are no longer absolutely entrenched in that view. A handful of individuals (mainly Stevin and Gilbert, then joined by the half a generation younger Galileo and Kepler) finally appeared who provided a seed enthusiastic about spreading the Copernican view. Galileo's discovery with the telescope (which made economy more striking, discomfort less severe) probably moved the situation to put a tipping point within reach. Now even without a great commitment of effort, anyone could see something of what made the extravagant Copernican idea interesting. A person could see Earth-like features on the Moon, vast numbers of previously invisible (so apparently very distant) stars, sunspots whose changing appearance defied tradition and also showed rotation of the Sun itself. And a smaller scale version of the Copernican system could be seen in Jupiter and its moons. So a person could see a world that looked Copernican. The last ditch efforts of the Church over the balance of the century to stop at the Tychonic compromise provided the holdouts (among the tiny minority whose opinions counted on this matter) on the right of the diagram.

What makes the Copernican parallel with politics interesting is the existence of the Tychonic compromise, since indeed in political contexts there is commonly a phase in which the idea that the existing system is somehow unacceptable becomes widespread, but not acceptance of the radical alternative, and more often in politics than in science the compromise actually proves to be viable.

2 Googling "Montgomery Bus Boycott" will yield multiple accounts.

## Chapter 6: Adverse defaults

1 What has become the classic example is Kahneman and Tversky's "taxi" problem. See the still-instructive debate in *Behavioral and Brain Sciences* (Cohen *et al.* 1981), where – as elsewhere in discussions of this problem – prominent, highly qualified academics go carefully through the Bayesian calculation to show they grasp it perfectly, then endorse the illusory base-rate neglecting common intuition anyway.

2 The main exception to claims turning on difficulty with modus tollens is Laming's (Gebauer and Laming 1997), where subjects misread the rule, responding as if "if the letter side has an A . . ." means "if the first side has an A . . .", yielding choices that would coincide with what would occur if modus tollens is neglected in the way proposed here. So the question of why a huge majority miss the simple logic is replaced by the question of why a huge majority misread the simple language. But if in fact a modus tollens neglect default is in play, subjects will behave as if they misread the question.

3 Early on Wason and Johnson-Laird (1972) found strong remedial effects in an experiment (RAST) using repeated choices from sets of not-p and not-q cards. But they did not try the simpler manipulation here of just removing the two easy cards

from the usual four-card display. A reader familiar with my 1987 discussion of Wason will notice that it was also in terms of defaulting, but with respect to a categories/instances pair.

4 The problem has been a favorite among statisticians for a long time. It was published at least as far back as 1889, in a version that postulated three boxes, each with two drawers, one containing a gold coin in each drawer, a second with silver coins, and the last one gold and one silver. The discussion here elaborates on Margolis (1996, Ch. 3), where it was presented in terms of three poker chips with red and white dots on the sides. The problem was bought to the attention of cognitive psychologists by Falk and Bar Hillel (1982).

5 I am about to suggest accounts of the 1/3, 1/2, and 2/3 choices. But where do the "others" come from? Although a side-issue for this chapter, the account here would interpret them as responses from subjects anchored on one of the three salient choices, adjusted for awareness of other possibilities.

6 The full results are: 1/2 = 24%, 1/3 = 35%, 2/3 = 27%, others = 14%.

7 Three recent Monty Hall discussions are Krauss and Wang (2003), Burns and Wieth (2004), and Fox and Levav (2004), all in the *Journal of Experimental Psychology* (*General*). Krauss and Wang report a substantial correction of the illusion, but using a "guided intuition" manipulation which is very elaborate compared to the MH* argument here. Burns and Wieth point to a "collider effect" as the key to the difficulty, and indeed this effect is interesting, but it seems to apply as much to XMH as to MH, without causing any difficulty for XMH. Fox and Levav treat a wider range of problems, including the "sides" variation of the three card problem already discussed.

8 Cognitive illusions affecting experts in their domain of expertise can be noticed elsewhere when nothing very important is at risk, or when an issue first arises, or when there is strong motivation to favor the intuition. For 400 years the very best experts in early astronomy (from Kepler through Thomas Kuhn and beyond) uniformly misjudged a very simple technical issue due to a stubborn but logically trivial cognitive illusion (Margolis 1998). But one or another of the side conditions applied to each of the victims of the illusion.

9 Within the trapezoid, $\Delta BAD = \Delta CAD$, since they share a common base and equal altitudes. Subtract the common area $\Delta AMD$, and we are left with $\Delta ABM = \Delta DMC$. How can sophisticated subjects fail to quickly see that? Faced with this really trivial puzzle, nearly everyone responds as if blind to what is in plain sight. What is beyond the two triangles directly in play is neglected. But just this sort of neglect defaulting will play a central role in the account of apparent indifference to reciprocity in Chapter 9. I first encountered this curious problem at a dinner with Robyn Dawes.

### Chapter 7: Anomalies in experimental economics

1 In one version, Saijo/Nakamura provided players with "rough" payoff tables which showed payoffs to self for a few combinations of others/own contribution. In others "detailed" payoff tables showed payoffs to self for all possible combinations others' contributions and own contribution. With seven players, each choosing a contribution of 0 to 10 tokens, this made the detailed tables a 60 × 11 payoff block of 660 three or four digit numbers. The difference in results using the alternative tables was large, with detailed tables yielding results close to what would be expected from perfect self-interest. But given the intense focus on the maximum payoff number to self found after navigating the mass of numbers, this is hardly a neutral presentation of the choice. I use the "rough" table results here.

2 And a player who declines the penalty and then either does not have a cooperate/ defect choice (the round is not played out) or has a choice and defects, also might or

might not be starting from the zero-sum frame. There is no way to tell. If he declines the penalty but then cooperates anyway, then he cannot have started from the zero-sum frame. This occasionally happened, but far too rarely to conflict with the possibility that frequently players did start from the zero-sum frame.

### Chapter 8: NSNX effects in the Public Goods game

1 Fehr and Gachter (2000) and Isaac, Walker, and Williams (1994). And later, Croson, Fatas, and Neugebauer (2006).
2 Data is sparse for choices other than divisible by 5. Give = 0 cases are absent since fractiondown is then automatically 0. To get a clean separation across categories, high gavg here is > 1.3, low <0.7, and the neutral zone is 0.9 to 1.1.
3 Since in a "strangers" game, the group affected by the choice in this round is not the same as the group involved in the previous round, an updown effect might seem inappropriate. But unless the chooser's sense of context changes, which could hardly happen here, a player feeling out of equilibrium coming out of the prior round will respond to that in her next choice.
4 In terms of the NSNX formalism, if *nsdl* were very small, W might decrease and certainly will not increase (no player would feel exploited), and S' (the cost to the chooser of contributing a token) is unaffected. But G', hence the value ratio G'/S', will improve with this indication of coordination, since the social value of doing one's share must be larger as it seems more likely that that cooperation might be sustained.
5 The Fehr and Gachter series used an (unannounced) restart to compare choices with and without a punishment arrangement intended to deter free-riding. In FG5 the punishment series came second, so could not effect choices in the standard condition. In FG4 punishment rounds preceded the standard condition. FG4 also shows the firstgrand effect, but attenuated relative to the unconditioned trials in FG5.
6 A player in IWW 4.3 who gave 50 while the mean *give* of others was 20 would get a payoff of $0.3 \times (3 \times 20 + 50) = 0.3 \times 110 = 33$, for a net loss of 17. But in IWW 4.75, payoff would be $0.75 \times 110 = 81$, for a net gain of 31.
7 The total *give* would be four times the average *give*. Each of the four players earns half of that, which is two times the average *give*.
8 If *all* gave 0, no one would be excluded (as when all give any other amount), but there would be nothing in the pool to be excluded from.
9 Players would earn triple the endowment in rounds where they do not contribute, and double their endowment from the one round in four in which a player is the designated contributor.
10 Both BSM-EX and BSM-EX-R show experience effects in the restart series (rounds 11–20), but as can be noticed, the relation between them is about the same.
11 Add 10 cents to each WLM payoff, and change the endowment from 50 tokens to 60 cents, but with *gives* restricted to units of 10 cents. Then the WLM game here would be identical to the Minimum game of Chapter 7. A player would choose how many dimes to send to the pool from his endowment, and receive a payoff of whatever dimes he kept plus 2 dimes for each dime of the "weakest link" *give*. A payoff table in the format of the Minimum game in Chapter 7 would be identical to the Minimum game table, except that the choice of a number (1, 2, 3, . . . 7) to report is replaced by a choice of how many dimes (0,1,2 . . . 6) to give.

The degenerate variant examined in Chapter 7 was the Weakest Link game here, but with a "money-back guarantee" that made it logically trivial to see that contributing the maximum was the only sensible choice. But players mostly missed it anyway.

**Chapter 9: Reciprocity puzzles**

1  For positive appraisals of experimental evidence for reciprocity, see (among others) Cox and Deck (2005), Fehr and Fischbacher (2003).

2  Players recorded choices in (usually) four games, one of which was chosen by lot as their payoff game at the end of the session.

3  In 6 of the 32 games a third party (C) chooses payoffs for A and B. To handle this, in these games 1/3 of the players are passive, as reflected in the smaller number of players shown for "C" games relative to other games within the session.

4  Returning to an earlier remark about choices by bystanders, we get an explanation of why we do not see clear failures of reciprocity in C choices. A player in the referee role who is paying attention at all cannot be caught by the neglect default.

5  CR21 in Berkeley used parameters between those of CR3 and 4 in Barcelona, and yielded a (only barely noticeable, though still in the right direction) truncated effect. I cannot offer an explanation, and indeed it would be hard to explain on any account, since on any account the fraction of generous choices would be expected to lie between those of CR3 and CR4, but it is not even very close to that. Three other games that allow clear comparisons show no such divergence between Barcelona and Berkeley results. CR2 and 17 yielded almost identical results. Two others (CR9 and 25, CR1 and 13) showed more generosity in Berkeley but nothing like the disparity between CR21 and CR3 and 4.

6  This is so even for the 0,800 or 400,400 choice though only 22 percent make the generous choice with A as bystander. It is hardly ungenerous that only 22 percent give away half their tokens to an anonymous stranger who has done nothing to warrant such generosity. But the truncated situation response is to an A who has chosen to provide B with this choice, though it neglects to notice A's alternative to doing that.

**Chapter 11: Notes on terrorism**

1  I thank Ethan Bueno de Mesquita for bringing this issue to my attention and for other helpful comments on this chapter.

2  Saddam thought the purported weapons were important as a deterrent against Iran as well as the US, and within Iraq against both Shiites and Kurds (who were *de facto* independent but were a threat against the oil-rich Kirkuk region). And admitting he had been bluffing might trigger a coup by his own generals.

# References

Andreoni, J. (1995) Cooperation in public goods experiments: kindness or confusion? *American Economic Review*, 85:4 (September): 891–904.

Basu, K. (1994) The Traveler's Dilemma. *American Economic Review*, 84: 391–3.

—— (2007) Game theory: The Traveler's Dilemma. *Scientific American*, June.

Binmore, K. (1994) *Game Theory and the Social Contract*. MIT Press.

Brunton, D., Hasan, R., and Mestelman, S. (2001) The "spite" dilemma: spite or no spite, is there a dilemma? *Economics Letters*, 71: 405–412.

Burns, B. D. and Wieth, M. (2004) The collider principle in causal reasoning: why the Monty Hall dilemma is so hard. *Journal of Experimental Psychology: General*, 133: 434–449.

Camerer, C. (2003) *Behavioral Game Theory*. Princeton University Press.

Capra, C. M., Goeree, J. K., Gomez, R., and Holt, C. A. (1999) Anomalous behavior in the Traveler's Dilemma. *American Economic Review*, 89: 678–960.

Charness, G. and Rabin, M. (2002). Understanding social preferences with simple tests. *The Quarterly Journal of Economics*, 117(3) (August): 817–869.

Chaudhuri, A., Schotter, A., and Sopher, B. (2002) Talking ourselves to efficiency: coordination in inter-generational minimum games with private, almost common and common knowledge of advice. NYU Working Paper.

—— and Graziano, S. (2003) Social learning and norms in an experimental public goods game with inter-generational advice. NYU Working Paper.

Cohen, L. J. (1981) Can human irrationality be experimentally demonstrated? *Behavioral and Brain Sciences*, 4: 317–331.

Collard, D. (1978) *Altruism and Economics*. Oxford University Press.

Cookson, R. (2000) Framing effects in public goods experiments. *Experimental Economics*, 3: 55–79.

Cosimedes, L. (1989) The logic of social exchange. *Cognition*, 31: 187–276.

Cox, J. and Deck, C. (2005) On the nature of reciprocal motives. *Economic Inquiry*, 43: 623–635.

Croson, R., Fatas, E., and Neugebauer, T. (2006) Excludability and contribution: a laboratory study in team production. Working Paper. University of Hannover.

Darwin, C. (1871) *Descent of Man*. Murray.

Downs, A. (1957) *An Economic Theory of Democracy*. Harper.

Elster, J. (1989) Social norms and economic theory. *Journal of Economic Perspectives*, 3: 99–117.

Evans, J. StB. T. (1989) *Bias in Human Reasoning*. Erlbaum.

Falk, R. and Bar Hillel, M. (1982) Some teasers concerning conditional probabilities. *Cognition*, 11: 109–122.

Falk, E., Fehr, E., and Fischbacher, U. *et al.* (2000) Testing theories of fairness – intentions matter. Working Paper 63, University of Zurich.

Fatas, E., Neugebauer, T., and Perote, O. (2001) Profit-sharing, free-riding and minimum effort incentives in partnerships. LINEEX Working Paper 4103. Universitat de Valencia.

Fehr, E. and Fischbacher, U. (2003) The nature of human altruism. *Nature*, 425: 785–791.

Fehr, E. and Gachter, S. (2000) Cooperation and punishment in public goods experiments. *American Economic Review*, 90: 980–994.

Ferraro, P. J. and Vossler, C. A. (2005) The dynamics of other-regarding behavior and confusion: what's really going on in voluntary contributions mechanism experiments? Experimental laboratory working paper series #2005–001. Department of Economics, Andrew Young School of Policy Studies, Georgia State University.

—— and Taylor, L. O. (2005) Do economists recognize an opportunity cost when they see one? A dismal performance from the dismal science. *Contributions to Economic Analysis and Policy*, vol. 4, no. 1, article 7.

Fischbacher, U. and Thoni, C. (2006) An experimental winner-take-all market. University of Zurich Working Paper.

Fox, C. R. and Levav, J. (2004) Partition–Edit–Count: naive extensional reasoning in judgment of conditional probability. *Journal of Experimental Psychology: General*, 133: 626–642.

—— and Rottenstreich, Y. (2003) Partition priming in judgment under uncertainty. *Psychological Science*, 13: 195–200.

Frisby, J. P. (1979) *Seeing: Illusion, Brain and Mind*. Oxford University Press.

Gebauer, G. and Laming, D. (1997) Rational choices in Wason's selection task. *Psychological Research*, 60: 284–293.

Gigerenzer, G., Todd, P. M., and ABC Research Group (1999) *Simple Heuristics that Make Us Smart*. Oxford University Press.

Gintis, H., Seabright, P., Ross, J. and Binmore, K. (2006) Symposium on natural justice. *Politics, Philosophy and Economics*, 5.

Gladwell, M. (2000) *The Tipping Point*. Little, Brown and Co.

—— (2005) *Blink: The Power of Thinking Without Thinking*. Little, Brown and Co.

Goeree, J. K. and Holt, C. A. (2005) An explanation of anomalous behavior in models of political participation. *American Political Science Review*, 99: 201–213.

Grice, P. (1989) *Studies in the Way of Words*. Harvard University Press.

Griggs, P. (1989) To see or not to see: that is the selection task. *Quarterly Journal of Experimental Psychology*, 41: 517–529.

Haile, P. A., Hortacsu, A., and Kosenok, G. (2006) On the empirical content of quantal response models. Cowles Foundation Discussion Paper #1432R.

Harrison, G. and List, John A. (2004) Field experiments. *Journal of Economic Literature*, 42(4) (December): 1009–1055.

Harrison, G. W. and Hirshleifer, J. (1989) An experimental evaluation of weakest link/best shot models of public goods. *Journal of Political Economy*, 97: 201–225.

Hoffman, B. (2006) *Inside Terrorism*. Columbia University Press.

Houser, D. and Kurzban, R. (2005) An experimental investigation of cooperative types in human groups. *Proceedings of the National Academy of Sciences*, 102: 1803–1807.

Isaac, R. M., Walker, J. M., and Williams, A. W. (1994) Group size and the voluntary provision of public goods: experimental evidence utilizing large groups. *Journal of Public Economics*, 54:1 (May): 1–36.

Isikoff, M. and Corn, D. (2006) *Hubris: The Inside Story of Spin, Scandal, and the Selling of the Iraq War*. Crown.

Kahneman, D. and Frederick, S. (2005) A model of heuristic judgment, in Holyoak, K. J. and Morrison, R. G. (eds) *The Cambridge Handbook of Thinking and Reasoning*. Cambridge University Press, pp. 267–293.

Koehler, J. J. (1996) The base rate fallacy reconsidered: descriptive, normative, and methodological challenges. *Behavioral and Brain Sciences*, 19(1): 1–53.

Krauss, S. and Wang, X. T. (2003) The psychology of the Monty Hall problem: discovering psychological mechanisms for solving a tenacious brain teaser. *Journal of Experimental Psychology*, 132: 3–22.

Kreps, D., Milgrom, P., Roberts, J., and Wilson, R. (1982) Rational cooperation in the finitely repeated prisons' dilemma. *Journal of Economic Theory*, 27: 245–252.

Kuran, T. (1997) *Private Truths, Public Lies: The Social Consequences of Preference Falsification*. Harvard University Press.

Ledyard, J. O. (1995) Public goods: a survey of experimental research, in Kagel, J. H. and Roth, A. (eds) *Handbook of Experimental Economics*. Princeton University Press.

Levi, M. (1988) *Of Rule and Revenue*. University of California Press.

Levine, D. K. and Palfrey, T. R. (2007) The paradox of voter participation? *American Political Science Review*, 101: 143–158.

List, J. A. and Levitt, S. D. (2005) What do laboratory experiments tell us about the real world? NBER Working Paper.

Luce, D. and Raiffa, H. (1957) *Games and Decisions*. Wiley.

Madison, J. [1787] (1999) 'Vices of the political system of the United States'. Library of America.

Margolis, H. (1977) Probability of a tie election. *Public Choice*, 31: 135–138

—— (1982) *Selfishness, Altruism and Rationality*. Cambridge University Press (hb); University of Chicago Press (1984) (pb).

—— (1987) *Patterns, Thinking and Cognition*. University of Chicago Press.

—— (1990a) Dual-utilities and rational choice, in J. Mansbridge (ed.) *Beyond Self-Interest*. University of Chicago Press, pp. 239–253.

—— (1990b) Equilibrium norms, in Symposium on Norms in Moral and Social Theory, *Ethics*, 100: 821–837.

—— (1991) Incomplete coercion, in K. Monroe (ed.) *The Economic Approach to Politics* (Downs festschrift). Harper & Row.

—— (1992) Free-riding vs. cooperation, in R. Zeckhauser (ed.) *Strategy and Choice* (Schelling festschrift). MIT Press.

—— (1996) *Dealing with Risk* (Chapter 3). University of Chicago Press.

—— (1997) Religion as paradigm. *Journal of Institutional and Theoretical Economics*, 153: 242–252.

—— (1998) Tycho's illusion. *Nature*, 392: 857.

—— (2002) Altruism and Darwinian rationality. *Behavioral and Brain Sciences*, 25: 269–270.

—— (2007) Are economists human? *Applied Economics Letters* (in press).

Maynard Smith, J. and Sugden, R. (1988) *The Economics of Rights, Cooperation, and Welfare*. Basil Blackwell.

McKelvey, R. and Palfrey, T. (1995) Quantal response equilibria for normal form games. *Games and Economic Behavior*, 10: 6–38.

Neugebauer, T. (2007) Can intermediaries assure contracts? Experimental evidence. Working Paper, University of Hanover.

Neustadt, R. E. (1983) *The Epidemic That Never Was*. Vintage Books.

—— (1999) *Report to JFK: The Skybolt Crisis in Perspective*. Cornell University Press.

Olson, M. (1965) *Logic of Collective Action*. Harvard University Press.

Quarantelli, E. L. and Dynes, R. R. (1977) Response to social crisis and disaster. *Annual Review of Sociology*, 3: 23–49.

Rabin, M. (1993) Incorporating fairness into game theory and economics. *American Economic Review*, 83(5) (December): 1281–1302.

Ricks, T. E. (2006) *Fiasco: The American Military Adventure in Iraq*. Penguin Press.

Robertson, D. (1956) What does the economist economize? *Economic Commentaries*. Staples Press.

Roth, J. A., Scholz, J. T. and Witte, A. D. (eds) (1988) *Taxpayer Compliance*. National Academy of Sciences Press.

Saijo, T. and Nakamura, H. (1995) The 'spite' dilemma in voluntary contribution mechanism experiments. *Journal of Conflict Resolution*, 39(3): 535–560.

Samuelson, P. A. (1963) Problems of methodology. *American Economic Review*, 53: 231–236.

Samuelson, P. (1972) Pure theory of public expenditure and taxation. In *Collected Scientific Papers*, Vol. 3. MIT Press.

Schelling, T. C. (1960) *The Strategy of Conflict*. Harvard University Press.

—— (1978) *Micromotives and Macrobehavior*. Norton.

Schotter, A. and Sopher, B. (2001) Advice and behavior in an inter-generational trust game. Center for Experimental Social Science, NYU.

Sen. Amartya, K. (1977) Rational fools: a critique of the behavioral foundations of economic theory. *Journal of Philosophy and Public Affairs*, 6: 317–344.

Shweder, R. *et al.* (1997) The 'Big Three' of morality (autonomy, community, divinity), and the 'Big Three' explanations of suffering, in P. Rozin and A. Brandt (eds) *Morality and Health*. Routledge.

Shweder, R. A., Much N. C., Mahapaira, M., and Park, I. (1997) The 'big three' of morality. In Brandt, A. A. and Rozin, P., *Morality and Health*. Routledge.

Sperber, D., Cara, F., and Girotto, V. (1995) Relevance theory explains the selection task. *Cognition*, 57: 31–95.

—— and Wilson, D. (1986) *Relevance*. Harvard University Press.

Stanovich, K. E. and West, R. F. (2000) Individual differences in reasoning: implications for the rationality debate? *Behavioral and Brain Sciences*, 23: 645–726.

Sundali, J. A., Rapaport, A., and Searle, D. A. (1995) Coordination in market entry games with symmetric players. *Organizational behavior and Human decision processes*, 64: 203–218.

Wason, P.C. and Johnson-Laird, P. (1972) *Psychology of Reasoning*. Harvard University Press.

Weber, R. A. (2006) Managing growth to achieve efficient coordination in large groups. *American Economic Review*, 96: 114–126.

Williams, G. C. (1966) *Adaptation and Natural Selection*. Princeton University Press.

Wilson, D. W. and Sober, E. (1998) *Unto Others*. Harvard University Press.

Woodward, B. (2006) *State of Denial*. Simon & Schuster.

Van Huyck, J., Battalio, R., and Beil, R. (1993) Asset markets as an equilibrium selection mechanism: Coordination failure, game form auctions, and tacit communication. *Games and Economic Behavior*, 5: 485–504.

Van Huyck, J. B. and Beil, R. (1990) Tacit coordination games, strategic uncertainty, and coordination failure. *American Economic Review*, 80: 234–248.

—— (1991) Strategic uncertainty equilibrium selection principles and coordination failure in average opinion games. *Quarterly Journal of Economics*, 106: 885–911.

Zajonc, R. (1980) *Emotions, Cognition, and Behavior*. Cambridge University Press.

# Index